Contents

First

Pu

NORTH WEST KENT COLLEGE

es

reeze,
Cronin
afford

D Y N A M I C
L E A R N I N G

HODDER
EDUCATION
AN HACHETTE UK COMPANY

£20.99

Orders: please contact Bookpoint Ltd, 130 Milton Park, Abingdon, Oxon OX14 4SB. Telephone: (44) 01235 827720. Fax: (44) 01235400454. Lines are open from 9.00–5.00, Monday to Saturday, with a 24 hour message answering service. You can also order through our website www.hoddereducation.co.uk.

British Library Cataloguing in Publication Data
A catalogue record for this title is available from the British Library

ISBN: 9781444112115

First Published 2010
Impression number 10 9 8 7 6 5 4 3 2 1
Year 2012 2011 2010

Hachette UK's policy is to use papers that are natural, renewable and recyclable products and made from wood grown in sustainable forests. The logging and manufacturing processes are expected to conform to the environmental regulations of the country of origin.

Cover photo © Win Initiative/The Image Bank/Getty Images
Artworks © Barking Dog Art
Typeset by Fakenham Photosetting, Fakenham, Norfolk
Printed in Italy for Hodder Education, an Hachette UK Company

Walkthrough

Prepare for what you are going to cover in this unit, and what you'll know by the end of it.

Learning outcomes:

By the end of this unit, you should:
1. Know the purpose and importance of public services skills

Helps you understand and remember key concepts and information.

Think about it!

Would you describe your class as a team? Or is it just a group of people in the same place at the same time?

Push your grade from a Pass to a Merit or Distinction with these handy hints!

How to upgrade to ...

M2 For M2, you need to explain in detail the work of a chosen job in the uniformed services. Talk to visiting speakers or anyone you know who is a member of the uniformed public services and ask them about their daily routine.

Reinforce concepts with hands-on learning and generate evidence for assignments.

Activity 1

How many other qualities of a good instructor can you think of? Make a table and write the quality in one column and a description in the other.

A little question to help you evaluate and link key points.

Ask Yourself!

Should police community support officers have powers to arrest people?

Key terms

SMART stands for specific, measurable, achievable, relevant and time constrained.

Revise all those new words and what they mean.

Reminds you what you need to do to meet a grading requirement.

(g) Grading Tip!

To achieve a pass grade the evidence must show that you are able to:

P3 For P3, you need to identify the different skills required by public service workers, as discussed above, and explain a little about them.

Understand how your learning fits into real life and working environments.

Case Study

Firms fined over Hatfield crash

Two firms have been fined a total of £13.5 million for breaching health and safety regulations over the Hatfield train crash in 2000, in which four people died.

The comprehensive guide to what assessors will be looking for in your work.

Grading criteria

To achieve a pass grade the evidence must show that you are able to:	To achieve a merit grade the evidence must show that, in addition to the pass criteria, you are able to:	To achieve a distinction grade the evidence must show that, in addition to the pass and merit criteria, you are able to:
P1 Outline the main purpose and roles of contrasting uniformed public services.	**M1** Explain in detail the role, purpose and responsibilities of contrasting uniformed public services.	Evaluate the role, purpose and responsibilities of a chosen uniformed public service.

This is your checklist for what you should know by the end of the unit!

End of Unit Knowledge check

1. List five ways in which public service employees can ensure they are in a fit state to carry out their duties.

About the authors

Marilyn Breeze had a long career in the public service sector, including working for the Police Service, the Education sector and Social Services before retraining as a lecturer in 1994. Marilyn is currently the Public Services Subject Leader and a lecturer at the University of Derby College, Buxton. She is also an external verifier for a major awarding body, a writer for new specifications and has recently been appointed and trained as a magistrate in her local area.

Margaret Cronin began working life as a police officer. She qualified as a teacher in 1992 and taught in English and Welsh schools, and achieved Master of Arts in Education in 1996. Margaret has also worked as a Registered Nursery Inspector carrying out inspections in pre-schools, day nurseries and independent schools. In 1997, she began lecturing in further education and was Programme Co-ordinator for Public Services. She is now an external verifier for a major awarding body and is involved in writing new specifications, from Level 1 to Level 5. Margaret is currently Director of her own training company.

Alan Spafford presently works with a major awarding body as an External Verifier on Public Service courses and as a Diploma Senior Assessment Associate for Diploma Principal Learning in Public Services. He has recently been appointed a Standards verifier and a Centre Quality Reviewer for the Midlands. He has been involved with sport and outdoor education all his working life for both private and Local Authority providers and is a former Departmental Head of Sport and Public Services at a Nottingham Further Education college. Alan has lectured on all levels of sport and public services courses for the last 18 years and presently lectures part time in Nottingham. He has also recently been involved in writing specifications. His inspiration for writing this book comes from his two sons Jack and William.

Photo credits

The author and publishers would like to thank the following for permission to reproduce material in this book:

p. 1 © Matt Cardy/Getty Images; 1.1 © PA Wire/Press Association Images; 1.2 © Rex Features 1.3 © Vince Bevan / Alamy; 1.4 © Shout / Rex Features; 1.6 © Robert Stainforth / Alamy; 1.10 © David Lee / Rex Features; p. 30 © Rex Features 2.1 © Ashley Cooper / SpecialistStock / SplashdownDirect / Rex Features; 2.4 © Jack Sullivan / Alamy; 2.5 © Geoff Moore / Rex Features; 2.6 © Rex Features; 2.7 © PA Wire/Press Association Images; 2.8 © Sally and Richard Greenhill / Alamy; 2.9 © Matt Cardy/Getty Images; 2.10 © Richard Gardner / Rex Features; p. 62 © Paula Solloway / Photofusion; 3.3 © David Rose / Rex Features; 3.4 © Alex Segre / Rex Features; 3.6 © Alexander Caminada / Alamy; p. 89 © Richard Gardner / Rex Features;

Unit 1
Public service skills

Introduction

Welcome to the first chapter of the book; this covers everything you will need to know to complete Unit 1: Public service skills.

This is a mandatory unit in the course, which means that everyone who studies towards the Certificate, Extended Certificate or Diploma in Public Services needs to complete this unit.

Members of the public services require excellent interpersonal skills; they also need to demonstrate outstanding communication skills and teamwork to enable the services to meet the expectations of the public.

In this unit, you will study the purpose and importance of public service skills. You will also explore teamwork, its purpose and why it is so important in the public services. You will identify some of the different qualities that are essential for effective teamwork and examine the characteristics needed for working as part of a team. You will take part in a range of practical team-building activities, allowing you to evaluate your own strengths and areas for improvement. You will also be involved in evaluating the performance of your team members.

In addition, you will explore methods of instruction and develop your interpersonal and communication skills, all of which are important for a career in any of the public services.

When you start out in the public services, you will follow numerous instructions; later on, as you progress in the service, you could be one of those issuing the instructions. In this unit, you will become familiar with a variety of methods of instruction that are employed in some of the public services. You will need to understand the principles and techniques of quality instruction. By the end of the unit, you will have the opportunity to put your knowledge into practice, by carrying out a short session with a small group of people.

You will also develop a range of professional and personal life skills that will serve you well in your future career. Following examination of your own skills, you will have a better understanding of how you can be successful in completing your studies for this course. This will stand you in good stead when you begin the process of applying to your chosen public service.

So how will you be able to achieve this unit? Every unit in the programme contains *learning outcomes*. These state what you should 'know', 'understand' or 'be able to' do.

Learning outcomes:

By the end of this unit, you should:

1. Know the purpose and importance of public service skills

2. Understand methods of instruction in public services

3. Be able to use a range of interpersonal communication skills.

Public service skills

P1 P2 M1 D1

Firstly, we will look at the skills that are needed in public service work. These include the skills that are necessary to carry out the job effectively – for example, punctuality and displaying the appropriate personal appearance and behaviour. These are examples of professional skills. Equally important are the skills that the individual develops; these include self-discipline, cooperation and the ability to deal with conflict.

Having identified the multitude of skills required by members of the public services, you now need to recognise *why* these skills are so important.

Take the skill of punctuality as an example; what does punctuality actually mean? Punctuality can mean being in a certain place at the right time – for example, arriving at work in plenty of time for the start of your shift.

In the public services, however, just 'being there' is not enough – you must display other skills and characteristics that mean the *purpose* of being on time has the desired effect. One of these purposes is to ensure that you are able to complete a required task within an agreed timescale. Another purpose could be to ensure that sufficient members of staff are available to carry out the task effectively. (You will learn more about how public service personnel work together later in this chapter.)

Discipline is essential for a career in the public services. Discipline can be described as 'obedience to authority', but this quality may be required in many different situations, such as giving (or receiving) orders or instruction, or as a means of threat. Often, discipline involves imposing and following rules and regulations and, if these rules are not adhered to, punishment (known as *disciplinary action*) could follow. Arguably the most important form of discipline is *self-discipline*, which means 'training and control of oneself and one's conduct.'

Activity

Working in pairs, write a list of as many skills as you can think of that are needed for public service work.

Now separate them into professional skills and personal skills.

Discuss your list with the rest of the class and then draw up a poster of these skills to display on the wall.

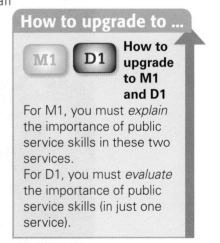

How to upgrade to …

M1 D1 | **How to upgrade to M1 and D1**

For M1, you must *explain* the importance of public service skills in these two services.
For D1, you must *evaluate* the importance of public service skills (in just one service).

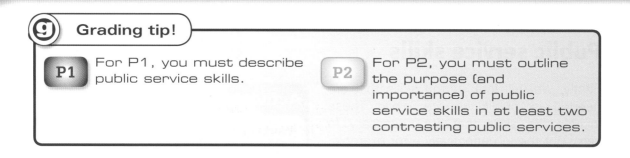

P3

(g) Grading tip!

P1 For P1, you must describe public service skills.

P2 For P2, you must outline the purpose (and importance) of public service skills in at least two contrasting public services.

Team-building activities

If you already possess the required skills and qualities to gain entry to your chosen public service and to progress in your career, well done – most people will need some help. During your studies, you will realise that high levels of teamwork are essential for those employed within public service organisations. (For example, see the case study below.)

⬭ Case study

Figure 1.1 'Operation Mista' involved 1,200 officers from the Metropolitan Police

Operation Mista

The size of this operation might suggest that a riot was in progress and the police had been called to calm things down. Figure 1.1 shows the scene when 600 officers marched down a North London street one spring morning. The total number involved, including officers from the Metropolitan Police, City of London Police and British Transport Police, totalled over 1,000.

Operation Mista targeted people suspected of drug dealing, money laundering, handling stolen goods and forgery. During the raids on 56 addresses, 37 people were arrested and a shopping street was closed.

Items recovered as a result of this activity included forged documents, such as passports and driving licences, 120 laptops, 32 iPods, 20 satnavs and 110 cameras.

What is a team?

An essential element of a team is that it comprises a group of people. Some teams are very small, such as two or three students working together to raise money for charity. Other teams might be very big, as in the example given in the case study above. Consider how many volunteers might be involved in searching for a missing child.

Does your sentence from the activity to the right take into account the ways in which the team members work together?

Did your group work as a team during the activity? Did one person take charge? Was everyone able to contribute to the discussion?

Teams vary in the time they stay together. A team might last a long time (e.g. a sports team) or a team might disband after just one operation – an example of this in the public services is a team that is set up to investigate a particular incident.

Not every group is necessarily a team; usually members of a team need different skills that complement each other – there would be no point in selecting a cricket

Activity

In groups, discuss the various teams that each of you are involved with or that you know about.

How many people are in the team? What (if any) are the personal benefits of being a member of the team?

Provide one sentence that describes all of these teams.

When you have completed your discussion, choose one member of your group to complete this sentence to display on a poster:

'A team is………'

Key term

A **team** could be described as 'a group of people linked in a common purpose'.

team that consisted wholly of fast bowlers if none of them could bat effectively. By utilising individual skills, the team can maximise its strengths and minimise its weaknesses.

> ### Think about it!
>
> Would you describe your class as a team? Or is it just a group of people in the same place at the same time?

> ### Key term
>
> **Teamwork** is the joint action of two or more people, where each contributes different skills, explores certain interests and is efficient in achieving common goals.

During your course you will play an active part in team-building activities, so you will have the opportunity to put teamwork into practice.

Teams often work together to achieve objectives set by the organisation in which they work. This might be a formal team created for a specific purpose – for example, trainers for a new fitness programme for new recruits. Alternatively, the team could be informal – for example, you and a few other students might start a discussion about ways in which you could contribute to the college's fundraising activities. An informal team is less structured than a formal team but is not necessarily less effective in its outcome.

Figure 1.2 Army regiment

The purpose of teamwork is to achieve the best possible results:

- in the quickest possible time
- with the least effort and expense
- without cheating or breaking the rules
- without destroying the team.

Public service teams

Every public service employs teams, for many reasons. Large teams might comprise several smaller teams that work together. Let us explore some teams you might already be familiar with, and some you might not.

Regiment

A regiment is a large group in the army; it is made up of smaller teams. A regiment usually comprises about 650 soldiers and is often considered the most important unit in the British Army. The regiment comprises smaller platoons.

Watch

A watch is a shift in the fire service. The same people always work together; therefore, it is a strong team. Fire service watches are given colours – for example, 'Blue' watch and 'Red' watch. Within the watch, each member of the team has his or her own role.

Crew

'Crew' is usually the name given to all the people who work on board a ship. This consists of officers and ratings; the officers provide leadership to the team and the ratings carry out the commands given by the officers.

The term 'crew' is also used on aircraft and in the ambulance service; it is used for rescue teams, particularly those that operate in helicopters.

Essential qualities for teamwork

Figure 1.3 A fire service watch

Figure 1.4 An RAF rescue crew

Every individual possesses certain qualities that make them good at what they do. However, teams are employed to accomplish goals that could not be achieved by individuals alone. In order for a team to work effectively, it is vital that these qualities merge to make the team efficient. A list of qualities is given below:

- Punctuality – the ability to organise yourself so that you are always where you should be when expected to be (and carry out your duties effectively).
- Well equipped – making sure that you have the right materials with you so you can perform to the best of your ability within the team.
- Accountability – accepting responsibility for the performance of the whole team. This includes when things do not go to plan, as well as when the team works effectively.
- Ability to summarise information quickly – essential for effective team performance.
- Concentration – vital to see the task through, especially when tiredness creeps in and you would rather be at home in bed!
- Good communication skills – you must be able to understand others and ensure your messages are understood and acted upon.
- Knowing the other team members – if you know the other team members by name, they will be responsive and will support each other.

Figure 1.5 Essential qualities for teamwork

- Willingness to identify problems – if the team members are aware of any problems, they can help solve them as a group.
- Resilience – the capacity to keep going and seeing failure as an opportunity to learn.

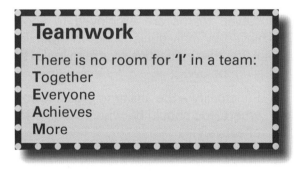

Teamwork

There is no room for 'I' in a team:
Together
Everyone
Achieves
More

---

g) Grading tip!

P3 To achieve P3, you will need to take part in *at least* two team-building activities.

To get the best out of your team-building activities, it is absolutely vital that you approach them in a positive way. You might have known some of your public services group before you began the course; if so, you will probably wish to be in the same team as them. Do not be too concerned, however, if your tutor chooses to put you in another team with people you do not yet know very well. Your tutor will select members of each team on the basis of personality and skills; each team needs the right combination of these to be successful.

Within the public services, any activity begins with all team members attending a *briefing*. This is similar to a meeting and is a proven way of getting information to all team members quickly and efficiently. A briefing is designed to provide the team with essential information about the activity; It should be conducted in an open manner and be a two-way process.

You will be given a briefing before you embark upon each of your activities. To be successful from the outset, you will need to be an *effective listener*, so you can understand exactly what the team is being asked to do (what the goal is). If you or others in your team do not fully understand what is required, this briefing is the time to ask questions – and get answers!

The goal outlined in the briefing needs to remain the focus for all team members throughout the activity. You and the other team members have to work together to plan and put into place the activity you have been given. It is good practice to discuss the problem at some length to ensure that every team member is agreed on what exactly the goal is and the way in which the problem should be tackled. It is also a good idea to regroup at regular intervals throughout the activity to consider whether the team is still on track to complete the activity successfully and to decide whether alternative action is necessary.

When you have completed each team-building activity, you will need to review its success. The questions given in 'Ask yourself' below might be useful in providing focus for this review.

Ask yourself!

1. When and where did the activity take place?
2. Was the briefing useful?
3. Did you know at the outset what was required?
4. How many members were there in your team?
5. What was your role in the team?
6. What other roles were there?
7. What methods of communication were used?
8. To what extent did your team achieve its goal?
9. Did your team need to change direction? If so, why?
10. Did team members support each other?
11. What (if anything) would you change if you did this activity again?

Qualities of a good instructor and methods of instruction

P4 M2

In this section, we will consider the second learning outcome, which is concerned with the qualities needed by an instructor and the methods of instruction used in the public services. You will have the opportunity to demonstrate your own instruction skills.

When you buy a new mobile phone, the packaging includes a set of operating instructions; you might read (or scan, or skim) these instructions until you feel confident to 'go it alone'. In the same way, you might have seen others (or been involved in) trying to assemble a piece of furniture, following instructions. These instructions are usually written in a particular format, designed to ensure that, if followed precisely, the outcome will be successful.

Wording of instructions

When you see instructions on signs, in manuals (e.g. a car or television manual) or in recipes, they are usually written in a form known as *imperative*; this means each stage must be followed in order to achieve a successful outcome. An example of an imperative is, 'Turn left at the job centre', as opposed to, 'When you get to the job centre, you should turn left.'

'You should not smoke here'	becomes	'**Do not** smoke here'
'You must not run'	becomes	'**Do not** run'
'You will need 200g flour'	becomes	'**Take** 200g flour'

Figure 1.6 Example of a sign giving an instruction

The type of instruction described here is not written as a full sentence; it is often written as a list. You begin at the top and work your way down. Equally, the list might contain numbers or bullet points. In public service organisations, it is vital that each stage of an operation is carried out in the order that provides the best chance of success. The person providing instruction must have the competence to issue the instructions accurately and, just as importantly, they must be confident that those following instruction have the ability to carry the operation out, without question.

Whatever field they work in, good instructors need to display a variety of qualities. This applies to a driving instructor, a sports instructor, someone involved in health and fitness and a range of other occupations, including working within the public services.

The list below contains a few qualities that are considered essential to be a good instructor:

- Knowledgeable – you cannot be expected to teach or train others in a skill that you do not excel at yourself.
- Competent – it is no good *knowing* about the topic if you are unable to demonstrate effectively how it should be carried out.
- Motivated – you must be enthusiastic about the subject and be able to enthuse your learners.
- Good communicator – there is more information about the art of communication in the final part of this chapter.

> **Activity**
>
> Working in pairs, give your partner a set of instructions for carrying out a task – for example, how to get from the classroom to the main reception area, or all the resources needed to make a favourite dish.
>
> Repeat the activity, with you receiving instruction from your partner.
>
> How successful were each of you in achieving the desired outcome?

> **Activity**
>
> How many other qualities of a good instructor can you think of? Make a table and write the quality in one column and a description in the other.

However, there are times when some methods of instruction are seen as 'over-stepping the mark', as in the case study overleaf.

◯ Case study

New bullying allegations rock Army

Friday 19 September 2008

'The British Army was rocked by a new bullying scandal yesterday after an undercover BBC investigation found that training instructors were physically abusing recruits at Catterick Army base.

Five corporals have been suspended as a result of the allegations brought forth by the BBC. All five were training instructors at the barracks and now face court martial.

The film, entitled "Undercover Soldier" aired on the BBC on Thursday 18 September. In the documentary, Russell Sharp, a BBC journalist, enlists in the Army in order to uncover abuse and bullying by instructors, nearly six years after the Army had promised to put an end to any and all bullying as a result of the Deepcut deaths.

Sharp reportedly saw recruits punched and kicked for conducting their training in an improper manner. In one instance a recruit had his hand smashed while in another incident a recruit was urinated on by training instructors.

It is believed that he used tiny cameras as well as his mobile phone to film the documentary and gather evidence on the bullying allegations. Sharp clearly never had any intention of actually serving in (the) Army, rather he was there solely to make a documentary at the expense of the Army.

He was living dual lives and had to conceal his role as an undercover reporter during the six months he served in the Army.

The MoD said that the bullying allegations have been under investigation for some time.

General Sir Richard Dannatt said that robust training was acceptable but that there was no place for bullying in the Army.

"The army does not allow bullying in any shape or form. There will always be some who get it wrong – my aim is to reduce it to an absolute minimum."

Liberal Democrat shadow Defence Secretary Nick Harvey said that the latest claims of bullying were proof that the Army had failed to eradicate it despite a zero tolerance policy.

"With one in ten soldiers reporting being the subject of bullying at some point over the last year, incidents remain unacceptably high.

"Bullying is not confined to the Army and the MoD must do far more to tackle bullying across the services.

"Our soldiers deserve to be treated with dignity and respect," Harvey said.'

Source: www.publicservice.co.uk

Methods of instruction

In most organisations (including public services), there are three main methods of instruction employed; these are generally referred to as 'step-by-step', 'talk-through' and 'by-the-numbers'. A good instructor will select the appropriate method, based on what particular aspect of the skill is being taught.

In most instances, marching movements are taught using the step-by-step method; this is so that every member of the team is given the same information at the same time. Where a number of actions are being carried out consecutively or at the same time, the best method to employ is talk-through. The by-the-numbers method is usually employed when movement requiring two or more counts are being taught.

Regardless of the method used, the instructor should be consistent in the approach to the task. Each task should be presented in the following stages: explanation, demonstration and practice.

Explanation

In the explanation stage, it is vital that the instructor provides (a) the name of the movement, (b) the practical use for the movement (why it is needed), and (c) the commands for the movement.

Demonstration

Step-by-step method: in this system, the explanation and demonstration are delivered together, but the movements are taught one step at a time.

Talk-through method: the explanation and demonstration are carried out while the instructor explains the process.

By-the-numbers method: in this method, the explanation by the instructor and the demonstration are also combined. However, the movements are explained and demonstrated by individual count, one count per movement.

Demonstration stage

During the demonstration stage, the instructor may ask another person to demonstrate or they might demonstrate the movement personally; to do so, he or she might need to adjust their own position to maintain eye-to-eye contact with the personnel being taught.

Remember, there can be no alternative for knowing what you are delivering – you must be sure of the facts *and possess the skills* to carry the activity out. It is vital that you allow sufficient time to complete the activity; this includes ensuring that in each section you cover the relevant part of the lesson.

Once you are aware of the audience you are instructing and whether they have any previous knowledge of the subject, you can decide if the teaching needs to start at the absolute beginning or if you can build on existing knowledge and skills. Regardless of whether your learners possess prior knowledge, you must provide an introduction to the lesson and describe what the objectives are – in this way, they will be better equipped to understand what is required of them.

You might find that, when you get towards the middle of the lesson, some of your learners appear to lose focus. It is at this stage that you should tell them the reason this activity needs to be completed and possibly offer encouragement or a reward for successful completion.

When you have explained and demonstrated the skill, and the learners have practised enough to demonstrate that they have understood what is required, you can bring the session to a close. Remember, you need to summarise what has been achieved and also give the learners the opportunity to be involved in the feedback.

(g) Grading tip!

P4 P4 requires an explanation of the qualities of a good instructor and how these qualities are used.

How to upgrade to …

M2 To achieve M2, you will need to *demonstrate* effective instruction skills; this could be when you carried out your team-building activities. If you have the opportunity elsewhere to demonstrate these skills, you will need to provide evidence that the skills you demonstrated were effective – this might involve a video recording of you in action or a written 'witness statement' from someone in authority who has seen you demonstrate those skills.

Remember, many people have to work very hard at becoming an effective instructor, while others achieve it relatively easily. Do not be put off at the first hurdle – the effort will be worth it!

Interpersonal communication skills

Now that you have deliberated over the methods of instruction and had the opportunity to demonstrate your skills during your team-building activities, we will consider the ways in which these skills are employed within a public service of your choice.

In all public services there is a need to use interpersonal skills and to communicate effectively in many different circumstances. These range from communicating in a one-to-one situation with a colleague or a member of the public, through to addressing a very large crowd (e.g. following a disaster).

To achieve the final learning outcome, you need to investigate various *interpersonal skills* and be able to demonstrate effective interpersonal *communication* skills.

Communication is an essential part of most people's everyday lives; ask someone to describe communication and they would probably tell you it is about talking with another person. However, it is also vital that the skills of effective listening are developed. Studies have revealed that, during the communication process, the average person spends between 45 and 55 per cent of the time listening. So it would seem that to be the most effective communicator, you should ensure that you speak and listen.

There are four stages in effective communication; each is linked to the statement in the 'Key term' box.

Activity

List as many situations as you can think of where effective communication is needed in one public service.

When you have written down as many as you can, compare with another person in the group who has chosen the same service. Are there any more to add?

Key term

Communication is the giving *and* receiving of information.

Transmission   **Reception**

Feedback   **Understanding**

Figure 1.7 Stages of effective communication

1. Transmission: how information is sent – spoken, written, signals, body language.
2. Reception: how information is received – hearing, reading, watching, feeling.
3. Understanding: does the receiver understand the information? Has the information been sent using an appropriate method? Can it be easily understood?
4. Feedback: this is the response you receive, confirming understanding.

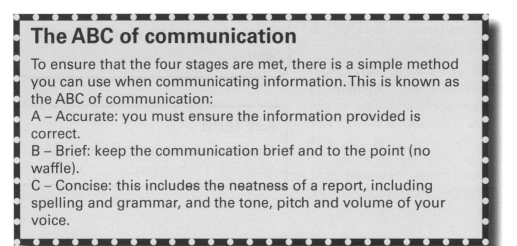

The ABC of communication

To ensure that the four stages are met, there is a simple method you can use when communicating information. This is known as the ABC of communication:

A – Accurate: you must ensure the information provided is correct.

B – Brief: keep the communication brief and to the point (no waffle).

C – Concise: this includes the neatness of a report, including spelling and grammar, and the tone, pitch and volume of your voice.

Methods of communication used in public services

There are many ways in which members of the public services communicate, both within the organisation and when dealing with other agencies and members of the public. These include:

- landline telephones
- e-mail or computer messaging services
- mobile telephones
- pagers
- radios
- intercoms/public addresses
- alarm activations
- incident reports
- witness statements
- fire reports
- search registers
- accident logs/reports
- briefings/meetings
- staff meetings
- memoranda
- bulletins
- newsletters
- posters
- signs
- signals
- notice boards
- postal/courier services.

The phonetic alphabet and radio transmissions

One of the most common pieces of equipment employed by the public services to enable them to communicate with each other is the radio. There are set procedures for radio use.

The first thing to be aware of is the phonetic alphabet. This is used by all public services, as well as in other employment. It is a tried and tested method of communicating and is designed to eliminate errors on the part of the person receiving the information.

The phonetic alphabet is as follows:

A	Alpha	J	Juliet	S	Sierra
B	Bravo	K	Kilo	T	Tango
C	Charlie	L	Lima	U	Uniform
D	Delta	M	Mike	V	Victor
E	Echo	N	November	W	Whisky
F	Foxtrot	O	Oscar	X	X-ray
G	Golf	P	Papa	Y	Yankee
H	Hotel	Q	Quebec	Z	Zulu
I	India	R	Romeo		

There is also a correct way of pronouncing numbers:

0	Ze-ro	4	For-wer	8	Ate
1	Wun	5	Fi-yiv	9	Niner
2	Too	6	Six	10	Wun-zero
3	Thruh-ree	7	Seven		

Activity

Working in pairs, both write a short message that you wish to transmit to your partner.

Make sure the message includes numbers and letters that need to be spelled out – for example, time of day, registration plate, date of birth.

Now, with one of you sitting each side of a screen, relay the message to your partner. (They must write down the message they receive.)

Repeat the exercise, with your partner transmitting and you receiving the message.

How straightforward did you find the activity? Did you both manage to record the message as it had been transmitted?

If you just need to transmit information, then understanding and being able to use the phonetic alphabet effectively is probably sufficient. However, within most organisations (including the public services), you need to know that the information that was transmitted was received accurately (without meeting the other person to check). There is also a need to exchange information, thereby operating a two-way conversation. You also need to make it clear to the listener that you have finished transmitting and that you are waiting for their response.

Pro words

Easily pronounced words or phrases may be used to convey an exact meaning between operators, thus avoiding unnecessary repetition. For example, RECEIVED is used to signify 'I have received and understood your last transmission.'

Some commonly used pro words are shown in Table 1.1.

Pro word	Meaning
OVER	This is the end of my transmission to you and *a response is necessary*.
OUT	This is the end of my transmission – *no reply is necessary*.
OUT TO YOU	I am finished with you and am about to call another station – *do not reply*.
RECEIVED	I have received *and understood* your last transmission – it will be acted upon where necessary.
SAY AGAIN	Repeat your last transmission.
WAIT or STANDBY	I am unable to reply immediately – normally followed by an indication of time, e.g. WAIT = one minute.
ETA	Estimated time of arrival.
ETD	Estimated time of departure.

Table 1.1 Commonly used pro words

The importance of good communication

The importance of good communication cannot be over-emphasised. Within the public services, poor communication could have devastating effects, even resulting in injury or death.

Good communication provides many benefits, including the ability to deal with organisational matters and the ability to interact with colleagues, other agencies and members of the public.

The benefits might also include the following:

- Reports are completed on time.
- Customers are dealt with promptly, thereby reducing tension.
- Those receiving the information have a clearer understanding.
- Time wastage from needing to repeat information is cut back.
- Problems are dealt with more efficiently.
- Tasks are carried out more efficiently.
- Details of situations are passed to the appropriate person promptly.
- Investigations and enquiries can be concluded in reasonable time.

Barriers to communication

There are several reasons why people fail to receive or understand information transmitted to them, and you should be fully aware of these.

First, you need to consider the type of communication to be transmitted, its circulation and how it is best communicated. For example, if there has been a spill of a hazardous chemical on a motorway and the road needs to be closed, the information will usually be broadcast on radio stations. The information is then likely to be received by many motorists (those who will be affected) far quicker than using other methods of transmission. In this way, some motorists will take another route to avoid the scene, thereby reducing the time taken to clear the backlog of traffic after the spill has been dealt with.

Barriers to communication include:

- poor or faulty equipment
- inadequate training
- poor literacy skills
- speech impediments
- accents/dialects
- incorrect documents used
- failure to complete documents
- slang
- jargon
- damage to signs/notices
- nervousness
- anxiety
- complacency.

We can now move on to examine the ways in which information may be processed. This includes verbal and non-verbal communication, reading, writing and listening, and also communication by technical means.

- Reading – used for receiving information.
- Writing – used for giving information.
- Verbal communication – used for giving information.
- Listening – used for receiving information.
- Non-verbal communication – used for giving and receiving information.
- Technical skills – used for giving and receiving information.

Activity

In pairs, think about the communication you have sent and received today. Copy and complete Table 1.2 below.

Type of communication	Sent or received	Message
Visual		
Written		
Verbal		
Non-verbal		
Technical		

Table 1.2 Types of communication

Each of these types of communication can be broken down further and might include the following:

- Language (spoken) – face-to-face, by telephone, video, web cam.
- Signing – British Sign Language, pointing, 'thumbs-up'.
- Body language – hand gestures, frowns, smiles, shrugging of shoulders.
- Written language – letters, texts, e-mails, reports, newspapers.
- Technical – e-mails, texts, radio, fax.

Verbal communication

Now we have identified methods of communication, we will focus on how effective these are in different situations.

High levels of communication and interpersonal skills are essential in order to work in the public services. These are the skills that are needed to build strong relationships, not only with members of your own team, but with others inside the organisation and also members of the public. The incorrect passage of information can have disastrous effects on the outcome. Therefore, it is important for us to communicate information effectively, and to the appropriate person.

Verbal communication comprises three main features – words, the way they are used and associated body language. Research has demonstrated that these features are made up as shown in Figure 1.8.

Non-verbal communication

This is the way we communicate with each other without the need for words to be uttered. Non-verbal communication is also known as body language.

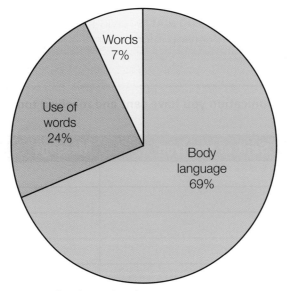

Figure 1.8 The communication wheel

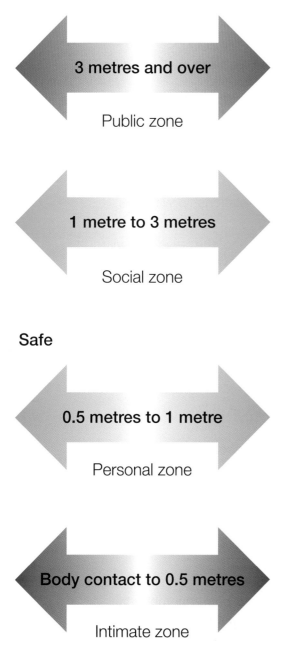

Public zone
As strangers in public areas, we feel most comfortable with a gap between us of 3 metres and over

Social zone
This is the area in which we are happy to interact with stragers.

Personal zone
This is the space in which people operate in a personal (but not intimate) relationship. If strangers come within this space, we are likely to feel uncomfortable.

Intimate zone
In a close and intimate relationship, we will be comfortable interacting from body contact to 0.5 metres.

Figure 1.9 Four zones of interaction

Body language can be divided into the following main areas:

- Gesture – any action that sends a visual signal to an onlooker.
- Touch – how, who and where we touch all convey meaning.
- Posture – how we stand or walk can convey information.
- Facial expression – the face can convey a great deal of information.
- Dress – in all societies, clothes send out all sorts of information about the wearer.
- Eye contact – patterns of gaze play an important role in establishing relations between people.
- Proxemics – this is our personal space; how close we let people approach can convey much information about our relationship with them.

Non-verbal communication has become a science and the seven main areas listed above can be sub-divided even further. However, all these areas interact with each other and should not be considered in isolation.

Proxemics

Everyone has his or her own personal territorial needs. These may vary from time to time depending on several factors and they also differ between cultures. The term 'proxemics' was first introduced by the American anthropologist Edward Hall, in 1963, to describe measurable distances between people as they interact. Hall's work has led to the identification of four zones of interaction.

You should always be conscious of the space between yourself and potential conflict. There is a relationship between distance and the time you need to react to a situation; this is called the reactionary gap.

- To cover two metres takes less than half a second.
- To cover four metres takes less than one second.
- To cover six metres takes less than one-and-a-half seconds.

Behaviour patterns

Another aspect of communication concerns *behaviour patterns*; these fall into three main categories. Being able to identify the patterns associated with each type of behaviour will allow you to cope with a range of situations. Within the public services, it is important that these behaviours are identified at an early stage to prevent any situation escalating into violence.

Behaviour patterns can be broken down into three categories: aggressive behaviour, passive behaviour and assertive behaviour.

Aggressive behaviour includes the following:

- finger-wagging
- putting others down
- making assumptions

- interrupting
- glaring
- threatening
- shouting
- being sarcastic
- stating opinion as fact
- blaming
- giving orders.

When faced with aggressive behaviour, the situation should be approached with caution, as it could soon become confrontational. However, attempts could be made to diffuse the situation before it escalates.

These might include saying, 'I understand what you are saying', 'Yes, I know, how can I help?' or 'Please don't shout, I'm here to help.'

Passive behaviour can be identified by the presence of any of the following:

- apologising a lot
- not making eye contact
- rambling speech
- agreeing to things they do not want to do
- fidgeting
- backing down
- using negative phrases
- always smiling
- putting themselves down.

This type of behaviour can be deceptive and care should be taken not to 'go along with' what is being said or suggested. This type of behaviour is commonly associated with guilt and the person is trying to make you feel sorry for them.

Assertive behaviour is about making it clear what you want; it might include giving reasons for why you want this, and stating the consequences of not getting it. The following traits are examples of assertive behaviour:

- having a relaxed posture and facial expression – standing your ground
- making others aware of your feelings or thoughts – being firm but fair
- discussing possible solutions to a problem – being courteous and polite
- providing possible solutions to a problem – using positive language
- acknowledging others' viewpoints – using clear, steady speech.

Assertiveness is the preferred behaviour for those employed in the public services. It demonstrates a high degree of professionalism and it gets the job done. People tend to listen more intently to someone who is being assertive, so they will have a clearer understanding of the message that is being put across. They will also feel more comfortable with the person who is displaying assertive behaviour because assertiveness can also indicate self-control and confidence. This, in turn, will lead to the public having more confidence in and respect for the public services.

Writing

It is important to remember that communication is the interaction and sending and receiving of messages between people. The person who has provided the information might not always be present when the receiver accepts it. You might write a letter to a prospective employer but you will hope that, when the letter is read, the employer will obtain from it what you intended. When communicating in writing, it is essential that the information is clear and that the reader will understand.

Within the public services, there are many occasions when written communication is employed; the style of writing will vary, depending on the nature of document and the intended audience. For example, a letter in response to a complaint from a member of the public will differ from a memorandum sent by a police sergeant to members of the rota, advising them of changes to their duty the next day.

Some members of the public services need to write reports to senior officers, following incidents or investigations. These documents need to be more formal than e-mail, in which the officer may provide basic information that was requested or notes taken at a meeting. Another example of written communication in the public services is a press release, which can be accessed by many thousands of people.

Rules for writing

Whatever the reason for the written communication, it is vital that spelling and grammar are correct. There are so many rules associated with writing that it would not be possible to list them all here, so here are a few basic ones to get you started.

- Do not abbreviate (not everyone will understand).
- Make sure there are no words left out (it is very easy to do).
- Be careful to use adjectives and adverbs correctly.
- No double negatives!
- Be very careful with commas (plurals do not need them).
- Talking of plurals, remember (usually) 'y' becomes 'i' and add 'es'.
- 'i' before 'e' except after 'c' (there are other exceptions!).

Can you think of any other 'rules' that help you when you are writing something? Remember, when you send your application form to your chosen service, you will want to ensure that the person reading it is very impressed with what you have produced and, as a result, will call you for interview.

Public service documents

Letters

Each public service has its own particular way of writing documents; this includes the layout and the way in which the information is organised. Most of the letters are formal in manner, although this might be toned down a little if a senior officer is expressing their thanks to another within the same organisation – for example, when the recipient has performed a task in a way that has led to a successful outcome for the service.

Memo

A memo (short for memorandum – plural, memoranda) is a document, usually brief in nature, sent inside organisations. In your school or college, this could be your teacher or tutor sending a memo to the head of department or head of house. The purpose of a memo is to pass on information in a concise manner and in a way that can be understood by the recipient. As with letters, the layout of a memo is determined by the organisation in which it is used; this could include a pre-printed pad (for handwritten messages) or a template that is used for sending a memo electronically (e.g. via e-mail).

Although the memo is less formal than a letter, there is usually a degree of formality in the layout. Memos are usually brief but can extend to two or more pages. In some cases, it might be necessary to include sub-headings within a lengthy memo.

Reports

The purpose of a report can be to make others aware of the outcome of an incident or investigation; on the other hand, it could be used to inform the entire workforce of a change in policy. A report is always written in a formal manner and might include tables or charts (e.g. if used to provide statistics).

Rules for report writing

Reports should include:
- the time and date the report was completed
- the author of the report
- the addressee
- a title.

The box opposite includes a set of rules for report writing, although these rules apply equally to all forms of written communication.

Whatever the reason for producing a written document, there are some standards that must always be maintained. These include the need for *accuracy* in spelling and punctuation. The *facts* must be as you believe them to be true (if unsure, you should always make the effort to test the facts out).

The language used in the document should be clear, precise and instantly recognisable by the reader; regional slang must be avoided. The writer should maintain the appropriate format for the document. If the document goes over more than one page, the pages should be numbered and any quotes should be referenced.

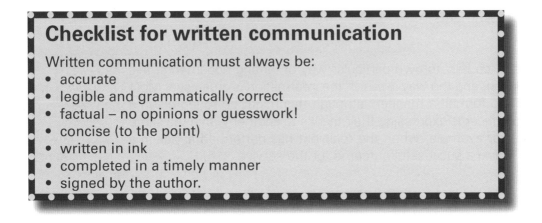

Checklist for written communication

Written communication must always be:
- accurate
- legible and grammatically correct
- factual – no opinions or guesswork!
- concise (to the point)
- written in ink
- completed in a timely manner
- signed by the author.

Reading

For every piece of written communication, there is a reader. Within the public services, there is a need to read and disseminate a wealth of information in this way. Examples include the complaint letter that was mentioned earlier, your application form, a newspaper article or a new piece of legislation that affects the way in which the public services operate.

Effective readers learn to use many styles of reading for different purposes, depending on the purpose of reading. For example, if you are exploring or reviewing a document to use in your assignments, you might *skim* it; if you are searching for particular information, you might *scan* the document until you recognise a particular word or phrase that relates to your subject. When reading large quantities of information, these techniques are more practical than reading every word within the document.

Skimming is used to identify quickly the main ideas that are contained within a document. When you read an article in a magazine, you probably do not read every word; instead, you are skimming the surface. Skimming is about three or four times faster than if you read every word. People might skim when they have a number of documents to read in a defined space of time.

There are many strategies that people use when skimming. Some might read the first and last paragraph; others might read the title, sub-headings and look at the illustrations. It is useful to read the first sentence of each paragraph; in this way, you can identify, for example, dates, names and places. Skimming is particularly useful when used to review tables, graphs or charts.

When you look through a telephone directory or dictionary, you are scanning the pages; usually you know what you are looking for and have a reasonable idea of where you will find it. When you scan, your eyes move quickly down the page in search of specific words or phrases. Once you have scanned the document, if you have found anything you think is useful, you might go back and skim it for more detail.

It is becoming more common to receive documents electronically, as a text or e-mail that can be read on a BlackBerry® or computer screen. Although reading a document on screen can be achieved at the same speed as on paper, research has shown that people have more difficulty in skimming a document on screen and it is a much slower process.

Figure 1.10 It is now quite common to read documents on electronic devices, such as a BlackBerry®

Tips for reading

- Use skimming when carrying out research for your assignments; this will enable you to decide if the content is suitable to meet the criteria.
- Scanning is a useful tool when you first find a resource to help you decide whether it is worth a closer look.
- Some authors use numbers, letters or the words 'first', 'second', or 'next' to distinguish important points.
- Look for words that are printed in **bold**, CAPITALS, *italics*, or in a different font or colour.

Listening

In the public services, it is essential that all communication skills are employed to good effect. Possibly the most important of all is the ability to listen. By being a good listener, you can be sure that the information is received effectively. This is absolutely vital when taking a statement of what someone has seen. You are also more likely to be able to carry out orders to good effect and to use the correct terminology when passing on information.

 Grading tip!

P5 P5 requires you to report on the effectiveness of various methods of interpersonal communication skills.

P6 For P6, you need to use the correct terminology employed in one of the public services.

P7 To achieve P7, you need to use interpersonal skills to communicate with personnel in public service situations.

End of unit knowledge check

1. Describe the communication cycle.
2. Explain six barriers to effective communication.
3. What is the step-by-step method of instruction?
4. Explain when you would use the skills of skimming and scanning.
5. Describe when you would use a memorandum.

How to upgrade to ...

 M3 To achieve M3, you need to *explain* the application of interpersonal communication skills in a chosen public service.

 D2 For D2, you need to *evaluate* the effective use of interpersonal and communication skills in a given public service.

Grading criteria

In order to pass this unit, the evidence that the learner presents for assessment needs to demonstrate that they can meet all the learning outcomes for the unit. The assessment criteria for a pass grade describe the level of achievement required to pass this unit.

Grading criteria		
To achieve a pass grade the evidence must show that the learner is able to:	**To achieve a merit grade the evidence must show that, in addition to the pass criteria, the learner is able to:**	**To achieve a distinction grade the evidence must show that, in addition to the pass and merit criteria, the learner is able to:**
P1 Describe public service skills		
P2 Outline the purpose and importance of public service skills using examples from at least two contrasting public services	**M1** Explain the importance of public service skills in at least two contrasting public services	**D1** Evaluate the importance of public service skills in a specified public service
P3 Contribute to different team-building activities		
P4 Explain the qualities of a good instructor and how they are used	**M2** Demonstrate effective instruction skills	
P5 Report on the effectiveness of various methods of interpersonal communication skills	**M3** Explain the application of interpersonal communication skills in a given public service	**D2** Evaluate the effective use of interpersonal communication skills in a given public service
P6 Use correct terminology in a given public service communication context		
P7 Use interpersonal skills to communicate with personnel in public service situations		

Unit 2
Employment in the uniformed public services

Introduction

If you are reading this, it probably means that you are interested in joining one of the uniformed public services. This may be for one of several reasons. It could be something you have always wanted to do; it could be because a relative of yours was in the public services and you are following in their footsteps; or it could be because you have seen the action-packed 'fly on the wall' television programmes that show the services in everyday situations. Whatever the reason, you are probably attracted to the idea of wearing a uniform and doing a job that is exciting and varied – chasing criminals, fighting fires or patrolling the streets in a foreign country on a peacekeeping mission.

Even if you have a clear idea of which service you want to join, it is important that you find out as much as you can about the service so that you can be fully prepared when the time comes to apply. You also need to know about all of the other services as you may find another service out there that appeals to you that you were previously unaware of.

You will probably be aware of some of the work carried out by the police, the fire service or the Army. However, these services carry out other work that you may not be aware of. Do you know what the UK Border Agency service does? Do you know the difference between the Royal Navy and the Royal Marines?

This unit will give you an overview of the different uniformed services in order to help you to make your career choice. You can then carry out your own research and study some of these in more detail. You will learn about the different jobs that exist within the services, what would be expected of you if you were to join and what you would receive in return.

Figure 2.1 Firefighters

Learning outcomes:

By the end of this unit, you should:

1. Know the main roles of different uniformed public services

2. Understand the main responsibilities of different uniformed public services

3. Understand the different employment opportunities available in the uniformed public services

4. Know the conditions of service for different public service jobs.

What is a public service?

A public service is a non-profit making organisation, which has been set up to protect or help people. Most public services are funded by the government, using money paid in tax by members of the public. These public services are classed as 'statutory' services, which means they are required to exist by law. Non-statutory services are those services that are not required by law and that are usually self-funded, such as charities. Both statutory and non-statutory services can be either uniformed or non-uniformed, which can be confusing!

Take a look at Table 2.1, which lists the main public services.

Uniformed services	Non-uniformed services
Police service	Social Services
Ambulance service	Education service
Fire service	Probation service
Army	Youth services
Royal Air Force	Refuse collection services
Royal Navy	Leisure services
Royal Marines	Civil service
Customs and Excise	Victim Support
Mountain/cave rescue	Environmental health
Coastguard	Highways service
Prison service	Housing services
National Health Service	National Health Service

Table 2.1 Main public services

Sometimes there is a cross-over between uniformed and non-uniformed services, and between statutory and non-statutory services. For example, think about the National Health Service. Is this funded by public taxes? Yes, absolutely, so this is definitely a statutory service. But is it uniformed or non-uniformed? Nurses wear a uniform, some hospital doctors wear a uniform, but many consultants in hospitals and doctors in local surgeries do not normally wear one. You will see that the mountain and cave rescue service is listed under 'uniformed services'. Members of this service do wear a uniform but this is not a statutory service. This service is funded by charitable donations and the service is operated by volunteers.

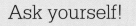

Ask yourself!

What do you think a public service is? How many examples can you think of?

Ask yourself!

Which of the services listed in Table 2.1 are statutory and which are non-statutory?

Purposes, roles and responsibilities   P1 P2 M1 D1

Every uniformed public service has a main purpose, roles and responsibilities.

> ## Key terms
>
> The **purpose** of a public service is the overall aim of the service, which is laid down by law.
>
> A **role** is the behaviour or duty expected of an individual or organisation. For a public service, this is what they actually do.
>
> A **responsibility** is a duty, obligation or liability for which someone is accountable. The responsibilities of a public service are to carry out their duties fairly, effectively and efficiently.

Let us look at these in more detail.

Purpose – overall aim of the service, laid down by law

In the UK, we have laws that govern the powers and responsibilities of the main public services. Examples of such laws are the Police and Criminal Evidence Act 1984, the Police Reform Act 2002 and the Armed Forces Discipline Act 2004.

Many services have a mission statement or 'vision' which sets out what their main purpose is. We will take a look at some of these later.

Roles – what the service actually does

Most of the public services perform more than one role. For instance, you may think the main role of the fire service is to put out fires, but there are many other roles within the fire service. These include the prevention of fires, educating people about how to avoid fires, visiting schools and colleges to talk about fire safety, inspecting premises and gathering evidence for court. Similarly, the armed forces are trained to fight when necessary, but they also provide an important peacekeeping role and can also be called on to perform other duties, such as refuse collection and firefighting in the event of industrial disputes, and also humanitarian roles in the event of earthquakes.

Responsibilities – how the service performs

Public services are paid for mainly by the public through taxation, including income tax, VAT and local council taxes. This brings certain responsibilities and makes the services 'answerable' or 'accountable' to the public, who need to know they are getting good value for their money. This means that public services need to keep written records of everything they do for other people to inspect. The uniformed public services have to show account-ability in three ways:

1. Legally, which means strictly following the law.

2. Professionally, which means doing the job in a fair, efficient and conscientious manner.
3. Politically, which means following government order, irrespective of which political party is in power.

Public services are governed by councils or committees who monitor their performance to ensure that they are acting fairly, effectively and efficiently. There are other groups who also keep an eye on the services and how they are performing. These include pressure groups such as Greenpeace, the Commission for Racial Equality and Members of Parliament. It is important to remember, however, that the public services are responsible to society generally, and are monitored closely by central government and local government, who set performance targets and ensure that the services meet their responsibilities.

Public services are subject to cuts in funding. Increased workload and shortage of money and resources can have a detrimental effect on the public services. Also, the responsibilities of the public services can change as society and public opinion changes.

Assignment tip

Uniformed services can be split into emergency services (fire, police, ambulance), armed services (Army, Royal Navy, Royal Marines, Royal Air Force) and other services (for example prison service, coastguard service). Sometimes your assignment task will ask you to describe 'contrasting services'. This means choosing services from the different types of service.

NB – when using the internet for research, always add 'UK' to your search to make sure you find services in the UK.

Activity

Is your local police service giving good value for money? Go online and find out how the service performed last year? Have crime rates in your area fallen? What were their performance rates?

Emergency services – the police service

Purpose of the police service

The Police and Criminal Evidence Act 1984 is a law that governs police powers; the Police Reform Act 2002 was brought in to make the police more efficient and cost effective and to give powers to community support officers. In recent years, the police service, along with other public services, has become more accountable and answerable to the public, who provide funding to pay for such services.

There are 43 police services in England and Wales and they all share the same purpose.

The purpose of the police service is:

- to uphold the law fairly and firmly
- to prevent crime
- to pursue and bring to justice those who break the law
- to keep the Queen's Peace
- to protect, help and reassure the community
- to be seen to do all this with integrity, common sense and sound judgement.

Mission statements

Most police services have a mission statement, which sets out how they will achieve their purpose and what that particular service sees as its own priorities, which may differ from area to area. Let us look at one of these. The following is the City of London Police mission statement.

Figure 2.2 Policeman

'*Policing the City 24 hours*

We will provide a high quality police service in the City of London and work with the community, other organisations and agencies, to promote a safe, peaceful and crime free environment.

Our values:
- To be sensitive, open and fair to the public and our own staff
- To encourage equal opportunities
- To encourage participation and consult the public and our staff
- To treat people as individuals
- To act with honesty, compassion, courtesy and patience.

Force priorities:
- **Deter criminal terrorist activity**
  Responsibility: Head of counter terrorism and serious crime
- **Deter economic crime activity**
  Responsibility: Head of economic crime
- **Prevent, deter and positively respond to public disorder**
  Responsibility: Head of counter terrorism and serious crime
- **Provide high quality community policing**
  Responsibility: Head of territorial policing.'

Source: www.cityoflondon.police.uk © Crown copyright material is reproduced with the permission of the Controller of HMSO and the Queen's Printer for Scotland.

Roles of the police service

When we talk about the roles of the police, we mean the work that they do and services that they provide. Most of us know that the police 'catch criminals', but do you know about all the other work that they do?

How many roles did you think of? The following list contains just some of the roles – there are others. Roles of the police include:

- responding to emergencies
- crime prevention
- crime investigation
- paperwork
- anti-terrorism
- giving evidence in court
- visiting schools
- reducing the fear of crime
- improving community relations
- escorting abnormal loads
- licensing of pubs and clubs
- providing government statistics
- investigating missing persons
- community safety
- firearms licensing
- drugs raids.

Figure 2.3 Don't stop that thief – it's too much paperwork!

Responsibilities of the police service

The 'Responsibilities' section at the beginning of this unit (page 33) mentions the legal, professional and political responsibilities of public services. The police are also accountable and answerable to the local police authority and the government. The mission statement of each service usually details how the service aims to deliver its policing in order to meet these responsibilities. The police are banned from striking or taking other industrial action by an Act of Parliament.

The police have been criticised for their handling of certain incidents and have been accused of failing to meet their responsibilities (see case study).

Case study

One case where the police were criticised involved the killing of a black British teenager from South-east London called Stephen Lawrence. Stephen was stabbed to death while waiting for a bus on the evening of 22 April 1993. The Metropolitan Police investigated the murder but no-one was ever convicted and the police were accused of negligence and of handling the case badly. An inquiry into this case stated that the Metropolitan Police Force was 'institutionally racist' and new policies and procedures were introduced nationally to govern police conduct.

- Carry out research to find out the full details of this case.
- What do you think is meant by 'institutionally racist'?
- What has been the effect of this case on the UK's police forces?

The government has now introduced a new national Policing Pledge, which demonstrates how the police are accountable to the public.

The Policing Pledge is a new set of promises from the police on the service they should provide and every force has committed to keeping those promises. The police promise to listen to your concerns, act on these concerns and then keep you informed of the progress they have made. Each neighbourhood will have local priorities, as agreed by the community.

Activity

The following list is made up of purposes, roles and responsibilities of the police service. State which are purposes, which are roles and which are responsibilities.

- **Reduce crime and bring offenders to justice.**
- **Work to create safer communities.**
- **Give good value for money.**
- **Uphold the law.**
- **Patrol the streets.**
- **Reduce crime.**
- **Create a safer community.**
- **Improve public confidence.**
- **Police the roads.**
- **Target violent crime.**
- **Carry out drugs raids.**
- **Advise on security.**

Ask yourself!

Should the police have targets for the number of bookings or arrests they make?

Grading tip!

P1 For P1, you need to choose two contrasting services and describe their main roles and purpose as shown above.

P2 For P2, you should talk about the responsibilities and accountabilities of these two services.

M1 For M1, a more detailed explanation of the above

two services is required (i.e. how and why the services do what they do).

D1 For D1, you need to evaluate the roles, purpose and responsibilities of one service. This means looking at how well the service performs its roles and responsibilities. You could find statistics to help with this.

How to upgrade to M1 if your chosen service is the police

M1 When upgrading to M1, you could explain in detail the main purpose and roles of the police. What methods do the police use to prevent crime? What things do they do to make communities safer? How do they improve public confidence? How much time do police officers spend on completing paperwork? Look on the different police websites and find out what the priorities and objectives of each constabulary are. How do they compare? Do they give good value for money? Find statistics on performance targets and compare these. Refer to and discuss cases, such as the Stephen Lawrence case or the G20 Summit incidents.

How to upgrade to D1 if your chosen service is the police

D1 To achieve the D1 grade, you should focus on one of your two services and provide some evaluation on this service. When writing about the police, you could look at the McPherson Report into the Stephen Lawrence case and discuss the implications of this. Explain if and how the police have changed their policies and practices since publication of the report. When examining performance targets, you could discuss the implications of police having targets to meet. Should there be more police officers on the beat? Should their time be spent completing paperwork? What do you think about the role of the police community support officers?

Emergency services – the fire and rescue service

Purpose of the fire and rescue service

Why do we have fire and rescue services? The Fire and Rescue Services Act 2004 governs the fire and rescue services, formerly known as the fire services. There are 45 fire and rescue services in England and they all have similar aims and purposes, as follows:

- firefighting
- fire safety
- protecting life and property
- attending road traffic accidents
- other rescues.

Figure 2.4 Fire and rescue services

Most fire and rescue services have a mission statement or vision. Greater Manchester Fire and Rescue Service state their vision as follows:

'Our vision is to make Greater Manchester a safer place by being a modern, community focused and influential Fire and Rescue Authority.'

Source: www.manchesterfire.gov.uk © Crown copyright material is reproduced with the permission of the Controller of HMSO and the Queen's Printer for Scotland.

Activity

Find three other mission statements from fire and rescue services and compare them.

Roles of the fire and rescue service

What exactly do the fire and rescue services do? We all know that the fire and rescue services attend fires, but they also undertake many other roles. The roles of the service include:

- putting out fires
- preventing fires
- investigating fires
- inspecting premises for fire regulations
- fire safety education
- rescuing people from road traffic accidents
- flood rescue
- decontamination training
- attending court to give evidence
- protecting the environment

- disaster management
- animal rescue
- fitting smoke detectors in homes.

Responsibilities of the fire and rescue service

Activity

Carry out research to find out exactly what is involved in carrying out the roles of the fire and rescue services.

All fire and rescue services have a professional responsibility to provide an efficient and effective service to the public. They should ensure that they recruit fairly and that their workforce is as diverse as possible. They are accountable to the taxpayers who help to pay for these services and they should keep records to show that taxpayers' money is being spent efficiently. They are also accountable to the local authority and central government, which also provide funding and monitor their overall performance.

All 45 services have legal responsibilities and have to abide by the laws that govern them. The main piece of law is the Fire and Rescue Services Act 2004.

Fire and rescue services also have a political responsibility in that they have to follow the policies of whichever government is in power. Unlike the police, the fire and rescue services can take industrial action, including going on strike. When this happens, the armed forces have to be called in to take over their firefighting role.

Ask yourself!

Do you think that the fire and rescue services should be allowed to go on strike?

How to upgrade to M1 if your chosen service is the fire and rescue service

M1 To get a higher grade, when talking about the responsibilities of the fire and rescue service, you could search on the internet and find the performance reports of two different fire and rescue services. You should find facts and figures for each service. You could then compare and contrast the two services.

When talking about roles, you should explain in detail the different roles of the service and give examples. For instance, instead of just saying that one of the roles is educating the community about fire safety, you should explain how they do this (i.e. by going into schools and colleges, old people's homes, hospitals, etc.).

You should also explain in detail what their other roles involve. For example, the name 'fire and rescue service', which changed from the 'fire service', reflects the many rescue operations that the service is involved in every year. What are the daily routine tasks that firefighters undertake? Firefighters are frequently called out to cut injured people out of vehicles that have been involved in collisions. This requires specialist equipment and training so as not to further injure the occupants of the vehicle. A typical rescue operation for the service could involve using metal cutters to free someone who has managed to get their head stuck between some railings!

How to upgrade to M1 if your chosen service is the fire and rescue service (continued)

What are the risks and dangers involved in fighting fires? Can you find some statistics showing how many firefighters lose their lives doing their job? Give some examples of incidents the fire and rescue services have been involved in and describe how they work closely with the other emergency services.

Fire inspections of public premises involve annual visits from the service to check that all fire procedures and equipment are adequate in case of a fire. If systems or equipment are not satisfactory, the building can be closed down by the service.

How to upgrade to D1 if your chosen service is the fire and rescue service

D1 For this grade, you need to evaluate the roles, purpose and responsibilities of one service. This means looking at how well one service performs its role and responsibilities. How well do you think this service is performing? You could compare and contrast government statistics on performance of different services for the M1 grade, then focus on one of these services for the D1 grade. How does the service spend its funding from the government? What are their priorities and objectives? How do these differ from other fire and rescue services? What is the service doing to ensure that they recruit a diverse workforce? What changes are taking place within the service, if any?

Emergency services – the paramedic/ambulance service

P1 **P2** **M1** **D1**

Purpose of the paramedic/ambulance service

The main purposes of the paramedic/ambulance service are:

- responding to emergency calls
- responding to less serious calls
- infection prevention and control
- taking patients to hospital for appointments
- dealing with major incidents.

Figure 2.5 Paramedics

Roles of the paramedic/ambulance service

Roles of the paramedic/ambulance service include:

- responding to 999 calls for medical assistance at accidents, emergencies and other incidents
- treating patients in the ambulance while they are being transferred to hospital from the scene
- driving and crewing an ambulance or other rapid response vehicle
- administering medical help at the scene of the emergency.

Responsibilities of the paramedic/ambulance service

As with other public services, paramedics have the same professional, legal and political responsibilities as other services, described earlier. Professional responsibilities include:

- meeting targets for response times and saving of lives
- being available for emergency cover at all times
- being accountable to the primary healthcare trust
- acting fairly and efficiently.

How to upgrade to M1 if your chosen service is the paramedic/ambulance service

M1 To get an M1 grade, you should expand on the information above and explain in more detail about the responsibilities of the service. You should explain in more detail about the professional, legal and political responsibilities, describing how the service should keep records that show how they are meeting their targets for response times, etc. You should look at more than one paramedic/ambulance service and compare and contrast these, using statistics from their websites or information obtained directly from the services.

When talking about the roles of the service, you should explain in detail exactly what is involved in the day-to-day routine tasks. Give examples of incidents that the service may be involved in and how they work closely with the other emergency services.

How to upgrade to D1 if your chosen service is the paramedic/ambulance service

D1 For the D1 grade, you should focus on just one of the two services you have written about and provide some evaluation. This means you could carry out research and explain what the priorities or objectives of the service are and how the service is meeting its performance targets. You could also describe how the paramedics work closely with the other emergency services and give examples of such incidents.

Case study

'Name: Bianca Smith
Job Title: Paramedic
Location: Borders

Bianca, is 30 and works in the Scottish Borders as a paramedic. She comes from the Borders and is as proud of her roots there as she is of her job. "I've been with the Scottish Ambulance Service for over nine years and I'm very proud to be part of it," she says. Recently, she has taken on new responsibilities for training within her station. She also goes out to deliver emergency first-aid instruction to local community groups and organisations. Outside work, her job with the NHS leaves her enough time and energy to enjoy walking, swimming, cycling and "a deep involvement in a local youth organisation". Last summer, she led a group of 24 young people and 10 adults on an expedition to Vietnam where they helped carry out community, environmental and cultural work. Why does she do the job she does? "It's a mixture of the pleasure gained from helping people," says Bianca. "That, and the interest that each day brings and having an ability to pass on my skills and knowledge of first aid to the local community."'

Source: www.infoscotland.com

Armed forces

The Ministry of Defence (MoD) is the headquarters of the British armed forces – that is, the Army, the Royal Navy (including the Royal Marines) and the Royal Air Force.

Purpose of the armed forces

The MoD has an overall vision, which applies to all the armed forces. Each service usually has its own mission statement, which says how they will carry out the MoD vision. The MoD vision is achieved over land (the Army), in the air (the Royal Air Force) and on the sea (the Royal Navy), but all three services frequently work together to achieve their aims.

Figure 2.6 Armed forces personnel

'The key principles which provide the basis of work for Defence:

- Defending the United Kingdom and its interests.
- Strengthening international peace and stability.

A force for good in the world

- Providing strategy that matches new threats and instabilities.
- Maintaining flexible force structures.
- Reaching out into the wider world.
- Investing in our people.

By holding true to these principles we will move forward together to maintain and enhance our capability.'

Source: www.mod.uk © Crown copyright material is reproduced with the permission of the Controller of HMSO and the Queen's Printer for Scotland.

Main role of the armed forces

The main role of the armed forces is to defend our country. This could be by acting as a deterrent because other countries can see that we have a strong Army, Navy and RAF. It could also mean fighting for our country, if necessary. Currently, our services are fighting a group called the Taliban in Afghanistan. They also carry out peacekeeping activities to prevent fighting in certain countries where there is a risk of unrest.

The British armed forces carry out humanitarian work after major disasters such as earthquakes or floods.

The Royal Air Force

The Royal Air Force (RAF) is the United Kingdom's air force and is the oldest air force in the world. The RAF played a significant part in the Second World War and has played a major role in more recent conflicts.

Purpose of the Royal Air Force

'The Royal Air Force's role, in conjunction with the Defence organisations, is to deliver the UK Defence Vision:

- Defend the UK and its interests.
- Strengthen international peace and stability.
- Be a force for good in the world.

We achieve this aim by working together on our core task to produce battle-winning people and equipment. The Royal Air Force will build upon the successes of our past and on the characteristics that make air power essential across the full spectrum of operations in order to contribute to the Defence Vision. Our people lie at the heart of this capability. We rely upon their professionalism, dedication and courage. We must train them well and enable them to leverage the potential of technology to achieve our vision of: "An **agile, adaptable** and **capable** Air Force that, person for person, is second to none, and that makes a decisive air power contribution in support of the UK Defence Mission."'

Roles of the Royal Air Force

The Royal Air Force plays a vital part in the world by delivering flexible air power anywhere in the world. The RAF must be able to respond quickly and effectively to any challenges or threats that this country and our allies may face. Although prepared and ready for any combat situation that may arise, the RAF's main role now is to help police the skies and support peacekeeping and reconstruction initiatives and to bring aid to the victims of war and natural disasters.

The RAF must be properly equipped with the latest technology and trained manpower in order to do this.

Responsibilities of the Royal Air Force

The Royal Air Force must operate in a cost-effective way and ensure that they are making the very best use of their resources and equipment, and not wasting taxpayers' money; that is why the RAF often works jointly as a team with the Royal Navy and the Army, making more efficient use of British defence resources. The Air Force Act 1955 is the law that governs the Royal Air Force.

British Army

P1   P2   M1   D1

We hear a lot in the news about the British Army's current deployment against the Taliban group in Afghanistan. Other roles include peacekeeping, providing humanitarian aid, enforcing anti-terrorism measures and helping to combat the international drugs trade.

Purpose of the Army

The main purposes of the Army are the same as the other armed forces:

- Defend the UK and its interests.
- Strengthen international peace and stability.
- Be a force for good in the world.

Roles of the Army

There are many different regiments and divisions in the Army and they all carry out different roles in order to achieve the main purposes of the service, as shown above. Table 2.2 lists some of the main divisions and their roles.

Army division	Role
Royal Regiment of Artillery	Defence of troops, target acquisition and surveillance using weaponry
Royal Corps of Engineers	Construction of camps, building bridges, clearing mines, laying mines
Royal Logistics Corps	Distribution of all equipment and provisions
Royal Electrical and Mechanical Engineers	Equipment maintenance
Royal Army Medical Corps	Medical care of soldiers and families
Army Air Corps	Airborne combat
Household Cavalry	Ceremonial duties and reconnaissance

Table 2.2 Army divisions and roles

Responsibilities of the Army

The Army has a legal responsibility to comply with the laws that govern the service. These laws are the Army Act 1955 and the Armed Forces Act 2001. They also have the same professional and political responsibilities as other uniformed services, described earlier.

Activity

There have been many discussions recently about whether our armed forces have been provided with adequate equipment to enable them to carry out their duties. Find and read a recent newspaper article about this.

Royal Navy

The Royal Navy is the oldest of the British armed forces and has played a crucial part in times of conflict, both as a fighting force and as a means of providing provisions and equipment to the other armed services. Current roles include seizing illegal drugs, disaster relief, supporting troops in Afghanistan and helping in the fight against world terrorism. The Royal Marines are part of the Royal Navy.

Purpose of the Royal Navy

The eight defence missions of the Royal Navy are as follows:

- 'Contribute to the security of the UK and its citizens world-wide in peacetime, including providing military aid to civil authorities.
- Participate in the Defence Diplomacy initiative through the building of international trust.

- Participate in Peace Support and Humanitarian Operations.

- Maintain capability to mount a response to a regional conflict outside NATO which could adversely affect European Security or UK interests.

- Contribute to the internal and external security of the UK's Overseas Territories, e.g. Bermuda, Gibraltar and the Falklands.

- Support British interests, influence and standing abroad extending to the support of defence exports.

- Provide forces required to counter a strategic attack on NATO.

- Provide forces needed to respond to a regional conflict inside NATO where an Ally calls for assistance under Article 5 of the Washington Treaty.'

Source: www.royalnavy.mod.uk © Crown copyright material is reproduced with the permission of the Controller of HMSO and the Queen's Printer for Scotland.

Roles of the Royal Navy

The main roles of the Royal Navy are:

- maintenance of the UK Nuclear Deterrent
- delivery of the UK Commando force
- supplying of assets to other forces
- patrolling areas which the UK is responsible for
- removal of mines
- sea exploration, weather research and other science projects
- protection of UK and EU fishing sites.

Responsibilities of the Royal Navy

The Royal Navy has the same professional, legal and political responsibilities as the other services. The Navy must ensure that they provide an efficient and effective service in a way that is fair and honourable.

The Royal Marines

The Royal Marines' Commandos are the amphibious infantry of the Royal Navy. This means that they are trained and equipped to operate on land, sea and air. They are trained and ready to deploy at a moment's notice in any emergency, in support of UK military operations, to carry out peacekeeping duties, provide disaster relief or help police the seas. They are recognised as one of the world's most elite fighting forces.

Figure 2.7 Royal Marine

They are an independent unit with their own

training centre and recruits have to undertake the lengthiest and most rigorous training programme of any of the armed forces. Only the fittest, the most determined and the most highly motivated recruits, who have the necessary state of mind, will earn the Royal Marines' coveted green beret.

How to upgrade to M1 if your chosen service is one of the armed services

M1 When upgrading to M1 and writing about any of the armed services, you could talk about the roles that each service is carrying out at the moment. If you are writing about the Army, you could explain the current deployment in Afghanistan and carry out research to find out where else they are currently deployed. You should explain what main role they are carrying out in each deployment. If choosing to write about any of the other armed services, you should carry out similar research to discover what their current deployments and roles are. You will probably find that all the services are involved in the same operations because they support one another.

How to upgrade to D1 if your chosen service is one of the armed services

D1 To achieve the D1 grade, you should evaluate the performance of one service. You could carry out research and examine news articles about the war in Afghanistan and discuss the roles of the Army or the Royal Marines. You could discuss the topic of whether our armed services are properly equipped for such a war. Should the government be spending more money on our armed services?

Other specialist/uniformed services – HM Prison Service

Purpose of HM Prison Service

All 138 prisons in this country are under the control of central government. The vision of Her Majesty's Prison Service is:

- to provide the very best prison services so that we are the provider of choice
- to work towards this vision by securing key objectives (as outlined in the 'Roles' section below).

Figure 2.8 Prison officer

Roles of HM Prison Service

The main roles of HM Prison Service are:

- to hold prisoners securely
- to reduce the risk of prisoners re-offending
- to provide safe and well-ordered establishments in which we treat prisoners humanely, decently and lawfully.

Responsibilities of HM Prison Service

Prisons are regulated, ensuring that they are run securely and safely, with the welfare of both prisoners and staff a prime concern. HM Prison Service is responsible to central government. Her Majesty's Inspectorate of Prisons is an independent body that inspects prisons and makes recommendations to the Home Secretary. HM Prison Service also carries professional and financial responsibilities to ensure that resources are being used effectively and that the taxpayer is getting value for money.

How to upgrade to M1 if your chosen service is HM Prison Service

M1 For the M1 grade, you should discuss the purpose and main roles of HM Prison Service. Are our prisons adequate? Are they achieving their main aims and objectives? How well do they perform? You could carry out research and find case studies to support your discussions.

How to upgrade to D1 if your chosen service is HM Prison Service

D1 For the D1 grade, you could evaluate the use and effectiveness of our prisons. How many offenders re-offend after leaving prison?

> **Ask yourself!**
>
> **The Prison Governors Association are calling for sentences of less than one year to be scrapped to help the prison overcrowding situation. What do you think?**

Other specialist/uniformed services – the UK Border Agency

This agency is fairly new and was formed when parts of the Border and Immigration Agency and parts of the HM Revenue and Customs Agency merged.

Purpose of the UK Border Agency

The purpose of the Independent Chief Inspector of the UK Border Agency is:

- to ensure independent scrutiny of the work of the UK Border Agency, delivering confidence and assurance that it is effective and efficient
- to see that the United Kingdom Border Agency delivers fair, consistent and respectful services, continuously driving improvement, so that their operation is thorough and effective.

Roles of the UK Border Agency

'The UK Border Agency is responsible for securing the United Kingdom borders and controlling migration in the United Kingdom. We manage border control for the United Kingdom, enforcing immigration and customs regulations. We also consider applications for permission to enter or stay in the United Kingdom, citizenship and asylum.'

Source: www.ukba.homeoffice.gov.uk © Crown copyright material is reproduced with the permission of the Controller of HMSO and the Queen's Printer for Scotland.

The agency is responsible for the issuing of visas for entry to this country. It is also responsible for border control, including the checking of passports and customs checks. The agency also deals with immigration, including the processing of applications from people seeking asylum in this country.

Responsibilities of the UK Border Agency

The UK Border Agency has a responsibility to be:

- high quality, rigorous and respected
- fair and transparent
- delivery focused
- frank and straightforward
- impartial and objective.

How to upgrade to M1 if your chosen service is the UK Border Agency

M1   To achieve the M1 grade, you could explain in detail how the UK Border Agency carries out its main roles. What is involved in border control, immigration control and customs control? You should explain how the agency deals with applications for citizenship and asylum.

How to upgrade to D1 if your chosen service is the UK Border Agency

D1   You will find lots of information in recent news articles to help you to upgrade to D1. You could look at government targets for immigration and how these are implemented. You could also look at recent developments and the change to the laws for UK citizenship. You could also refer to case studies on the UK Border Agency website.

Individual job roles in the uniformed services

Different job opportunities in the uniformed public services

There is a huge range of job opportunities within the uniformed public services. In addition to the high-profile, front-line jobs that you may be aware of, there are also the support staff who work behind the scenes. These include roles such as cleaning staff, medical staff, catering staff, administration, etc. In this section, we will look at some of these roles in more detail.

Job descriptions

Anyone who is applying for a particular job needs to see the job description for that job. A job description describes the job role and lists the duties that an employee will be required to do.

> **(g) Grading tip!**
>
> **P3** For P3, you need to carry out relevant research and provide an outline of the different job opportunities within a selection of uniformed services.
>
> **P4** For the P4 grade, you need to describe the conditions of service for two jobs in contrasting public services.

> **How to upgrade to M2**
>
> **M2** For M2, you need to explain in detail the work of a chosen job in the uniformed services. Talk to visiting speakers or anyone you know who is a member of the uniformed public services and ask them about their daily routine.

Job roles in the Army

P3 P4 M2

When asked about career choices, young people may reply that they want to join the Army and be a 'soldier'. They may not realise just how many different job roles there are within the Army and other uniformed services. Everyone who joins the Army trains to be a soldier first, but then may train in another specialist area. So, after completing your initial soldier training, you can choose to train for the career of your choice, as a chef, an engineer, a tank driver, an electrician, a dentist, etc. The Army is a community in itself and just like any other community, the Army needs plumbers, doctors, nurses, clerks, dentists, chaplains, drivers, musicians, bricklayers and many other specialists. Mechanics are required to maintain all the Army vehicles and logistics officers plan and implement all the transportation and accommodation requirements for Army deployments.

Figure 2.9 Army chef

Table 2.3 shows some of the job roles that are available in the Army. There are many others.

Chef	Gunner
Tank driver	Musician
Dentist	Postal courier
Clerk	Logistics specialist
Mechanic	Ammunition technician
Doctor	Communication systems operator
Nurse	Chaplain
Engineer	Human resource specialist
Electrician	Lawyer
Plumber	Medical scientist
Firefighter	Physiotherapist
Military police	Optician
Infantry soldier	Dental nurse
Mounted cavalry	Pharmacist
Vet	

Table 2.3 Job roles in the Army

Activity

Choose several of the job roles given in Table 2.3, then log on to the Army website and find out as much as you can about these jobs.

Job description for an aircraft technician

'Royal Electrical and Mechanical Engineers

Soldier
Responsible for keeping all of the Army's aircraft in the air, with inspections, repairs and servicing.

The job
Aircraft technicians are responsible for the inspection, repair and servicing of airframes and gas turbine engines on the Army's aircraft. These are mainly helicopters, but include fixed-wing aircraft. Technicians sign off aircraft as ready to fly after maintenance, so the role is key to flight safety. Responsibility extends to fitting weapons and pyrotechnics, and maintaining ground support equipment.

   This is a job for someone who has the ability to focus for long periods of training in a technical subject. You will need to be good with your hands because practical, technical skills are the bread and butter of this trade. With responsibility for deciding when an airframe is ready to fly, integrity and an honest nature are essential requirements for this job.

What skills will you learn?
You will learn how to maintain and inspect the airframes and gas turbines of military helicopters and fixed-wing aircraft, identifying repairs that need to be carried out, completing them and then passing the aircraft as fit to fly. Fitting aircraft weapons systems will form part of your responsibilities, and you will also become familiar with ground support equipment. The ability to deliver high standards of engineering and flight safety with complex documentation, while doing your job as a soldier in the field, will become an essential skill.'

Source: www.armyjobs.mod.uk © Crown copyright material is reproduced with the permission of the Controller of HMSO and the Queen's Printer for Scotland.

How to upgrade to M2

M2 To achieve the M2 grade, you will need to explain one job role in greater detail. You should describe the daily routine tasks of that job role and discuss the personal aspects of the role. What are the positive and negative aspects of the job? For example, joining the Army involves moving away from home, leaving family and friends and there is a real risk of injury or even death. However, most Army soldiers would say that the friendships they form and the opportunities and experiences they receive more than make up for the negatives of the job.

Job roles in the police service

P3 P4 M2

New police recruits are required to work a probationary two-year period on the beat after their initial training. After this period, they can continue to work as a beat officer or they can choose to specialise and carry out further training to work in a choice of jobs. These could include working in the criminal investigation department (CID) as a detective, working in the road traffic department as a traffic police officer or working as a dog handler.

Figure 2.10 Police community support officers

There are also many civilian roles in the uniformed services, particularly in the police. Many jobs such as control-room operators and scene of crime officers are now carried out by civilian staff. (Civilian members of staff are mainly support staff who are not regular police officers.)

Police constable

A police constable may carry out the following tasks in their day-to-day routine:

- Foot patrol – members of the public like to see police officers on foot, patrolling the streets. The presence of police officers can reassure the public and can act as a deterrent to criminals.
- Crime prevention – officers on the beat also take part in crime reduction initiatives, such as targeting anti-social behaviour or street binge drinking.
- Assisting in emergency incidents – beat officers may be called upon to attend accidents, fighting on the streets or domestic violence.
- Attending court – police officers will need to attend court to give evidence in cases they have been involved in.
- Information gathering – officers may be required to carry out investigation of serious crimes, which can involve making house-to-house enquiries.
- Paperwork – all police officers will need to complete a large amount of paperwork as part of their routine work.

Police community support officer

You may have seen the police community support officers patrolling your area. These officers wear a similar uniform to regular police officers, but they are also civilian employees and do not have the same powers as regular police officers. They do not have the power to arrest. They should not be confused with police specials, who are police volunteers.

> **Ask yourself!**
>
> **Should police community support officers have powers to arrest people?**

Although police specials do not get paid, they do have the same powers as regular police officers, including the power to arrest.

> ### Activity
>
> **Make a list of the job roles of a regular police officer, a police community support officer and a police special (or special constable), and then compare these.**

Job roles in the Maritime and Coastguard Agency

A typical job description for a Coastguard would look as follows:

Job description for the Coastguard Agency

'Coastguards work for the Maritime and Coastguard Agency (MCA), as part of the service which co-ordinates search and rescue along the British coast, and investigates illegal shipping activities and pollution incidents.

The coastguard service employs coastguard watch assistants, coastguard watch officers and coastguard rescue officer volunteers.

You would usually start as a coastguard watch assistant, providing administrative support and staffing operations rooms.

Typical responsibilities:

- Receiving and handling 999 calls.
- Monitoring equipment.
- Providing information to the general public.
- Updating logs and completing general administration.

As a coastguard watch officer, you would be involved in all aspects of the service. Your work would include:

- assisting in staffing operational centres
- taking part in cliff rescues, coastal searches and boat work (in some posts).

As a coastguard rescue officer volunteer, you would be trained to respond to coastal incidents and be paid for the hours you work.'

Source: www.careers-guide.com

Job roles in the prison service

A typical job description for a prison officer would look as follows:

Job description for a prison officer

Typical work activities for a prison officer will include:

- carrying out security duties as required, contributing effectively to the safe and secure custody of Prisoners.
- ensuring that all incidents are reported and dealt with effectively, including bullying, assaults, substance misuse and self harm.
- preparing reports as required in a timely manner.
- following set procedures for dealing with Prisoner applications.
- encouraging Prisoners to deal with personal challenges through offending behaviour programmes.
- completing searching in adherence to local and national policy.
- encouraging Prisoners to follow regime activities.
- complying with audit requirements.
- upholding respect for Prisoners, their property, rights and dignity.
- applying authorised control and restraint procedures where appropriate.
- ensuring Control and Restraint training (C & R) is completed each year as required.
- completing observation book entries.
- monitoring vulnerable Prisoners appropriately.
- acting as Personal Officer to a group of Prisoners.
- ensuring standards of hygiene and cleanliness are maintained.
- ensuring Suicide and Self Harm processes are complied with.
- ensuring information system for Prisoners is effective.
- contributing to own development through the Staff Performance & Development Record.
- ensuring all work is carried out to a high professional standard.

Source: www.hmprisonservice.gov.uk

Job roles in the ambulance service

A typical job description for a paramedic would look as follows:

Job description for a paramedic

'Paramedics are the senior ambulance service healthcare professionals at an accident or a medical emergency. On arriving at the scene of an incident they assess the patient's condition and then give essential treatment. They use high-tech equipment, such as defibrillators (which restore the heart's rhythm), spinal and traction splints and intravenous drips, as well as administering oxygen and drugs.

Paramedics are often the first people to arrive at the scene of an accident. They can work alone or with an ambulance technician, using a motorbike, emergency response car or even a bicycle to reach their patients. With extra training, they could also become members of an air ambulance crew.

They are trained to drive what is in effect a mobile emergency clinic and to resuscitate and/or stabilise patients using sophisticated techniques, equipment and drugs. They can be called out to any emergency incident and they work closely with the other emergency services. They also work closely with doctors and nurses in hospital accident and emergency departments. As well as contact with patients, they also deal with patients' relatives and members of the public, some of whom may be hysterical or aggressive.'

Source: www.nhscareers.nhs.uk © Crown copyright material is reproduced with the permission of the Controller of HMSO and the Queen's Printer for Scotland.

How to upgrade to M2

M2 For the M2 grade, you should identify the day-to-day duties of one job role (as above) then go on to explain more about each duty, e.g. looking at the sample job description for a prison officer above, what exactly would 'performing security checks and search procedures' involve?. You could explain that checks and searches need to be carried out in prisons to check for drugs, weapons, etc. to prevent prisoners escaping or harming themselves or others. You could also carry out some research to find out what rehabilitation of prisoners means.

Activity

Write down six questions that you would like to ask a visiting speaker, either from the Army or the police service. The questions should be related to their job role, and not about salary, holidays or pensions etc., which are part of their conditions of service (covered in the next section).

Conditions of service

P4

When we talk about conditions of service, these are what some people might call the benefits or 'the perks' of a job – that is, the pay, pensions, security, holidays, sickness benefits, etc. and how well the employer looks after its employees. These conditions should always be set out at the start of employment and are legally binding on both the employee and the employer. Public service jobs tend to have good conditions of service. This could be to compensate for the fact that uniformed public service jobs usually contain some element of risk or danger and involve working unsociable hours. However, jobs in the public services are traditionally more secure than private jobs and holidays and pensions etc. are usually better.

Salary

Salaries vary between the different uniformed public services, and usually rise according to the length of service of an employee. Table 2.4 shows the starting salaries of some of the uniformed services. Salaries in the armed forces are often paid in addition to free or low-cost accommodation and include all meals.

Fire and rescue	Royal Navy	Army	HM Prison Service	Police service	Paramedic	RAF
£20,896	£16,227	£13,337.24	£17,744	£23,259	£19,683	£16,266

Table 2.4 Starting salaries

Annual leave (or holiday entitlement)

Holiday entitlement also varies from service to service and can rise in accordance with length of service. Members of the armed forces are entitled to 30 days of leave per year. Members of the police and prison services usually receive between 22 and 30 days of annual leave, depending on length of service.

Pension

Most uniformed public service workers will be entitled to a pension when they retire from the service. Uniformed public service workers can usually retire and draw their pension at a younger age than private sector workers. Members of the police service and the Army can retire with a full pension at the age of 55.

Training

Many uniformed public services have their own initial training programmes, which new recruits take part in. Training is often ongoing throughout the length of employment.

Working hours

Conditions of service should include details of the working hours of employees. Uniformed public service employees usually need to work unsociable hours and shifts in order to provide a 24-hour service, seven days a week.

Accommodation

Some uniformed public services (i.e. the armed services) provide free or low-cost accommodation for their members. Sometimes an allowance is given to help to pay for accommodation.

Initial training programmes

All uniformed public services require new recruits to undergo a period of initial training. The length of training varies from service to service. After completing the initial training period, recruits often then complete a probationary period and further training is usually ongoing throughout the length of service. Table 2.5 shows the length of initial training periods for different public services.

Public service	Initial training period
Royal Air Force	29 weeks
Police	15 weeks (can vary)
Fire service	16 weeks
Royal Marines	32 weeks

Table 2.5 Length of initial training periods

Activity

Carry out research to find the training programme for the service you are interested in. How do you think you would cope with the training?

Figure 2.11 below is an example of a training programme for Royal Air Force recruits.

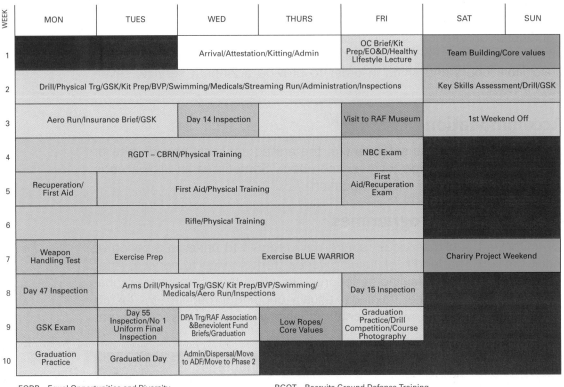

WEEK	MON	TUES	WED	THURS	FRI	SAT	SUN
1			Arrival/Attestation/Kitting/Admin		OC Brief/Kit Prep/EO&D/Healthy Llfestyle Lecture	Team Building/Core values	
2	Drill/Physical Trg/GSK/Kit Prep/BVP/Swimming/Medicals/Streaming Run/Administration/Inspections					Key Skills Assessment/Drill/GSK	
3	Aero Run/Insurance Brief/GSK		Day 14 Inspection		Visit to RAF Museum	1st Weekend Off	
4	RGDT – CBRN/Physical Training				NBC Exam		
5	Recuperation/First Aid	First Aid/Physical Training			First Aid/Recuperation Exam		
6	Rifle/Physical Training						
7	Weapon Handling Test	Exercise Prep	Exercise BLUE WARRIOR			Chariry Project Weekend	
8	Day 47 Inspection	Arms Drill/Physical Trg/GSK/ Kit Prep/BVP/Swimming/ Medicals/Aero Run/Inspections			Day 15 Inspection		
9	GSK Exam	Day 55 Inspection/No 1 Uniform Final Inspection	DPA Trg/RAF Association &Beneviolent Fund Briefs/Graduation	Low Ropes/Core Values	Graduation Practice/Drill Competition/Course Photography		
10	Graduation Practice	Graduation Day	Admin/Dispersal/Move to ADF/Move to Phase 2				

EODB – Equal Opportunities and Diversity
EODB – Equal Opportunities and Diversity
GSK – General Service Knowledge

RGOT – Recruits Ground Defence Training
CBRN – Chemical Biological Radiological or Nuclear
JPA – Joint Personnell Adminstration

Figure 2.11 Example RAF training programme

Source: www.raf.mod.uk

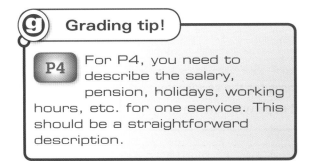

Grading tip!

P4 For P4, you need to describe the salary, pension, holidays, working hours, etc. for one service. This should be a straightforward description.

End of unit knowledge check

1. Identify three roles of the police service.
2. What does 'accountability' mean?
3. What is a mission statement?
4. What is the main role of the Royal Air Force?
5. What are 'conditions of service'?

Grading criteria

In order to pass this unit, the evidence that the learner presents for assessment needs to demonstrate that they can meet all the learning outcomes for the unit. The assessment criteria for a pass grade describe the level of achievement required to pass this unit.

Grading criteria		
To achieve a pass grade the evidence must show that the learner is able to:	To achieve a merit grade the evidence must show that, in addition to the pass criteria, the learner is able to:	To achieve a distinction grade the evidence must show that, in addition to the pass and merit criteria, the learner is able to:
P1 Outline the main purpose and roles of contrasting uniformed public services	**M1** Explain in detail the role, purpose and responsibilities of contrasting uniformed public services	**D1** Evaluate the role, purpose and responsibilities of a chosen uniformed public service
P2 Discuss the main responsibilities of two contrasting uniformed public services		
P3 Outline the different employment opportunities available in the uniformed public services	**M2** Explain in detail the work of a chosen job in the uniformed services	
P4 Describe the current conditions of service for two jobs within contrasting uniformed public services		

Unit 3
Employment in the non-uniformed public services

Introduction

The public service sector employs more people in this country than any other sector. These are essential services that are usually paid for, wholly or partly, by the government. They include vital services such as health, education and social services, without which a modern society could not function. There are many, many jobs in these services, which you may not know much about at the moment.

Public service jobs can be divided into different categories. There are uniformed public services and non-uniformed public services. There are statutory public services, non-statutory public services and voluntary public services.

This unit will give you the opportunity to find out more about the non-uniformed services and to broaden your knowledge of a whole range of careers. This should then enable you to make the correct career choice based on the knowledge you have gained.

This unit will also provide information about the vast range of different job opportunities within these services and you can investigate the kind of work that public service workers do on a day-to-day basis.

When thinking about a career, you will want to know about the conditions of service – that means knowing how much you will be paid, how many hours you will work, etc. In this unit, you will learn about these conditions of service and find out how they differ among the different services.

Public service sector employers take the subject of equal opportunities very seriously and try to recruit a workforce from many different sections of society.

Learning outcomes:

By the end of this unit, you should:

1. Know the main roles of different public services

2. Understand the main responsibilities of different non-uniformed public services

3. Understand the different employment opportunities available in the non-uniformed public services

4. Know the conditions of service for public sector jobs.

What is a public service?

Public services are non-profit making organisations, which have been set up to protect or help people. Many of these people are vulnerable members of our society who cannot help themselves, such as people who are very sick, disabled or elderly.

Most public services are funded by the government, using money paid in tax by members of the public. These public services are classed as 'statutory' services, which means they are required to exist by law. Non-statutory services are those services that are not required by law and that are usually self-funded, such as charities. Both statutory and non-statutory services can be either uniformed or non-uniformed, which can be confusing! For example, think about the National Health Service. Is this funded by public taxes? Yes, absolutely, so this is definitely a statutory service. Are doctors and nurses members of the uniformed services or the non-uniformed services? Nurses wear a uniform and so do some junior doctors, while consultants in hospitals and local doctors tend not to. When we think of uniformed public services, we generally think of services such as the emergency services or the military services. These types of services are covered in Unit 2, so this unit will concentrate on the services generally known as 'non-uniformed'.

Ask yourself!

What do you think a public service is? How many examples can you think of?

Activity

How many non-uniformed public services do you know? Make a list of these.

How many non-uniformed public services did you think of in the activity? Table 3.1 below lists some of these services – there may be others.

Non-uniformed services
Social services
Education service
Probation service
Youth services
Refuse collection services
Leisure services
Civil service
Victim Support
Environmental health
Highways services
Housing services
National Health Service
Planning department

Table 3.1 Non-uniformed public services

Activity

Look at Table 3.1. Write a short explanation of what you think each service does.

Purposes, roles and responsibilities

P1   P2   M1   D1

Every public service has a main purpose, roles and responsibilities.

Let us look at these in more detail below.

Purpose – overall aim of the service, laid down by law

Most public services have a vision or statement, which sets out what their main purpose is. We will take a look at some of these later.

Roles – what the service actually does

We may think we know what the main public services do, but quite often they may have other roles that we may not be aware of.

> **Key terms**
>
> The **purpose** of a public service is the overall aim of the service, which is laid down by law.
>
> A **role** is the behaviour or duty expected of an individual or organisation, for a public service, this is what they actually do.
>
> A **responsibility** is a duty, obligation or liability for which someone is accountable. The responsibilities of a public service are to carry out their duties fairly, effectively and efficiently.

Responsibilities – to perform duties fairly, effectively and efficiently

Public services are mainly paid for by the public through taxation, including income tax, VAT and local council taxes. This brings certain responsibilities and makes the services 'answerable' or 'accountable' to the public, who need to know that they are getting good value for their money. This means that they need to keep written records of everything they do for other people to inspect. The public services have to show accountability in three ways:

1. Legally, which means strictly following the law.
2. Professionally, which means doing the job in a fair, efficient and conscientious manner.
3. Politically, which means they should follow the instructions of the government, irrespective of which political party is in power.

Public services are governed by councils or committees who monitor their performance to ensure that they are giving good value for money. It is important to remember, however, that the public services are responsible to society, generally, and are monitored closely by central government and local government, who ensure that the services meet their responsibilities. Whenever public money is involved, there never seems to be enough to go around. Shortage of money and resources can have a detrimental effect on the public services.

Grading tip!

P1 For P1, you need to choose two different non-uniformed services and describe their main roles and purpose.

P2 For P2, you should talk about the responsibilities and accountabilities of these two services.

How to upgrade to M1 and D1

M1 An M1 grade requires a more detailed explanation of the above two services (i.e. how and why the services do what they do).

D1 For a D1 grade, you need to evaluate the roles, purpose and responsibilities of one service. This means looking at how well the service performs its role and responsibilities. You could find statistics to help with this.

Let us now take a look at some of the job opportunities available in the non-uniformed public services.

Health and social care services   P1 P2 M1 D1

Purpose of health and social care

The Department of Health is the government department that is responsible for the provision of health and social care in this country. The overall purpose of the Department of Health is to 'improve the health and well-being of people in England'. The department's aims are:

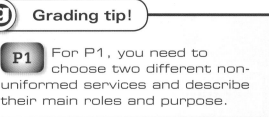

- better health and well-being for all: helping people stay healthy and well; empowering people to live independently; and tackling health inequalities

Figure 3.1 Hospital nurses at work

- better care for all: the best possible health and social care that offers safe and effective care, when and where people need it; and empowering people in their choices
- better value for all: delivering affordable, efficient and sustainable services; contributing to the wider economy and the nation.

This sector employs the largest number of people in the UK.

There are many different organisations in this country that look after people's health, while others look after their social care needs. They often work together. These services include:

- statutory services – these are services that are required by law and are funded by the government, e.g. the National Health Service
- voluntary services – these are services that are paid for by public donations. Although these services are voluntary, members of staff working in these organisations are usually paid
- private services – these services are paid for by the people who use them
- informal services – many services are provided by other carers, such as family members, friends or people in the community.

Activity

Read the following case study and decide how many types of services from the above categories are being used.

○ Case study

Anne is a 56-year-old lady who suffers from multiple sclerosis, which means she needs 24-hour care. She lives in her own home. Anne's medical needs are provided by her local doctor and other specialists. Anne's main carer at home is her husband – her two daughters also visit every day. Anne and her husband also pay for some daily help and the family receive support from the Multiple Sclerosis Society.

Assignment tip

Remember not to cut and paste or copy work from other sources into your assignments. This is known as plagiarism, which means stealing someone else's words or ideas! Read the text, and then write about the subject *in your own words*.

Roles of health and social care services

The basis of the National Health Service is that everyone in this country should have access to free health care if they need it. This care is provided by the following bodies.

Primary care trusts

Primary care is the medical care that you receive from your local doctor, optician or dentist. These services are managed by the primary care trust in your area.

NHS (National Health Service) trusts

Hospitals are managed by NHS trusts. NHS trusts employ hospital staff and other health workers and are responsible for ensuring that hospitals provide good service.

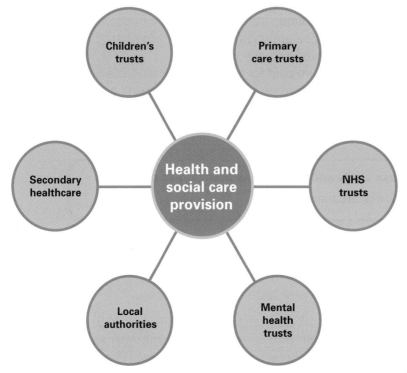

Figure 3.2 Health and social care provision

Mental health trusts

These trusts provide services for people with mental health problems.

Local authorities

Local authorities around the country are responsible for providing social services in the community. Social services departments work very closely with the health services to provide this care. (See the next section for more information on social services.)

Secondary health care

If your doctor refers you to a specialist, for example, for physiotherapy or counselling, this is classed as secondary care.

Children's trusts

Children's trusts aim to improve the health of all children and they bring together all the services that work for children and young people in a particular area.

Responsibilities of health and social care services

The Department of Health passes some of its powers and money to the trusts and organisations mentioned above to provide the necessary services. They then have to provide annual reports, stating how they have performed and how they have spent their money. It is their responsibility to give the public value for money and to provide high-quality services. Are they employing enough doctors or nursing staff? Are they buying the right equipment? This is their professional responsibility. They also have a political responsibility to carry out the policies and plans of the government.

In a recent Opening of Parliament speech, the Prime Minister, Gordon Brown, promised free nursing care for the elderly. The Health and Social Care Act 2001 is the law that governs all health and social care provision and local authorities must ensure that they abide by this act. The NHS and Community Care Act 1990 places a legal responsibility on the health and social care services to enable people to live safely in the community.

Activity

Gordon Brown's plan to provide free nursing care for the elderly sounds like a good idea. However, some people and agencies have expressed concerns about this plan. Can you find out why this is?

How to upgrade to M1 if your chosen service is the health and social care sector

M1 To upgrade to M1, you should carry out research into all of the above-mentioned services and explain about them in detail. How are they funded? What is the structure of the service? How are they performing? Look for more information on their websites.

How to upgrade to D1 if your chosen service is the health and social care sector

D1 To upgrade to D1, you should evaluate the purpose, roles and responsibilities of the above services. How are these services performing? Can you find any relevant statistics? Carry out research on the Department of Health website for further information and find newspaper articles about the services and discuss these. Much has been written about cases of poor care in hospitals, MSRA infections, dirty facilities and the mistreatment of elderly patients. Discuss these in your evaluation.

Local authority employment

> **Key terms**
>
> The terms **local authority, local council** and **local government** all basically mean the same thing. They are the organisations that receive money from central government and from local council taxes to provide our local public services.

Local councils affect everyone's lives. They provide vital services, such as education, social services, housing, refuse collection, leisure facilities, libraries, parks and gardens. There is a huge range of job opportunities in the local authority sector.

> **Activity**
>
> **How many different jobs within local authority employment can you think of? Write these down.**

Social services

The Department of Health provides the framework and policies for local authorities to provide social services across the country.

Social services departments are responsible for ensuring the care and well-being of vulnerable people in our society. This includes young children who may be in a situation of abuse or neglect, children and young people who are living in care, the sick, the elderly and people with mental health problems. Social services departments are responsible for the running of care homes for these people. Sometimes care homes and nursing homes are privately owned, but social services are still responsible for monitoring the quality of care that is offered.

Social services departments try to care for people in their own homes, wherever possible, by providing care workers to visit them. Social services will follow up the care provided by the NHS when patients leave hospital and the two services work very closely together. Partnerships are often formed between primary care trusts, NHS trusts, social services and voluntary agencies.

Purpose of social services

The main purpose of social services is 'to deliver a social care system that provides care equally for all, whilst enabling people to retain their independence, control and dignity'. This means that the service will try to ensure that people who wish to remain in their home can do so by providing the help that they need. It also means that if someone does go into a care home, they should be treated with respect and dignity.

> ### Key term
>
> A **financial means test** is a system used to find out how much people can afford to pay for services.

Roles of social services

Since 1993, social services departments have had a duty to assess people's needs for community care services and, where they have agreed that there is a need, to provide an appropriate service. 'Assessing needs' simply means finding out what help or support you may need. Social services departments should then provide services that support people in their own homes or provide a placement in a care home. In either case, subject to a financial means test, people may have to pay for this service.

⬭ Case study

There have been several high-profile cases resulting in social services being criticised. One of these, involving the death of a 17-month-old toddler known as 'Baby P' resulted in an inquiry into the case. In his report following the inquiry, Lord Laming criticised failings in information sharing between agencies, the poor training and support given to 'overstretched' front-line staff and the red tape 'hampering' social workers.

Carry out some research to find out the details of this case and why social services staff were seen to be at fault.

Responsibilities of social services

There are national guidelines in place, under the Fair Access to Care Services (FACS) system, to monitor the provision of social services in this country. Social services also have professional responsibilities to ensure that they are using resources wisely and efficiently. They also have legal responsibilities to abide by the laws that have been made to ensure that people are treated fairly. The main laws that govern social services are as follows:

● The Human Rights Act 1998/2000 makes it unlawful for any local authority to act in any way that is against a person's human rights and gives a right to receive fair treatment.

- The Mental Health Act 1983 (updated 2007) safeguards people who are receiving treatment for a mental health disorder.
- The Children Act 1989/2004 states how children's services should be organised.
- The Care Standards Act 2000 and the Nursing and Residential Care Home Regulations set out national minimum standards that are required for care homes.
- The NHS and Community Care Act 1990 places a legal responsibility on health and social care services to enable people to live safely in the community.

How to upgrade to M1 if your chosen service is social services

M1 In order to upgrade and meet the M1 criteria, you could undertake further research into the different roles carried out by social services in this country. Go online and look at the websites of different local authorities and find out what services they offer. Do they all offer the same services? How do they compare with each other? For example, do some authorities offer more help, or cheaper help, to the elderly in their community?

How to upgrade to D1 if your chosen service is social services

D1 You should find plenty of information to use for the D1 criteria. There has been much written in the press and on the internet about cases where social services have been seen to fail its clients. The case of 'Baby P' was mentioned earlier in this chapter. There are other similar cases, which you could find information on. You could mention a report in which Birmingham Social Services were heavily criticised.

Education service – Department for Children, Schools and Families

P1   P2   M1   D1

Purpose of the Department for Children, Schools and Families

The Department for Children, Schools and Families is a government department that is responsible for the education of all children in this country.

The purpose of the Department for Children, Schools and Families is to make this the best

Figure 3.3 Primary school class

place in the world for children and young people to grow up. The main aims are to:

- make children and young people happy and healthy
- keep them safe and sound
- give them a top-class education
- help them stay on track.

The department aims to:

- secure the well-being and health of children and young people
- safeguard the young and vulnerable
- ensure an excellent education for all our children and young people
- keep them on the path to success
- provide more places for children to play safely.

Roles of the Department for Children, Schools and Families

The role of the department is to oversee the education and upbringing of all children in this country, from early years education in nurseries and playgroups, all the way through to schools and colleges, up to higher education at university. The department is responsible for making policies and decisions, such as setting the school leaving age and deciding what subjects should be taught in the national curriculum. They then pass on their powers and responsibilities to local authorities to provide schools and education. There are also some private schools where parents pay fees for their children's education.

Responsibilities of the Department for Children, Schools and Families

As with other public services, money for education comes from the taxpayer. This means that the department must act responsibly and wisely when deciding how the children in this country should be educated. Schools and colleges are closely monitored through the use of league tables and other statistics to see how well they are performing. The Every Child Matters programme, which the government introduced, aims to ensure that all children are healthy, stay safe, enjoy and achieve, make a positive contribution and enjoy economic well-being.

Local authorities around the country are accountable to the government to make sure that schools are performing well and that children and parents are getting the best education. Local authorities are responsible for employing teachers and other school staff in their area. They carry a professional responsibility to ensure that schools are well resourced, that they are performing well and that the teaching is good.

Local authorities also have a legal responsibility under the Education Act. This act was first introduced in 1880 to make it compulsory for children to attend school until the age of ten! The school leaving age has increased several times since then and was recently changed from 16 to 18 years of age. This means that all teenagers will have to stay at school and study A-levels, attend college or do an apprenticeship with some study and training included, until they are 18 years of age. All local authorities also have a political responsibility to ensure that they carry out the plans and policies of whichever government is in power.

How to upgrade to M1 if your chosen service is the education service

M1 In order to upgrade to an M1, you should carry out research on the Department of Children, Schools and Families, which has its own website. Here, you will find more information about the department, and this will help you to explain in more detail what the purpose, roles and responsibilities of the department are. You should look at the purpose and the aims of the department and explain more about these. You could also talk about the Children, Schools and Families Bill, which is a new law brought out by the Department of Children, Schools and Families and which covers all aspects of education.

How to upgrade to D1 if your chosen service is the education service

D1 In order to upgrade to a D1, you will need to evaluate the purpose, roles and responsibilities of the department. How is the department performing? Can you find any relevant statistics? Carry out research to find newspaper articles about the department and discuss these. You will find many tables and statistics on the department's website where parents can see how well different schools are performing. Take a look at the achievement and attainment tables – are these helpful to parents?

Leisure services sector

What are leisure services? 'Leisure services' is the collective name given by local government to a whole set of responsibilities.

Purpose of the leisure services sector

The main purpose of leisure services is to protect and promote public health. The aims of leisure services are:

- to protect and enhance public parks and open spaces and make them accessible to all
- to offer and maintain sporting facilities for people of all ages and interests
- to encourage and financially support artistic events such as theatre and music performances
- to maintain and develop museums and galleries which reflect the cultural life of the area
- to promote tourism to bring visitors to the area
- to maintain libraries, which support education and learning, encourage creativity and give the general public free access to a wide range of information.

The various leisure services all have common benefits in that they encourage education, social inclusion and community spirit. They bring people from different backgrounds into contact, be it through competitive sport, cooperative performance or simply by meeting at events. These facilities also give people a chance to improve skills and talents in activities that fall outside the bounds of a standard education.

Roles of leisure services

There are several different roles, which include:

- encouraging physical activity participation
- reducing obesity, coronary heart disease, diabetes and high blood pressure
- developing facilities and resources
- increasing community participation
- increasing young people's participation and reducing the risk of youth offending
- increasing self-esteem and reducing social isolation
- increasing cultural knowledge by providing libraries and museums.

Figure 3.4 One role of leisure services is to provide and maintain museums, galleries and libraries

Responsibilities of leisure services

Local authorities have a responsibility to provide leisure services at a subsidised cost. They distribute their leisure service responsibilities across a variety of different departments. For example, the library service buys books, the environmental service employs gardeners and arts resources may provide DJ equipment for events. Many new leisure

Ask yourself!

How many different kinds of sporting and arts facilities are available in your town?

centres are 'dual use' – this means that they are built close to a school, so that during the day pupils can use the facilities as part of their education and they are then open to the general public for the rest of the time. Often, the changing rooms are built with separate areas for the pupils and the public.

Many councils now pass on the responsibility for running some leisure facilities to non-profit making companies. There are also many privately run leisure centres, but these may be too expensive to attend for a large proportion of the general public.

> **Ask yourself!**
>
> **What do you think would happen if there were no council-run leisure services?**

How to upgrade to M1 if your chosen service is the leisure services sector

M1   To meet the M1 grade, you should look at the main roles and responsibilities of the leisure services in more detail and explain how they can help protect and promote general health.

How to upgrade to D1 if your chosen service is the leisure services sector

D1   To upgrade to a D1, you should carry out research and find any statistics to prove that providing leisure services does promote good health in the community. Should these services be free? If so, where could the money come from?

Individual job roles in the non-uniformed public services

Different job opportunities in the non-uniformed public services

As with any organisation, all public services employ a huge number of people to provide the service. As well as front-line employees who actually deliver the particular service, there are many, many others who work in the background, carrying out job roles that are just as vital and important. These employees are usually known as 'support staff'.

> **Activity**
>
> How many 'support' jobs can you think of that would be needed in a public service organisation, such as a hospital or a school?

How many support jobs did you think of in the activity above? There are far too many to list here individually, but your list should have included roles such as:

- cleaners
- cooks
- finance staff
- secretarial staff
- caretakers
- porters.

Job descriptions

Anyone who is applying for a job needs to see the job description for that job. A job description describes the job role and lists the duties that an employee will be required to do. The assessment for the P4 grade requires you to produce a job description for a job of your choice and to describe the role in your own words. You will usually find job descriptions in the recruitment section of the services' websites.

Grading tip!

P3 P3 requires you to explain different employment opportunities available in the non-uniformed public services. To achieve this grade, you should look at several services.

P4 P4 requires you to produce a job description for a job role in a non-uniformed public service.

For this grade, you should carry out research and look at a number of job descriptions. Then, choose one particular job that you may be interested in and create your own job description, describing, in your own words, what the main duties of that role involve.

How to upgrade to M2

M2 For M2, you need to explain in detail the work of a chosen job in the uniformed services. For this grade, you should discuss the roles, talk about the positive and negative aspects and which parts of the job you would find interesting or rewarding, etc. Talk to visiting speakers or anyone you know who is a member of the uniformed public services and ask them about their daily routine.

Job roles in health and social care

P3 **P4** **M2**

The range of jobs in health and social care is vast. Although health care agencies and social services work closely together, the roles of the workers are clearly separate. Health care workers usually look after patients who have health-related problems or conditions. People who work in social care usually deal with clients who have a range of personal and social needs.

Activity

Look at the following list of jobs. Which are health care jobs and which are social care jobs?

- **Health visitor**
- **District nurse**
- **Dentist**
- **Pharmacist**
- **Social worker**
- **Care assistant**

Table 3.2 lists some of the jobs in the NHS.

Nurse	Counsellor
Doctor	Occupational therapist
Pharmacist	Psychologist
Midwife	Scientist
Health visitor	Receptionist
Physiotherapist	Porter
Cleaner	Information technology worker
Engineer	Caterer
Domestic staff	Security staff
Speech therapist	Health care assistant

Table 3.2 Jobs in the NHS

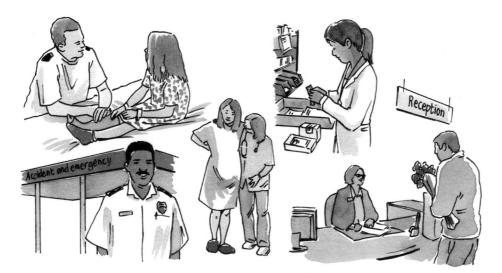

Figure 3.5 Some of the jobs available in the NHS

A typical job description for a health care assistant could look like the following:

Job description for a health care assistant

Patient care
1. Help with nursing care as instructed by nursing staff, including bathing, bed making, lifting patients and helping with meals as necessary.
2. Caring for patients' personal clothing and other property in accordance with agreed policies relating to security and confidentiality.
3. Cleaning of beds and cleaning of lockers.

Ward responsibilities
1. Assisting the nursing staff to keep the ward tidy, including equipment and treatment rooms.
2. Assisting and checking, unpacking and storing of items delivered to the ward.
3. Answering the telephone and taking messages as required.
4. Being familiar with procedures related to health and safety, fire and other emergencies.

General
1. Observing complete confidentiality of information and records at all times, both on and offsite.
2. Complying with all the trust policies as they relate to staff, patients, relatives and visitors.
3. Undertaking errands as required.
4. Maintaining good working relations amongst staff.
5. Establishing and maintaining good relations with visitors and relatives, helping them to find their way around the hospital site.

Medical receptionist

A medical receptionist plays a very important role as he or she is the first point of contact that patients and visitors have when they go to a GP practice, health centre or hospital. Medical receptionists are responsible for ensuring that people are in the right place at the right time.

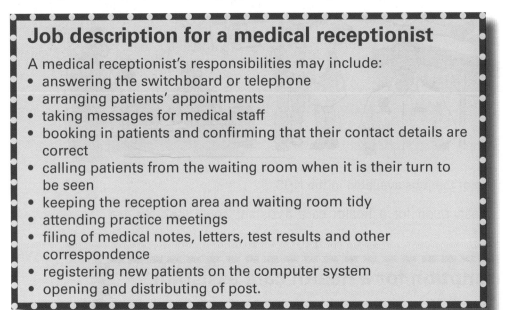

Job description for a medical receptionist

A medical receptionist's responsibilities may include:
- answering the switchboard or telephone
- arranging patients' appointments
- taking messages for medical staff
- booking in patients and confirming that their contact details are correct
- calling patients from the waiting room when it is their turn to be seen
- keeping the reception area and waiting room tidy
- attending practice meetings
- filing of medical notes, letters, test results and other correspondence
- registering new patients on the computer system
- opening and distributing of post.

Job roles in education

P3 P4 M2

If you are interested in working in education, there is a wide range of jobs to consider. Table 3.3 shows some of them, but there may be others!

Special needs teacher	School librarian
Primary school teacher	School nurse
Secondary school teacher	Administrative assistant
College lecturer	IT technician
Kitchen assistant	Lunchtime supervisor
Teaching assistant	Nursery nurse
Cleaner	Caretaker

Table 3.3 Jobs in education

Activity

Carry out some research to find out what the jobs listed in Table 3.3 involve.

Teaching assistant

Teaching assistants play an important role in helping schools to run smoothly and efficiently and in helping to provide support for teachers so that they can concentrate on teaching. The term 'teaching assistant' is an umbrella term used to include classroom assistants, learning support assistants and others whose primary role is to assist the teacher in the classroom.

Figure 3.6 Teaching assistant in class

Job description for a teaching assistant

Responsible to: Head Teacher

Duties
This job description describes in general terms the normal duties that the post-holder will be expected to undertake. However, the job or duties described may vary or be amended from time to time without changing the level of responsibility associated with the post.

Teaching and learning
1. Assist in the educational and social development of pupils under the direction and guidance of the head teacher, special educational needs coordinator and class teachers.
2. Assist in the implementation of Individual Education Programmes for students and help monitor their progress.
3. Provide support for individual students inside and outside the classroom to enable them to fully participate in activities.
4. Work with other professionals, such as speech therapists and occupational therapists, as necessary.
5. Assist class teachers with maintaining appropriate records.
6. Support students with emotional or behavioural problems and help develop their social skills.

Administrative duties
1. Prepare and present displays of students' work.
2. Support class teachers in photocopying and other tasks in order to support teaching.
3. Undertake other duties from time to time as the Head Teacher requires.

Source: Adapted from www.teachernet.gov.uk

Job roles in social services

P3 P4 M2

Some job roles in social services are listed in Table 3.4.

Residential home care worker	Social worker for children and families
Community support worker	Personal care worker
Social worker for the elderly	Care assistant
Occupational therapist	Community support organiser

Table 3.4 Jobs in social services

Social worker

A social worker works with people who have been socially excluded or who are experiencing a crisis. Social workers work in a variety of settings, supporting individuals, families and groups within the community. Qualified social work professionals are often supported by social work assistants. They also work closely with other health and social care staff.

Over 50 per cent of social workers work with young people and their families. They may also work with the following groups:

- young offenders
- people with mental health problems
- school non-attenders
- drug and alcohol abusers
- people with learning and physical disabilities
- the elderly.

Job description for a social worker

A social worker's duties may include:

- helping clients of all ages to identify their problems and come to terms with them
- interviewing clients and their families, and advising and supervising them
- conducting group sessions for people who have similar problems and establishing support groups

- arranging practical support, such as home helps, meals-on-wheels and financial assistance
- keeping records and writing reports
- liaising with other professionals, such as police officers, doctors and community workers
- writing assessments of individuals for court proceedings.

Source: www.get.hobsons.co.uk

Job roles in the leisure services sector

P3 P4 M2

If you are interested in working in the leisure services sector, Table 3.5 lists some of the jobs you could choose from.

Health promotion/education specialist	Leisure centre assistant
Health and fitness instructor	Sports physiotherapist
Leisure centre manager	Outdoor activities instructor
Pool/beach lifeguard	Sports coach

Table 3.5 Jobs in the leisure services

Health and fitness instructor

Health and fitness instructors are responsible for teaching people how to exercise in a safe and effective manner. They may work in private gyms, independent health clubs or leisure centres. Instructors may deliver group exercise classes, such as aerobics, or they may give one-to-one tuition.

Figure 3.7 Health and fitness instructor

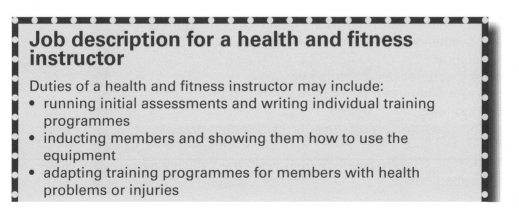

Job description for a health and fitness instructor

Duties of a health and fitness instructor may include:
- running initial assessments and writing individual training programmes
- inducting members and showing them how to use the equipment
- adapting training programmes for members with health problems or injuries

- offering advice and guidance on healthy eating and lifestyle
- implementing marketing initiatives.

Health and fitness instructors may instruct in a range of activities and in one or more centres. They may devise routines for their exercise classes, choose music and check that the necessary equipment is available, such as weights, steps and mats.

Job roles in other non-uniformed public services P3 P4 M2

We have already looked at some local authority jobs, but there are many others that are too numerous to discuss in detail. The following is a small selection of other jobs you may want to find out more about.

Environmental health officer

You may not be sure what an environmental health officer does, but if you have watched certain television programmes where you have felt very queasy at the sight of cockroaches and rodents, the chances are you have been watching an environmental health officer in action!

Environmental health officers use their specialist skills and knowledge to enforce public health policies. Their work involves ensuring public health and hygiene. Any business involved with food will receive regular inspections from the environmental health department. If they are not happy with the hygiene conditions, then they can close the business down!

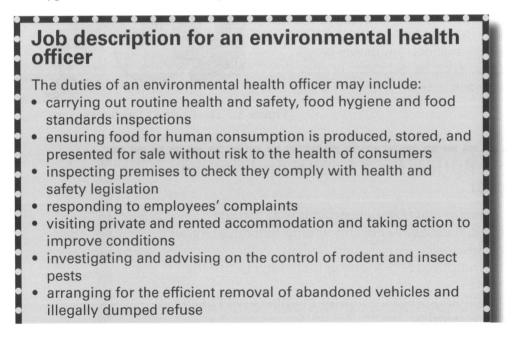

Job description for an environmental health officer

The duties of an environmental health officer may include:
- carrying out routine health and safety, food hygiene and food standards inspections
- ensuring food for human consumption is produced, stored, and presented for sale without risk to the health of consumers
- inspecting premises to check they comply with health and safety legislation
- responding to employees' complaints
- visiting private and rented accommodation and taking action to improve conditions
- investigating and advising on the control of rodent and insect pests
- arranging for the efficient removal of abandoned vehicles and illegally dumped refuse

- licensing pet shops, animal boarding places, zoos and riding establishments
- monitoring levels of noise, air, land and water pollution – this may include liaising with other professionals
- participating in legal proceedings
- keeping appropriate records.

Planning officer

The planning department controls the building of new developments or building extensions. Anyone who wishes to erect a new building must apply to the planning department for permission. This department will make sure that the building fits in with the surrounding area and that it does not intrude too much on the privacy of others, or that there is adequate access to the property. The planning officer will visit the site to check planning requirements are adhered to.

Figure 3.8 A planning officer conducts site visits to check on building work

Job description for a planning officer

The roles of a planning officer include:
- ensuring that any building development has planning permission
- ensuring that planning requirements are complied with
- providing clear guidance to homeowners and builders, etc.
- conducting site visits
- investigating breaches of planning
- where a solution cannot be negotiated, gathering evidence and presenting it to the planning committee, which can include councillors and magistrates.

How to upgrade to M2

M2 In order to upgrade to M2, you should talk about each aspect of your chosen role in more detail by stating what may be involved in the tasks. You should talk about the positive and negative parts of the job, why the job appeals to you and which aspects you would find interesting, etc.

Conditions of service

P4

When deciding on a career, one of the first things you will probably want to know is how much the job pays. The salary for any job is set out in the conditions of service. When we talk about conditions of service, this is what some people might call the benefits or 'the perks' of a job – that is, the pay, pensions, security, holidays, sickness benefits, etc. and how well the employer looks after its employees. These conditions should always be set out at the start of employment and are legally binding on both the employee and the employer. Public service jobs are usually considered to have good conditions of service.

Salary

Salaries vary between the different public services and usually rise according to the length of service of an employee. Table 3.6 shows the starting salaries of a few public service jobs – these are the salaries after training and these rise every year in service.

Nurse	Teacher	Fitness instructor	Teaching assistant	Social worker
£20,000	£21,102	£13,000	£15,000	£20,000

Table 3.6 Starting salaries

Annual leave (or holiday entitlement)

Holiday entitlement varies from service to service and can rise in accordance with length of service.

Pension

Most public service workers are entitled to contribute to a local government pension, which they will receive when they retire from the service.

Working hours

Conditions of service should include details of the working hours of employees. Many public service employees work unsociable hours and shifts in order to provide a 24-hour service, seven days a week.

Paid absence

This includes sickness absence, maternity or paternity leave and other paid absences.

Grading tip!

P4 For P4, you need to describe the salary, pension, holidays, and working hours, etc. for one non-uniformed public service job. This should be a straightforward description

How to upgrade to M3

M3 For M3, you should examine the conditions of service for two jobs from different non-uniformed public services and compare these. What are the differences? Which job carries the highest salary? What are the prospects for promotion? What are the pension arrangements? How many days holiday will you get? Which job has the most attractive conditions of service?

End of unit knowledge check

1. Identify three roles of a social worker.
2. What does 'accountability' mean?
3. Why is the role of medical receptionist so important?
4. What are 'conditions of service'?

Grading criteria

In order to pass this unit, the evidence that the learner presents for assessment needs to demonstrate that they can meet all the learning outcomes for the unit. The criteria for a pass grade describe the level of achievement required to pass this unit.

Grading criteria		
To achieve a pass grade the evidence must show that the learner is able to:	**To achieve a merit grade the evidence must show that, in addition to the pass criteria, the learner is able to:**	**To achieve a distinction grade the evidence must show that, in addition to the pass and merit criteria, the learner is able to:**
P1 Outline the main purpose and roles of different public services	**M1** Explain in detail the roles, purpose and responsibilities of different non-uniformed public services	**D1** Evaluate the roles, purpose and responsibilities of a chosen non-uniformed public service
P2 Discuss the main responsibilities of different non-uniformed public services		
P3 Outline the different employment opportunities available in the non-uniformed public services	**M2** Explain in detail the work of a chosen job in the non-uniformed services	
P4 Describe the current conditions of service for a given job within a non-uniformed public service		

Introduction

There are more people employed in the public service sector in this country than in any other sector and, although such services may be liable to public spending cuts and some privatisation, public services will always be required.

This means that public service jobs are still seen as relatively secure. Jobs in the uniformed public services may also be seen as fairly glamorous and exciting, appealing to many young people. 'Fly on the wall' documentaries and other television programmes tend to show the exciting parts of the job, rather than the routine duties, such as paperwork. Anyone who applies for a job in the public services will almost certainly face stiff competition from other applicants. The recruitment and selection process for most public service jobs is usually a lengthy one. It is particularly important that applicants are fully prepared before applying for a job to give themselves the best possible chance of success. If you are intending to apply for such employment, this chapter will help you.

In this chapter, we will examine the entry requirements and different routes of entry for different careers, which may then give you several options to consider for your future, such as going on to higher education or gaining relevant voluntary or paid work experience before applying to enter your chosen service.

Public service employees need to have particular skills and qualities that enable them to deal with the different situations they may encounter. Some public services require certain levels of fitness and stamina to carry out the physical work involved. Others may require particular qualifications and training.

We will investigate these requirements and you will be able to carry out a personal evaluation of your own skills and qualities. You can then produce a personal action plan to enable you to improve on any weak areas. Remember, the entry requirements given are the *minimum* that you will need. Having more than the minimum entry requirements will give you a better chance of success.

We will also look at the different application processes. This chapter should help you to complete the career-planning unit and show you how to improve your chances of getting through the required processes when applying to the public services for employment.

Figure 4.1 Call centre operators receiving emergency calls

Learning outcomes:

By the end of this unit, you should:

1. Know the application and selection process for public services employment

2. Know the skills and qualities required for a job in the public services

3. Be able to complete an application for a role in a chosen public service.

Application and selection process for different careers in the public services

As competition for most jobs has risen, more emphasis has been placed on the applications and recruitment processes. Many employers now require job applicants to attend multiple interviews and, in many cases, to complete various tests and possibly also to give a presentation to the interviewing panel.

Wherever possible, public service employers should seek to ensure that the workforce they recruit is as diverse as possible. This means that they should encourage applications from a diverse range of people, including different ethnic minorities and people with disabilities if this does not interfere with their ability to do the job. Employers should also ensure that males and females are recruited in equal numbers where possible.

The next section will look at the different entry requirements for several different public services.

Ask yourself!

Why is it important that the public services recruit a diverse workforce?

Key term

Privatisation is when an organisation that was 'owned' by the government and paid for by public money is sold to a private organisation. An example of this is British Rail.

Assignment tip

Remember not to cut and paste or copy work from other sources into your assignments. This is known as plagiarism, which is stealing someone else's words or ideas! Read the text, and then write about the subject *in your own words.*

The police service

P1   M1   D1

Figure 4.2 Police force badges

	Requirement
Age	You can apply at 18 years but cannot be appointed until you are 18 and a half.
Height	There is no minimum or maximum height requirement.
Fitness	You will be required to undergo a fitness test. 'Expect to be tested on two key fitness requirements: • Dynamic strength – involves performing five seated chest pushes and five seated back pulls on the Dyno machine to measure your strength. • Endurance – you will be asked to run to and fro along a 15-metre track in time with a series of bleeps, which become increasingly faster.' Source: www.policecouldyou.co.uk © Crown copyright material is reproduced with the permission of the Controller of HMSO and the Queen's Printer for Scotland.
Qualifications	The police service does not require any formal qualifications but a good standard of literacy and numeracy are necessary.
Health	You will undergo a physical examination, so you should be in a good state of health. Applicants may be rejected if they are obese, diabetic, asthmatic or have mental health problems.
Eyesight	A good level of vision is required – glasses or lenses may be worn.
Nationality	You must be a British citizen, member of the Commonwealth or member of the EU.
Criminal convictions	Having a criminal record will not necessarily prevent you from becoming a police officer, but generally you will be excluded if you have served a prison sentence or have committed a crime of violence. You must declare all criminal convictions.

Table 4.1 Police: entry requirements

There are 43 different police forces in this country, but they tend to have very similar selection and recruitment processes.

Every police force handles its own recruitment, but there are national entrance tests. In England and Wales, this is the 'police initial recruitment test' (PIRT).

A police career is well paid and varied, which is why the police recruitment process is thorough. You will be up against strong competition when you come to apply. Proper preparation will give you the best chance of landing a career in the police service. This section explains the process, including information on the PIRT.

Spending some time now to consider your future career could be key to whether your police application is successful. Once you are accepted into a police force and have completed your training period, you will have a wide range of different jobs from which to choose.

The fire service

Each fire service handles its own recruitment, but they all follow national fire service recruitment procedures and you should contact the personnel or recruitment department of the fire and rescue service to which you intend to apply.

	Requirement
Age	You must be at least 18 years old.
Height	There is no minimum or maximum height requirement.
Fitness	You will be tested on the following: 1. Enclosed space. 2. Ladder climb. 3. Casualty evacuation. 4. Ladder lift. 5. Equipment assembly. 6. Equipment carry.
Qualifications	Formal qualifications are not necessary but a good standard of literacy and numeracy are required. Personal qualities and physical attributes are more important than academic qualifications. The fire service look for the following qualities in applicants: • Willingness to adapt to shift work. • The ability to operate effectively in a close team. • Initiative. • Flexibility. • Honesty. • The ability to take orders. • Good communication skills to deal with people who are injured, in shock or under stress. • Sound judgement, courage, decisiveness, quick reactions and the ability to stay calm in difficult circumstances. • An interest in promoting community safety, education and risk prevention.

	Requirement
Health	You will undergo a physical examination, so you should be in a good state of health. You will be asked to complete a questionnaire covering your medical history and will then be subject to a series of tests.
Eyesight	A good level of vision is required and you will be tested for this.
Hearing	A good level of hearing is required and you will be tested for this.
Criminal record	You must declare all criminal convictions – having a criminal record will not necessarily prevent you from becoming a firefighter.

Table 4.2 Firefighter: entry requirements

The Army

	Requirement
Age	16–33
Qualifications	Formal qualifications are not necessary but a good standard of literacy and numeracy are required.
Health	Successful completion of GP questionnaire and a full Army medical.
Nationality	Must be a British citizen, a citizen of a Commonwealth country or have British Overseas Territories citizenship.
Criminal record	You must declare all criminal convictions – having a criminal record will not necessarily prevent you from joining the Army.

Table 4.3 Soldier: entry requirements

The social services

Figure 4.3 Social worker

	Requirement
Qualifications	Undergraduate entry via UCAS. Most universities ask for two A-levels or equivalent qualifications and experience of working with people as a volunteer or employee in social care. All students must have at least the equivalent of Key Skills Level 2 in English and maths and be able to communicate clearly in spoken and written English.
Criminal record	You must disclose any previous criminal convictions but this would not necessarily prevent you from becoming a social worker.

Table 4.4 Social worker: entry requirements

Education

	Requirement
Qualifications	Undergraduate entry via UCAS. Four GCSEs, including maths and English. Bachelor of Education degree, or other undergraduate degree plus a one-year Postgraduate Certificate in Education.
Criminal record	A Criminal Records Bureau (CRB) check will be required.

Table 4.5 Teacher: entry requirements

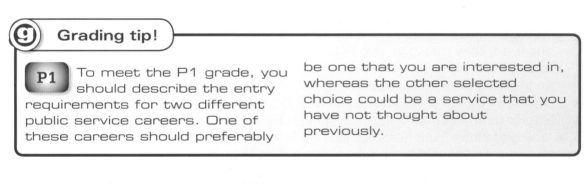

Grading tip!

P1 To meet the P1 grade, you should describe the entry requirements for two different public service careers. One of these careers should preferably be one that you are interested in, whereas the other selected choice could be a service that you have not thought about previously.

How to upgrade to M1

M1 To upgrade to M1, you should choose one of these careers and explain why the service is asking for particular entry requirements. For instance, if looking at the fire service, you should look at each requirement, such as fitness, then look at the required components of the fitness test and give examples of when they would be needed by a firefighter.

How to upgrade to D1

D1 To meet the D1 grade, you should carry out further research regarding the service's entry requirements. For example, what exactly are the eyesight requirements and what precisely do the fitness tests involve? Why is it so important that firefighters meet such rigorous requirements?

Application and selection processes

P2

Most jobs need to be applied for. All public service jobs have strict application processes that must be followed correctly. Practically all public service jobs ask for an application form to be completed. Some application forms may be lengthier than others. All job application forms must be completed accurately and neatly. This is your one chance to get through to the next stage – do not blow it! Many public services use a 'paper sift', which means that any form that is not completed correctly gets thrown into the bin straight away.

Tips for completing your application form

1. Make two or three photocopies of the form so that you can practise completing it in rough before completing the original form.
2. Read the guidance notes carefully before starting to complete the form. They may give you detailed instructions on how to answer each question. Check if you should complete the form in black ink or in block capitals.
3. Ask someone to check your spelling and grammar on the rough copies before completing the original form.
4. Always tell the truth in an application form. You will be questioned about everything you have written at the interview.
5. Do not rush when filling in the form – it is worth spending time to do it properly.

Some services, such as the police, will ask you to talk about your own experiences in dealing with certain situations. You should think very carefully how to answer such questions. You may feel you have not experienced the situation you are being asked to describe but you should try to relate this back to a situation you have experienced – for example, at home, in college, at work or when socialising.

Activity

Write down an example of when you have had to deliver some bad news to someone. Describe the events leading up to the situation and describe how you dealt with giving the bad news.

Personal statements

You will often be asked to provide a personal statement or other supporting information as part of your application. This is an extremely important part of your application; it is an opportunity to make your application stand out. You should give details of any past experience that is relevant to the job for which you are applying.

Curriculum vitae

At some point, you will probably be asked to provide a curriculum vitae (CV), which is a document that gives specific details about you and your experience. A CV should usually include the following details:

- your full name
- your address
- your date of birth
- your contact telephone numbers
- your e-mail address
- your education details (schools and colleges attended)
- your qualifications, with dates achieved
- your present employment details
- details of your past employment, voluntary work or work experience
- any other achievements, e.g. first aid qualifications, driving licence
- additional information – you could list your main hobbies and interests here
- names and addresses of two people who are willing to provide a reference for you.

A CV should be produced accurately and neatly and saved to disk so that it can be updated regularly. There are many different formats for writing a CV and you can find samples of these online.

Activity

Take a look at the following sample CV. There are several things wrong with it. See if you can spot what these are. Is anything missing? How could the CV be improved? Once you have done this, produce your own CV and ask your tutor to give you feedback on it.

Curriculum Vitae

Name:	P. Smith
Date of birth:	19.3.89
Telephone number:	0778567567
Education details: Fleetland	Fleetland Comprehensive Scool, Main Street, 1998–2003
	Fleetland College of Further Education 2003–2005

Past employment – I used to deliver papers.

Present employment – I wash pots at the Red lion pub on Fridays and serve at the local chip shop on Saturdays.

Other achievements –

Additional information – I like football and hanging around with my mates.

Applying to local authority jobs

Step 1 – Application

Vacancies for local authority positions (e.g. teachers, social workers, planning officers, administration workers and librarians) can usually be found on the websites of local councils. The website will give the general details of the advertised vacancies and will also normally include an online application form or details of how to request an application form. The website should provide the job description and details of all the required skills and qualities for the job. You will be given a closing date for the receipt of completed application forms.

Step 2 – Interview

If your application form meets the required standard, you will normally be invited to attend an interview. This will usually take place before a panel. You may be asked to carry out a presentation or some other activity, such as a psychometric test or a simulation activity (see page 104), which you would be given details of before the interview date. If you get through this stage, you may be asked to attend a second interview.

Step 3 – Job offer

After the interview process, you will be notified, either by telephone or by letter, of whether your application was successful. You will then need to decide whether to accept the job offer. It is wise to wait for written confirmation of any job offer before resigning from a previous job.

Figure 4.4 Steps for applying to local authority jobs

Case study

'Liz Holmes is a social worker for Northumberland County Council in the disabled children team.

"I qualified in 1994. I worked in general childcare until seven years ago when I began specialising in social work for children with disabilities.

Northumberland's a very big county. It covers a huge area filled with small villages. There are transport problems so services can be difficult and expensive for people to find and reach. I often spend 30 or 40 minutes travelling each way to see a family. I do 22 hours a week and have about 25 cases. I work with children who have moderate to severe learning and physical disabilities and sensory impairments – typically autism, cerebral palsy and muscular dystrophy. We also encounter rare syndromes and conditions.

I work closely with community nurses and the local school for children with special needs. I have a good relationship with the staff there – the physiotherapist, speech therapist, language therapist and school nurse. If a child I'm involved with is at the school, I will coordinate team-around-a-child meetings where we can update each other, avoid duplication and make sure there aren't any gaps in providing for that child's needs.

One of the things I do is organise placements providing overnight care for children with learning disabilities to give families respite and provide the child with an opportunity to socialise away from the family. I monitor and review the quality of placements, which means I visit the child and communicate with them, using sign language if necessary.

I'll observe the child to see how comfortable he or she is with staff and their peer group. I'll check the logbook to see their dietary requirements are being met, and I'll look out for problems such as whether they've been unsettled at night or upset by another child, especially if it becomes a pattern. I'll ask the child what they've been doing. But if you build a rapport and a relationship of trust, the child is more likely to communicate with you, so I also spend time communicating with the child more naturally by playing. We might go to the sensory room and get into the ballpool."'

Source: www.guardian.co.uk

Copyright Guardian News & Media 2009

Applying to the Royal Marines

Step 1 – Enquiry

To begin the application process, you should contact the Royal Marines' careers advisors. You can do this either online or by telephone. They will check if you are eligible to join and, if you are, they will arrange an appointment for you to visit the Armed Forces Careers Office.

Step 2 – Armed Forces Careers Office visit

During this visit, you will have the opportunity to chat with serving Royal Marines about life in the corps and what is required of you for the remainder of the application process.

Step 3 – Aptitude test

This short test is designed to assess your skills with language, numbers, reasoning and mechanical comprehension.

Step 4 – Interview and medical check

You will take part in an interview to find out more about why you want to join. You will then be given a medical check to make sure that you are in good health.

Step 5 – Pre-joining fitness test

In order to ensure that you, as a Royal Marines candidate, are able to complete a three-mile run, you will undertake a pre-joining fitness test. This consists of two 2.4km runs; the first run must be completed within 12 minutes 30 seconds and the second run, to be the candidate's best effort, must be within 10 minutes 30 seconds, with a minute's rest between the two runs. The runs are conducted on a two-degree inclination on a running machine.

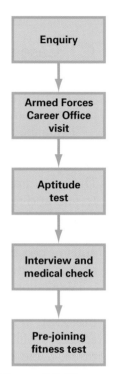

Figure 4.5 Steps for applying to the Royal Marines

Potential Royal Marines course (PRMC) and potential officers course (POC)

Over three days at the Commando Training Centre Royal Marines at Lympstone, you will go through a range of physical and mental tests in the gym, the classroom and on the assault course. You will also get to talk to recruits already in training. If you are a potential Royal Marines officer, you will also be examined on your leadership potential and your ability to work as part of a team. For more information about the PRMC or POC, you can visit the Royal Marines website, www.royalnavy.mod.uk/royalmarines.

Applying to the police service

Step 1 – Check that you meet the basic entry requirements

Go online and find out which forces in your area are recruiting. You should then request an application pack, by telephone, by post or online.

Step 2 – Application

On receiving your application form, the force that you have applied to will check that you are eligible and they will mark your answers to the questions. Your application form must be completed very neatly and accurately. Sixty per cent of candidates do not complete the form correctly and so are rejected at this stage. If your application is successful, you will be invited to attend an assessment centre

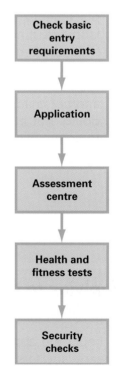

Figure 4.6 Steps for applying to the police service

Step 3 – Assessment centre

Two weeks before attending the centre, you will be sent material in preparation for the assessment. At the centre, you will be tested on your written English skills, verbal reasoning, oral skills and mathematical skills. This is called the 'police initial recruitment test' (PIRT).

There will also be an interview, role plays and written tests. During the interview, you will be asked questions about five 'competencies'. These competencies are:

- community and customer focus
- resilience
- teamworking
- respect for race and diversity
- oral communication.

The following boxes contain examples of a verbal reasoning test and a numeracy assessment test.

Verbal reasoning test

Scenario
Some time of the night of October 1st, the Copacabana Club was burnt to the ground. The police are treating the fire as suspicious. The only facts known at this stage are:

- The club was insured for more than its real value.
- The club belonged to John Hodges.
- Les Braithwaite was known to dislike John Hodges.
- Between October 1st and October 2nd, Les Braithwaite was away from home on a business trip.
- There were no fatalities.
- A plan of the club was found in Les Braithwaite's flat.

Question 1
A member of John Hodges' family died in the blaze.
- ○ True
- ○ False
- ○ Impossible to say

Question 2
If the insurance company pay out in full, John Hodges stands to profit from the fire.
- ○ True
- ○ False
- ○ Impossible to say

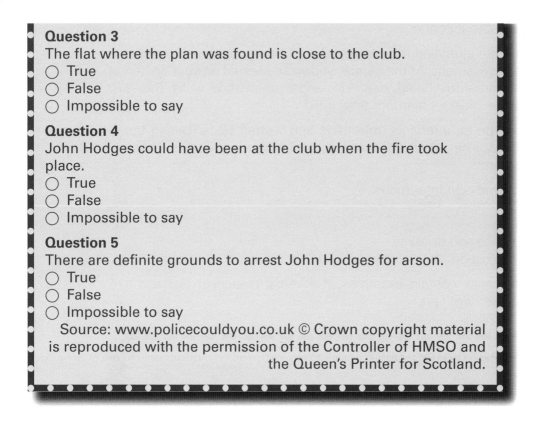

Question 3

The flat where the plan was found is close to the club.

○ True
○ False
○ Impossible to say

Question 4

John Hodges could have been at the club when the fire took place.

○ True
○ False
○ Impossible to say

Question 5

There are definite grounds to arrest John Hodges for arson.

○ True
○ False
○ Impossible to say

Source: www.policecouldyou.co.uk © Crown copyright material is reproduced with the permission of the Controller of HMSO and the Queen's Printer for Scotland.

Numeracy assessment test

Question 1

A purse was found with one £5 note, four 20p coins, and five 2p coins. How much did the purse contain altogether?

○ £5.10
○ £5.22
○ £5.82
○ £5.85
○ £5.90

Question 2

A car park has space for 220 cars per floor. How many can fit on 3 floors?

○ 440
○ 460
○ 640
○ 660
○ 680

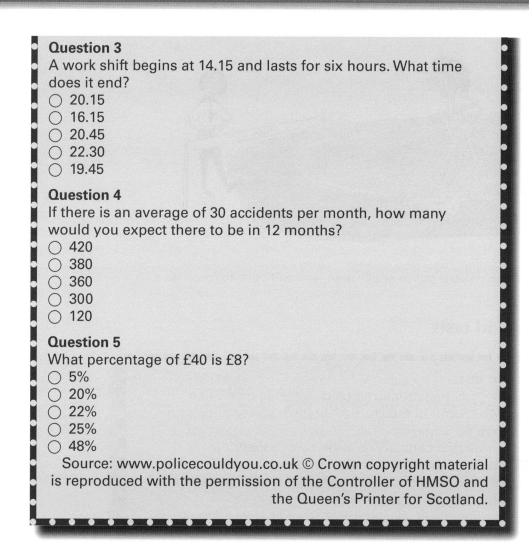

Question 3

A work shift begins at 14.15 and lasts for six hours. What time does it end?

○ 20.15
○ 16.15
○ 20.45
○ 22.30
○ 19.45

Question 4

If there is an average of 30 accidents per month, how many would you expect there to be in 12 months?

○ 420
○ 380
○ 360
○ 300
○ 120

Question 5

What percentage of £40 is £8?

○ 5%
○ 20%
○ 22%
○ 25%
○ 48%

Source: www.policecouldyou.co.uk © Crown copyright material is reproduced with the permission of the Controller of HMSO and the Queen's Printer for Scotland.

Step 4 – Health and fitness tests

You will need to pass the police fitness test, an eyesight test and a thorough medical. Refer to the Police Could You? website (www.policecouldyou. co.uk) for full details of these tests.

Step 5 – Security checks

Before you can be accepted as a police officer, you will be required to undergo rigorous security checks and background checks. This process can take several months (it could be up to 18 months) from start to finish. It is recommended that you seek alternative employment while waiting for your application to progress.

You should refer to the Police Could You? website (www.policecouldyou. co.uk) for helpful tips and information about all of the recruitment tests and processes.

Figure 4.7 As part of your police application, you will have to undergo a fitness test

Other types of tests

Psychometric tests

Psychometric tests are structured tests, taken in exam-like conditions, which aim to measure a person's ability or certain aspects of their personality.

Most psychometric tests are devised by occupational psychologists. Their aim is to provide employers with a reliable method of selecting the best applicants and to design tests carefully so that they are fair to all applicants.

All psychometric tests, except for personality tests, are strictly timed.

Simulations

Simulation exercises are designed to imitate particular workplace tasks, behaviour or skills. The most common types of simulation exercises include:

- group exercises/case studies
- presentations
- fact-finding exercises
- role plays
- in-tray priority exercises.

Interviews

Most people will need to go for a job interview at some point in their career. There are several different types of interview.

Formal interview

This is a structured interview, usually taking place before a panel who will ask you some set questions. You may be asked to prepare and deliver a presentation to the panel.

Informal interview

This is more relaxed than a formal interview and may consist of a chat with one or more people. You must not be too relaxed, however, as you are still 'on trial'.

Full-day interview

This can consist of several different parts. You may be asked to give a presentation to the panel, take part in one or more interviews and meet and interact with other candidates or existing employees. For certain jobs, you may be asked to do a task. For example, if applying for a teaching job, applicants may be asked to deliver a short lesson while being observed. You will be constantly assessed throughout the day, so you may feel quite exhausted by the end of it.

Preparing for interview

You have passed the application stage and been invited to attend an interview. This is your chance to sell yourself and prove that you are the right person for the post. It cannot be stressed enough just how important it is to prepare for your interview. You will usually be competing against many other applicants and you need to make sure that you stand out – for the right reasons! There are many things that you can do to prepare yourself for interview.

Research

Make sure that you research the public service you are applying to. Try to find out about any new developments or how the service has changed in recent years. If you are applying to an armed service, read up about any current deployments that they are involved in. Carry out research to find any organisational reports and to learn about the structure of the organisation. Take a look at the website for the service – you will probably find samples of the questions you may be asked. Think how you would answer these sample questions. Take part in any mock interviews that are arranged at your school or college to give you an idea of what to expect.

Plan

Make sure you know where and when the interview is to take place. If it is somewhere you have never visited before, make a practice journey before the day of the interview at a similar time so you know what to expect regarding volume of traffic, roadworks, bus/train times, parking, etc. Do not underestimate the time it will take you to reach the interview venue after parking or walking from the bus station and to find the room where the interview is to take place.

Plan your outfit and appearance for the interview. Public service interviews are always quite formal so a smart appearance is essential. This is probably not the time to show what a trendy dresser you are! You should not dress for an interview in the same way as you would for a night out! Tone down any distinctive hair colours and remove any facial piercings. Make sure your clothes are clean, pressed and ready before the day.

Figure 4.8 During an interview, it is important to create the right impression!

On the day

The more you have prepared for the interview, the less nervous you are likely to be. Nerves are perfectly natural, however, and most interviewers will make allowance for this. Do not over-compensate for nerves by appearing too confident or cocky. Most public service interviewers are looking for someone who can work well within a team and not be too domineering.

Some public service interviews will involve interaction with the other candidates, where you could be observed. How you react in such a situation could indicate whether you are a good team player or have the necessary social skills required for a public service job.

Be aware of your body language during the interview. Sit up straight during the interview and make eye contact with the panel. Try not to fidget! Listen carefully to the questions asked – if you do not understand the question, ask the interviewer to repeat it or clarify it. If it is something you think you may know the answer to but are not sure, then say what you know – it may be correct! If you really do not know the answer, however, simply apologise and say so. Do not waffle on about something you know absolutely nothing about!

Always tell the truth during an interview! Most public service interviewers will be experienced in judging whether a person is being honest. Also, checks will certainly be carried out, so any untrue stories will be discovered.

Do:
Prepare!
Plan your journey!
Plan your appearance!
Keep calm!

Don't:
Be late!
Be cocky!

Figure 4.9 Do's and don'ts for interviews

Interview questions

There are some standard questions that you will almost certainly be asked in any public service interview; it is important that you prepare your answers to these. The following is a list of sample questions that you could be asked.

1. Why do you want this job?

What not to say!	This sounds better!
I have wanted to be a police officer/soldier/firefighter since I was little.	It is something I have always had in mind but I have thought carefully about it now for some time. I know the job may not be as glamorous as people think and how some television programmes show it. I also realise that there are risks and responsibilities involved, but I think these would be balanced by the satisfaction of knowing that I could help individuals and maybe make a difference to the community. I think the job would be challenging and interesting and very character building.

2. What skills and qualities can you bring to the job?

What not to say!	This sounds better!
I don't know really. I just think I would be good at it.	I think I have good communication skills. I like talking to people and feel I am a good listener. I do enjoy helping people. I am hard-working and honest and feel I could remain calm in difficult situations. I enjoy working in a team and am reliable and committed. If I say I will do something, I like to do it and do not like to let people down. I have also done some voluntary work with people with disabilities. This has helped me to understand the problems that some people face, which I was not aware of before.

3. How can the public services ensure equal opportunities?

What not to say!	This sounds better!
Everyone has to be treated the same, whoever they are. Nobody should get special treatment.	I think it is very important that the public services reflect society in this country, so that means having a mix of ethnic minorities in the services. There should also be a good mix of males and females and there should not be any issues about people's sexual orientation. Recruitment processes need to show that they welcome applications from all sections of society.

4. Can you give me an example of when you have demonstrated good communication skills?

What not to say!	This sounds better!
Er, er! I can't think really.	The voluntary work that I do with people with disabilities sometimes involves working with people with poor speech and hearing. As part of my volunteer role, I have to attend meetings to discuss the needs of the people I am helping to look after. This means that I have to watch and listen very carefully to understand what someone is trying to say. It is important that I do this and that I can clearly communicate this information back to the meetings. I feel that my college course has helped me to develop good communication skills too as we have had to take part in class debates and discussions and also give presentations to the rest of the group.

5. When have you worked well as a member of a team?

What not to say!	This sounds better!
I have never really done it because I didn't like team sports at school and I prefer to do things on my own.	I have always enjoyed playing team sports, like football and rugby, even though I wasn't the world's best player! I work as a member of a team in my voluntary work where we have to work a rota system to make sure that there is full-time cover. We need to make sure there is good communication between us all or important information about the guests may not get passed on, which could have serious consequences. Also, in my part-time job where I work in a restaurant, teamwork is important. We each have our own sections and jobs to cover but we also help each other out if we see that someone else is really busy.

(g) Grading tip!

P2 To meet the P2 criteria, you should choose a service and outline the different stages a candidate will go through when applying to join the service and give a short explanation of what each stage involves.

Skills and qualities required for work in the public services

Most public services, uniformed or non-uniformed, require a range of different skills and qualities. Some of these skills are specifically required for certain jobs, but others are more general and are needed in most public service jobs. We will now take a look at some of these skills.

Skills required

Teamwork skills

Teamwork plays a very important part in the public services:

Together
Everyone
Achieves
More

Figure 4.10 Teamwork is very important in the public services

Being part of a team means looking out for others and sharing the workload. All public service jobs involve working in teams of one sort or another. The Army has several different regiments and the fire service has different watches, while the police service has different teams, such as the criminal investigation department (CID), traffic section and drugs squad.

Leadership skills

Leadership qualities are vital for many public service employees. Leaders need skills that enable them to direct others effectively. This can mean being assertive without being domineering, being fair but firm, and being positive and enthusiastic even if others are not. Good leaders are able to motivate others and know when to delegate, or pass down, certain tasks or responsibilities.

> ## Ask yourself!
>
> **Think of some examples of great leaders, past or present. What qualities do/did they have?**

Communication skills

Good communication skills are essential for public service employees. Speaking, listening, reading and writing are skills that they need every day during their working lives. Dealing with the public is a key role and the way in which public service members approach this is extremely important. It does not matter if you are a police officer, a social worker or a local planning officer, how you speak to members of the public can make a real difference to how you are perceived. Good communication skills should be developed wherever possible. Non-verbal communication skills (or body language) are also very important. Potentially aggressive situations can often be diffused if dealt with in a calm, controlled manner. It is, therefore, vital that you are aware of your body language and the message it sends out.

Time management skills

Punctuality is an absolute must-have in the public services! Public service workers must be able to manage their time effectively, whatever their role. This usually means being organised, looking ahead and planning your time effectively. You could use a diary or wall planner to help you plan your time; entering all your assignment deadlines will help you to ensure that these are handed in on time.

Problem-solving skills

Public service workers often have to deal with a wide range of problems and situations. Problem-solving is a skill that can be practised and developed in order to deal with such situations.

Qualities required

Qualities are slightly different from skills. They make us the people we are and we are usually born with them. However, some qualities can be

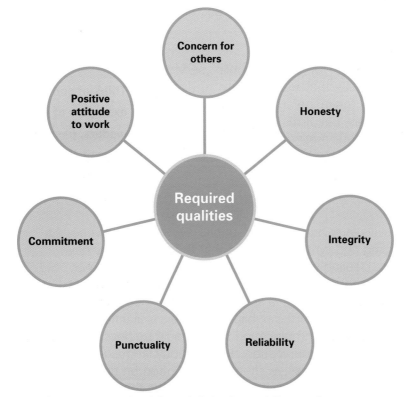

Figure 4.11 Qualities required for a job in the public services

acquired as we mature and develop. There are many important qualities required of public service workers (see Figure 4.11). A few of these are detailed below – do you think you have these qualities?

Honesty

It goes without saying that public service employees should be honest and law-abiding individuals. The public needs to know that they can trust and respect members of the public services.

Integrity

If a person has integrity, it means that they have good morals, know what is right and wrong and are of good character.

Commitment

Commitment, or dedication, is required by all public service employees. Most public service jobs are not 9:00 till 5:00. Many employees work far more hours than those they are contracted to work in order to get the job done. They are generally willing to do this for the benefit of other people who rely on them. Being committed usually means doing whatever is required and not letting people down.

Reliability

Being reliable means doing what you have said you will do when people are depending on you. This is an essential quality for public service employees.

Specific skills and qualities

The skills and qualities listed above are generic, which means that they are general skills that would be needed for most public services. In addition to these, there are skills required for specific jobs. For example, to join the Army as a soldier, you would need to be brave. Likewise, firefighters can find themselves in dangerous situations; most people would consider firefighters to be courageous since they must be willing to enter a burning building to save a life. Social workers, nurses and most other public service workers are often interested in improving the lives of others and, therefore, to enter these professions, you would need to be a caring person.

(g) Grading tip!

P3 For P3, you need to identify the different skills required by public service workers, as discussed above, and explain a little about them.

How to upgrade to M2

M2 For M2, you should explain the skills in greater detail, describing why such skills would be needed and giving examples of how and when they would be used by different public service workers. You could talk about how teamwork is used in the armed forces or the fire service and why it is so important. You could also explain why it is vital that police officers are seen to be totally honest.

Prepare an application for a role in a chosen public service

P4   P5   M3

P4   M3

Skills audit

It is important to know what skills and qualities you already possess. Many of us are often not aware of these until we actually sit down and think about them. It can be quite difficult to look at yourself and see how you measure up. When you are asked to rate yourself in a particular skill, think carefully and answer the question truthfully. Think about your strengths and weaknesses and how you compare with others.

For instance, you may have noticed that you are more likely to speak up in class than others, which indicates that you have good communication skills. Do you listen to others when they tell you about their own problems? Are you good at finding solutions to problems? When asked about your time management, ask yourself the following questions: do you arrive at college or work on time or are you frequently late? Are you good at handing in assignments by the deadline date?

ⓖ Grading tip!

P4 For P4, you should carry out a personal skills audit for one uniformed service of your choice and one non-uniformed service.

How to upgrade to M3

M3 For M3, you should produce your personal skills audit and then map the skills to a public service of your choice. Add some notes to explain how you rate yourself and why you feel you need to develop some skills or why you feel you already have the adequate skills.

Activity

Complete the following table (Table 4.6) and rate yourself accordingly using the following criteria:

1. I have no experience of using this skill.
2. I have some experience but feel I need to improve further.
3. I have experience of using this skill but still need to improve in certain aspects.
4. I am an expert and feel that this is not a priority for my development.

	1	2	3	4
Teamwork skills				
Leadership skills				
Time management skills				
Problem-solving skills				
Communication skills – reading				
Communication skills – speaking				
Communication skills – writing				
Communication skills – listening				
Communication skills – body language				

Table 4.6 Personal audit of skills

Action planning

Once you have carried out your skills audit, you will need to think about how to improve the skills that you have identified as needing development. You should draw up an action plan to outline how and when you are going to develop your skills.

Make sure that your action plan is SMART!
An action plan should be:

Specific – setting clear and specific targets will help you to be clear about the steps you need to take.

Measurable – objectives must be measurable, which means you will know when you have completed them.

Achievable – it is important that your objectives can actually be achieved and that you are not striving for something which may not be achievable.

Realistic – you should ensure that your objectives are realistic and that you are not setting targets for yourself which are too high, which could be demoralising and demotivating.

Time constrained – you should set yourself a time-limit to achieve your objectives otherwise you may never get to achieve the objective.

An example of a suitable action plan is shown in Table 4.7.

Skill to improve	How much to improve	How to improve	Deadline
Speaking skills	To achieve Level 2	Practise doing presentations at college. Complete Communications Key Skills Level 2.	July
Writing skills	To achieve Level 2	Attend and complete Communications Key Skills Level 2.	July
Reading skills	To achieve Level 2	Read books and magazines at home and college.	July
Time management	To ensure all assignments are handed in on time	Maintain diary with all assignment dates. Complete wall chart to display at home. Organise clothes and equipment the day before needed.	One week
Teamwork skills	To develop better skills	Take part in more teamwork activities. Think about my role in the team.	July

Table 4.7 Sample action plan

Prepare an application

P5

We have discussed the different application methods for the different public services earlier in this chapter. The third learning outcome of this unit requires you to prepare an application for a job role in the public services.

g **Grading tip!**

P5 For P5, you should carry out some research to find out what the application process is for a job you are interested in.

You will almost certainly be asked to complete an application form and you may need to download this from the service's website. You may need to include a personal statement as part of the form or as an additional document.

To complete P5, you should have a suitable application form completed neatly and accurately, and also an up-to-date CV. You should refer to your skills audit and map these skills to the job role in which you are interested. You should also produce your action plan for preparation before entry to a public service.

Well done! You have now completed this chapter. If you put the theory into practice, you will give yourself the best possible chance when you come to apply for a job in your chosen public service.

End of unit knowledge check

1. What do the initials 'CV' stand for?
2. Name two different types of interview.
3. Name three different skills required by public service workers.
4. Name three different types of communication skills.

Grading criteria

In order to pass this unit, the evidence that the learner presents for assessment needs to demonstrate that they can meet all the learning outcomes for the unit. The criteria for a pass grade describe the level of achievement required to pass this unit.

Grading criteria		
To achieve a pass grade the evidence must show that the learner is able to:	To achieve a merit grade the evidence must show that, in addition to the pass criteria, the learner is able to:	To achieve a distinction grade the evidence must show that, in addition to the pass and merit criteria, the learner is able to:
P1 Describe the current entry requirements for two public service jobs		
P2 Describe the application and selection process for two public service jobs		
P3 Identify the different skills and qualities required for a given public service role		
P4 Carry out a personal skills audit for a given public service role	**M1** Analyse your skills against a given public service role	**D1** Evaluate your skills against a given public service role
P5 Complete an application for a role in a specific public service		

Unit 5

Improving health and fitness for entry to the uniformed public services

Introduction

People working in the uniformed public services need to be fit to carry out their work, so in order for you to join the service of your choice, you need to get fit and stay fit. You will also have to realise the importance of personal health and lifestyle, which may have an impact on your fitness throughout your career.

The aim of this unit is to give you an overview of health and fitness in preparation for entry to the public services. You will be asked to study the anatomy and physiology of the main body systems and find out what the short-term and long-term effects of exercise are on your body. Your lifestyle and nutritional health also affect your health and fitness, so you will be required to keep a personal food diary and, perhaps, change the way you presently live.

The practical element of this unit tests your fitness using a variety of methods, and from this you will be able to assess your own levels of fitness in relation to your chosen service which, from the results, will help you to put together a training programme. Each public service has its own fitness test, which is generally quite easy to pass if you are already quite fit. Most of the services put you through a cardiovascular test, such as a run or a multi-stage fitness test, and test your muscular strength and endurance with a 'Dyno' machine or by asking you to do sit-ups, pull-ups and press-ups. The harder fitness challenges generally take place once you are recruited.

From all this information, you can produce a personal health improvement programme in which you can participate in preparation for entry into the uniformed public service of your choice.

Learning outcomes:

By the end of this unit, you should:

1. Know the major body systems associated with a healthy lifestyle

2. Understand the effect of basic nutrition and lifestyle factors on public service fitness

3. Be able to take part in fitness tests in order to appreciate the requirements of the uniformed public services

4. Be able to participate in a personal health improvement programme for uniformed public services.

The major body systems associated with a healthy lifestyle

Key terms associated with a healthy lifestyle

A healthy lifestyle means different things to different people. To gain a better understanding, you need to define all the words that are associated with 'healthy lifestyle'.

Fitness can be general or specific. General fitness means that you are healthy and can perform everyday activities without getting out of breath, you have a good body composition and you have plenty of cardiovascular and muscular endurance. Specific fitness is being able to play sport or physical recreation at a higher level; for this, you need more than just general fitness.

Health is the state of complete physical, mental and social well-being, not merely the absence of disease or infirmity – this is a definition from the World Health Organisation (WHO). Health is affected by your lifestyle and the environment in which you live.

Well-being is the condition of your body working well, of feeling contented with no stress or mental concerns and of being a part of society with family and friends.

Nutrition is the act or process of nourishing. Nutrition includes the kinds of food and drink that you consume, how much you eat and at what times of the day you eat your meals. Good nutrition requires a balanced diet of the main food groups.

Lifestyle is the particular attitudes, habits or behaviour associated with an individual or group. Social habits include drinking alcohol, smoking cigarettes, taking drugs and the way you spend your free time. Does stress or depression feature in your life and do you have family or friends upon whom you can rely and trust?

The effects of exercise on the body systems

The four main body systems associated with health are generally considered to be the skeletal system, the muscular system, the respiratory system and the cardiovascular system.

The skeletal system – the bones

Structure
The adult skeleton is made up of 206 bones. There are four different types of bone – long, short, flat and irregular. Many of the bones meet at joints to help us move. There are three different types of joint – immoveable, slightly

moveable and freely moveable. The five types of moveable joints are ball and socket, hinge, pivot, gliding and condyloid.

Function
The skeletal system has five main functions:

- It gives us our body shape.
- It supports the body.
- It protects the vital organs.
- It allows movement.
- It makes new blood cells.

The effects of exercise on the skeletal system
There are no real short-term effects of exercise on the skeletal system, but there are a few long-term benefits, such as your joints remaining flexible through regular use and the strengthening of cartilage, ligaments and tendons, which join the muscles to the bones, as long as you do not over-stretch them! The bones are also strengthened and this can improve your posture. In addition, there is a continuous formation of white blood cells from bone marrow; white blood cells help to fight disease by destroying bacteria.

The muscular system – the muscles

Structure
There are three different types of muscle – cardiac, involuntary and voluntary. Muscles are made up of many fibres; we all have the same number of fibres but different amounts of voluntary muscle fibres called fast twitch and slow twitch.

Function
The muscles pull on the bones of the skeletal system to provide movement. Muscles work in pairs that pull in opposite directions.

There are two types of muscle contraction – isometric and isotonic.

Figure 5.1 The muscular system

The effects of exercise on the muscular system
There is a slight improvement in muscle tone and strength each time you exercise, but you must be sure not to overuse the muscles during an exercise session as they can tear.

The respiratory system – breathing

Structure
The respiratory system is made up of six components – mouth and nose cavity, trachea, bronchi, bronchioles, alveoli and lungs.

Function
The function of the respiratory system is to breathe in oxygen from the air into our lungs where it exchanges with carbon dioxide, which we then breathe out

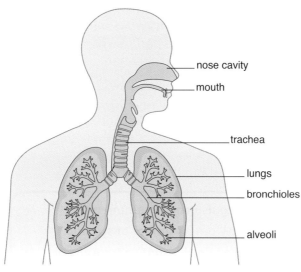

nose cavity
mouth
trachea
lungs
bronchioles
alveoli

Figure 5.2 The respiratory system

The effects of exercise on the respiratory system
As soon as you start to exercise, the respiratory system begins to work harder. You start to breathe more deeply and much faster, therefore taking in more oxygen and breathing out more carbon dioxide. As your oxygen intake increases, the muscles have to work harder.

Long-term benefits of exercise include the diaphragm and intercostal muscles becoming stronger which, in turn, makes your chest cavity larger. This enables you to breathe more air in and exchange gases much faster.

The circulatory system – blood and circulation

Structure
The circulatory system has three main functions – to transport blood around the body, to keep your body temperature under control and to protect you against disease by forming blood clots.

There are three types of blood vessel – arteries, veins and capillaries. Plasma carries platelets, red blood cells and white blood cells in the bloodstream.

Function
The heart pumps oxygenated blood around the body in arteries and returns deoxygenated blood back to the heart along veins. The deoxygenated blood flows from the heart to the lungs to be oxygenated and then returns to the heart to begin the process again. This is known as double circulation.

Capillaries carry food and oxygen to the tissues of the body and take waste away from them.

The effects of exercise on the circulatory system
Similarly to the respiratory system, the circulation of blood around the body starts to increase as soon as you start to exercise. Your heart starts to beat faster to circulate more blood and this is diverted from the minor organs of the body to the muscles so that they can work harder. As you get warmer, the blood moves closer to the skin and you begin to sweat.

Over time, exercise increases the number of red blood cells, your arteries become bigger and your heart increases in size so that it beats more slowly. Your heart rate returns to normal after exercise much more quickly after exercise too.

Activity

With a friend, take each other's resting pulse and breathing rate and record the results. Individually, carry out a number of specific cardiovascular exercises, such as running on the spot, star jumps or burpees, for a few minutes and then ask your partner to check your pulse and breathing rate immediately. Record the results. After a minute, ask them to take the results again and once more after three minutes. After your partner has finished the exercises, take their pulse and breathing rate as they did for you and then compare the results.

Who took the longest to get back to a resting heart rate and normal breathing rate? Did you feel the immediate effects of exercise and how did you feel afterwards?

P3

The benefits of exercise

Exercise is physical activity that you do to keep healthy and increase your fitness. It keeps your body in good physical condition and the more you do, the better the body works. It is recommended that you exercise for a minimum of 30 minutes, three times a week, in order to stay in good condition. As well as the benefits of exercise mentioned previously, with regard to the body systems, there are other benefits associated with exercise that affect your life and lifestyle.

Health benefits include reducing your risk of suffering from disease or injury and increasing your life expectancy. You will eat better and be able to digest your food much more easily. The body functions better overall and you will have fewer problems with muscles and joints and, therefore, less time off work or your studies due to illness or injury.

Exercise provides enjoyment and excitement, so some of the benefits can affect you mentally, which means that you will not be as stressed or depressed and you may have higher self-esteem and confidence. Stress puts an increased strain on your main body organs, such as your heart and your brain, and when suffering from stress, you will find it difficult to concentrate or think as clearly as normal. This, in time, can lead to far more serious health or mental issues.

Think about it!

Keeping fit also has a social benefit, helping you to make and meet friends. Plus, it makes you feel good about yourself. Sport is a positive use of time and an excellent way of releasing energy. It also helps you to work more efficiently. Exercising crosses the usual barriers of age, gender, race, religion and class.

M1

The impact of regular exercise on the body systems

Regular exercise could, in time, reduce your heart rate, and therefore your blood pressure, slow down your breathing rate and strengthen or tone many of your muscles. It could also control your weight, improve your digestion and increase your stamina. You will feel the immediate impact of exercise on the body as soon as you start exercising, but it will take more time for you to notice the long-term impact. Overall, you will feel healthier and less lethargic as your body adapts to frequent exercise.

The skeletal system will strengthen and the wearing out of your bones and joints, which occurs as you get older, will slow down. The tendons and ligaments will improve and cartilage will become thicker. Muscles will work harder and longer as they increase in size and strength. The heart will increase in size as it is a muscle and grows as it is exercised, and blood will carry more oxygen as blood volume increases. Breathing will become more efficient as the lung volume increases and more air is transferred from the air in the lungs to the capillaries.

How to upgrade from M1 to D1

D1 In order to turn your merit grade into a distinction, you will need to give much more detail of how each system mentioned previously, and others not mentioned, is affected by regular exercise, both in the short term and the long term. You will notice the short-term effects of exercise on the body systems immediately, while the long-term effects on the whole body are slower to emerge. Take each body system and mention both types of effects upon it after exercise in order to ensure that you cover all the relevant points for the top grade.

The short- and long-term benefits of regular sport and recreational activities

D1

When you exercise, you make your body work harder than normal and put a greater stress on your body; this in turn makes your major body systems respond and you will see and feel immediate changes to your breathing and heart rate. These are the short-term effects, or benefits, to your body. If you exercise on a regular basis, you will notice some longer-term effects on your body and the major body systems.

Short-term benefits

As you exercise, you start to breathe faster and more deeply. This means that your lungs and respiratory system are working harder to draw oxygen from the air and remove the carbon dioxide from your lungs. The oxygen goes to the muscles and muscular system so that they keep working to produce movement.

Your heart beats faster to circulate the oxygen in the blood (oxygenated blood, which is bright red) around the circulatory system. Blood that normally goes to some of your internal organs is diverted to the muscles to keep them moving.

The blood vessels widen to cope with the extra blood supply and keep your blood pressure at the correct level. This means the blood gets hotter and moves closer to the surface of the skin so that heat can escape.

Your skin turns red as you start to sweat; this helps you to keep cool and prevents you from overheating.

The circulatory and respiratory systems work together (cardiovascular system) to provide oxygen for the muscular system to continue working until you begin to rest.

Figure 5.3 Benefits of exercise

Long-term benefits

Your body systems will adapt and even change permanently as you participate in exercise, fitness or physical activities and you will become stronger, faster or more flexible, depending upon the types of work your body is made to do.

Circulatory system – the heart becomes larger and stronger as the walls get thicker and more blood is pumped per beat. Your resting heart rate falls as each heartbeat pumps more blood. Blood vessels increase in size and number and your body produces more red blood cells to transport oxygen more efficiently. Your heart beats more slowly but pumps the same amount of blood, so your blood pressure falls.

Respiratory system – the lungs get bigger and so increase their capacity to let in more oxygen. The rate of carbon dioxide being exhaled increases and the muscles used for breathing, including the diaphragm, make your chest cavity larger.

Cardiovascular system – the increase in efficiency of the circulatory and respiratory systems makes the exchange of gases much faster and, therefore, you can exercise for longer and at a higher tempo.

Muscular system – muscle tone is increased and body fat is reduced. The muscles adapt to use more energy and work more efficiently and for longer. A larger network of blood vessels is developed to feed more oxygen and energy to the muscles.

g) Grading tip!

P1 For P1, you need to define the key terms associated with a healthy lifestyle.

P2 For P2, you need to describe the effects of exercise on the body systems associated with health.

P3 For P3, you must outline the benefits of exercise.

M1 For M1, you need to explain the impact of regular exercise on the body systems associated with health.

D1 For D1, you should evaluate the short-term and long-term effects of regular exercise on the body systems associated with health.

The effect of basic nutrition and lifestyle factors on public service fitness

Keeping a personal food diary

A personal food diary will help you to control the types of food you eat and how much food and drink you actually consume. It will also make you realise what the best times of the day are for main meals and snacks. You must eat a balanced diet of all the food groups so that you consume all five nutrients in the correct amounts.

Carbohydrates

These nutrients are broken down into two types: simple and complex carbohydrates.

Simple carbohydrates are sugars found in cakes, sweets and jams and immediately supply energy, which you must use very quickly before they turn into fats.

Complex carbohydrate is starch, which is found in bread, pasta, rice and potatoes. As the name implies, these foods are not simply taken into the bloodstream but have to be broken down in a complex manner over a period of time. Then you are rewarded with a steady supply of energy with which to exercise. These should be the biggest part of any meal.

Proteins

Meat, fish, eggs and milk are some forms of protein that help the body to grow and repair itself on a continuous basis. They are made from chemicals called non-essential and essential amino acids, which your body needs in order to provide you with the energy required to exercise.

Fats

There are two main types of fats, which provide energy and help to keep us warm. Saturated fats are found in animal products. Monounsaturated and polyunsaturated fats are found in margarines, butter, oils and oily fish.

Vitamins

Vitamins help your bones, teeth and skin to grow and are found in nearly all foods. Some of them can be stored in the body until you need them but others cannot be stored so you need to eat them regularly to keep you healthy.

Minerals

All foods contain small traces of minerals as they are found in the soil and the air. You need small amounts regularly to strengthen your bones and keep your teeth healthy.

Of the three main nutrients that supply your energy, carbohydrates should account for 55 per cent of calorie intake, fats 30 per cent and protein 15 per cent.

Your diet should also contain a small amount of fibre to help your digestive system and plenty of water because you need to replace all the fluids that you lose or use.

Figure 5.4 Vitamins and minerals are found in these foods

Activity

Draw up a table for the next seven days and write down all the food and drink that you consume and when you consume it. This should include all takeaways, vending-machine confectionery and other snacks. The idea behind a personal food diary is to help you to plan ahead and ensure you eat a balanced diet. You can then look back at your food diary and see if it is working.

	Mon	Tue	Wed	Thur	Fri	Sat	Sun
AM							
PM							

Table 5.1 Weekly food diary

When you have completed your diary for a few weeks, it is important to look back at the entries and see how, or even if, it has affected your health and lifestyle. Have you lost or gained any weight? Do you have the energy to carry out your regular exercise? Because people are all different and have different metabolisms, they need to eat different foods, which is why you cannot have the same diet as someone else and get the same results. It is vital that you are aware of what you eat and how food can affect your body weight, especially when exercising or playing sport, as you need to adapt your diet to ensure your energy levels remain high enough to compete.

Effect of basic nutrition and lifestyle factors on fitness   P5   M2

To reach optimum fitness and to remain at your peak, it is important that you eat the correct balanced diet, take part in regular, moderate exercise, do not smoke or take illegal drugs and only drink alcohol in moderation (when you are old enough). If any of these factors are not in place or not in the correct amounts, then it will seriously affect your overall fitness and you will probably not be able to participate at the recommended 80 per cent of your maximum heart rate.

Basic nutrition

A balanced diet is one that contains all the nutrients in all the right amounts, which means you have to eat a varied diet with plenty of fresh fruit and vegetables and a choice of food from each of the groups mentioned earlier.

Fats, carbohydrates and proteins give you the energy you need to perform your daily tasks and the extra you need for when you exercise. Your height, shape and gender will determine your optimum weight and, by not moving too far from this, you can keep up your performance and enjoy good health.

Figure 5.5 Food pyramid

Different people need different amounts of food and a lot depends on your age, your job and the kind of exercise you take part in. How long your muscles can work for depends on your endurance, both cardiovascular and muscular.

Lifestyle factors

Stress

Most people experience stress at some time in their lives and it is a normal part of work. However, if the stress level gets too high, it can have a negative effect on health. You must ensure a good balance between work and leisure and make sure you get enough sleep. It is recommended that you have eight hours per night to rest the body and the mind. You should not take drugs or medicine to help you sleep or relax, or to affect your mood. If you have severe personal or emotional problems, you must seek help from the professionals, who can help you return to being a regular, happy person.

> **Key term**
>
> **Lifestyle factors**, with regards to health and fitness, include stress, smoking, alcohol and family history.

Smoking

Most people recognise that smoking cigarettes can damage your health. It is not easy to stop as it is habit forming, but it will bring health benefits if you cut down the number you smoke and eventually stop. Again, there are professionals who can help. The NHS has a free 'quit smoking' policy and can offer help in the form of patches, fake cigarettes and other methods designed to help you stop smoking.

Alcohol
Many people consider alcohol as a normal part of their diet. Often, an alcoholic drink at the end of the day helps people to relax. However, excess alcohol is harmful to health and can lead to very serious internal problems and, for some people, even death.

Family history
Some people suffer from an illness because of a family predisposition – for example, heart disease. You should find out about your parents' and grand-parents' health. Will they survive, or have they survived, to a long age?

How to upgrade to M2 and D2

M2   D2   To move up from a pass to a merit, you need to look closely at your personal food diary and assess the nutritional intake. You also need to analyse your lifestyle factors to ensure that you are maximising your fitness potential. You could review what you are presently doing and make recommendations on what you could improve – this would ensure a distinction grade.

Evaluating a personal food diary with areas for improvement   D2

Towards the end of this unit, you will need to stop recording your consumption of food and liquids on a regular basis and examine how worth-while it was and what you might do to improve it in the future. You will need to break down your food diary precisely into all the food groups and work out how much you consume of each one. You can then evaluate the foods you need to cut down on and, if necessary, increase the ones you need more of. The more descriptive you can be of the different foods you eat, the better your chance of gaining the distinction grade.

Questions to consider:

- Did you manage to cut down on the amount of fat, sugar and salt in your diet?
- Could you consume more fibre, fruit or vegetables?
- Which foods are you eating too much of and which are you not eating enough of?
- In other words, is your diet balanced and does it take into account your lifestyle?

If necessary, you could make adjustments to your diet so that you consume enough kilojoules (kJ) for the amount of energy you are generally using each day. On average, females require around 9,000kJ and males require 12,000kJ, depending on the nature and duration of exercise taken.

Body composition is the percentage of body weight which is fat, muscle and bone. Your composition affects the way you go about your daily life and it can be changed by reducing the amount of fat you eat and the proportion of lean muscle in your body. Males should be around 12–18 per cent fat and females 14–20 per cent fat. The rest of your body weight should be the lean body mass of bone, muscle, organs and connective tissue.

Ask yourself!

You need to balance your intake of food and liquid with the amount of exercise you take part in; the more you do, the more you need – of the right kind! So look at your diary and see where and when you would require more carbohydrates or protein, remove any snacks that do not provide you with the correct requirements and ensure that meals are taken at the right time of the day in order for the calories to be used up before relaxing and sleeping.

Grading tip!

P4 For P4, you need to keep a personal food and lifestyle diary.

P5 For P5, you need to describe the effect of basic nutrition and lifestyle factors on fitness.

M2 For M2, you must review the effect of basic nutrition and lifestyle factors on fitness taking account of your personal food and fitness diary.

D2 For D2, you should evaluate the effect of a personal food diary and suggest areas for improvement.

Taking part in fitness tests to appreciate the requirements of the uniformed public services

P6 P7 M3

P6

Components of fitness and testing methods of fitness

Most uniformed public services use physical fitness tests to establish the fitness levels of entrants before they are offered a position. Some are more demanding than others, depending upon the nature of the service.

Therefore, you must be prepared to undertake a number of fitness tests at the beginning of the unit to establish your 'base' level of fitness and to make you aware of the areas you need to work on and improve over the coming weeks and months. Towards the end of your study, you will once again participate in the same fitness tests and see where you have improved and by how much.

Components of fitness

Health-related fitness
Health-related fitness includes stamina, strength, suppleness and body composition.

Stamina (aerobic fitness or endurance) is how long your body can work until it is too tired to work any longer (fatigue). There are two types of stamina: cardiovascular endurance and muscular endurance. Cardiovascular endurance is your body's ability to cope with activity over a long period of time and muscular endurance is a particular muscle's ability to carry on working without getting tired.

Strength (muscular strength) is how much force a muscle, or muscles, can exert against a resistance. Three types of strength include explosive, dynamic and static.

Suppleness (flexibility) is the range of movement possible at a joint. Four types of stretching include static, passive, active and PNF (proprioceptive neuromuscular facilitation).

Body composition is the percentage of your body weight that is fat, muscle and bone.

> ### Key term
> The **'S' factors** are stamina, strength, suppleness, speed, spirit, sustenance, skill and sleep.

Skill-related fitness
Skill-related fitness includes speed, agility, balance, power, coordination and reaction.

Speed is the time taken for you to move a specified distance or to move all or part of your body as quickly as possible. This can also refer to the speed of your reactions.

Agility is the ability to change your body position under control.

Balance is to maintain a given posture in different situations.

Power (explosive strength) is strength × speed of movement or to contract your muscles with speed and force in one act.

Coordination is the ability to use your senses together to control your body.

Reaction is how quickly you can respond. If your reactions are fast, you respond more quickly.

Exercise methods

There are a number of methods you can use for exercising or training in your programme.

Aerobic or endurance training

This type of training will help you to keep going for longer and at a higher intensity. It improves the aerobic systems of the body, especially the cardiovascular and respiratory systems, as you are exercising continuously and do not stop. However, you do not work out at your maximum level; you should be able to talk as you exercise or at least not be short of breath. Activities include brisk walking, jogging, swimming, rowing and cycling. They can all be carried out indoors but it is much better if you can do some of your exercising outdoors to see the differences it can make.

Interval training

The purpose of this type of training is to develop both the anaerobic and aerobic systems as periods of exercise are followed by periods of rest. The rest periods are essential for recovery and will enable you to train for longer. You train at your maximum level and then rest for a few minutes before starting again. You could run six 100m sprints in 15 seconds or four 200m sprints with a minute's rest between each sprint.

Figure 5.6 Continuous training

Fartlek training

'Fartlek' is a Swedish word, meaning 'speed play'. This is usually continuous training but you vary the speed of your running from fast to slow and over different terrains, on the flat and over hills. It can improve both aerobic and anaerobic fitness.

Flexibility training

This involves stretching and moving your joints to just beyond the point of resistance. This stretches the tendons and ligaments so that your joints are more mobile. A variety of exercises can be used, such as static stretching, passive stretching, active stretching and PNF.

Weight training

In this type of training, you use machines or free weights to provide some resistance to your muscle groups. Weight training consists of repetitions and sets; the number of repetitions carried out is a set and you usually complete three sets of ten repetitions, using near maximum weight. You then progressively increase the weights on a weekly basis, if you can do this safely.

Plyometric training

This is a series of explosive movements used to improve muscular power. The muscles stretch then contract, giving you extra power. This type of training, which includes bounding, leaping, hopping, skipping and throwing, places a great deal of stress on the joints, so it should only be carried out for short periods of time.

Circuit training

This involves a series of exercises at different stations in a specific order, a circuit. You perform an exercise or a repetition of exercises at each of 8–10 stations in a given amount of time. The stations should be arranged so that you do not exercise the same muscle groups consecutively and the stations can be changed regularly to keep it interesting.

Fitness tests used by the public services

P7

Entry to the uniformed public services usually includes a fitness test. Each of the armed forces has their own way of testing fitness and the blue-light services have tests that vary from county to county. In either case, it is imperative that you are fit to join the public services.

The Fire and Rescue Service

In front-line positions in the fire service, you may need to use ladders, hoses and other equipment. It is not just about sheer strength but, by employing the right techniques and teamwork, you can achieve things you did not think possible. The fitness test will determine whether you have the required levels of aerobic fitness and strength to carry out the role of a firefighter. In addition, you will be required to carry out job-related awareness tasks. These are designed to simulate aspects of a firefighter's role and you will be required to wear a provided fire kit.

The fire service fitness tests include the following:

- Ladder climb – to test confidence and ability to follow instructions.
- Casualty evacuation – to test physical upper and lower body strength and coordination.
- Ladder lift – to test physical upper and lower body strength and coordination.
- Enclosed space – to test confidence, agility and identify claustrophobic tendencies.
- Equipment assembly – to test manual dexterity.
- Equipment carry – to test aerobic fitness, stamina, upper and lower body strength and coordination.

HM Prison Service

To gain entry to HM Prison Service as a prison officer you will need to pass the basic job-related fitness test which you will be required to pass on an annual basis throughout your career. The test and pass levels are the same for men and women, regardless of age. The standard of fitness required to reach the pass level reflects the physical demands of the job and is easily reached and maintained through regular aerobic exercise.

HM Prison Service fitness tests include the following:

- Grip strength – squeezing a dynamometer as tightly as possible to measure the strength of your forearm muscles and grip. Both hands are tested.

- Endurance shuttle run – running at a progressively faster pace over a 15-metre course until you reach the required level. This tests your aerobic endurance.

15m

Figure 5.7 The shuttle run

- Dyno strength – this measures the strength of the muscles in your upper body and upper arms, which are used in controlling and restraining. A machine is used to complete a series of pushes and pulls to reach a target level of force.
- Speed agility run – measuring your ability to run at pace as well as to negotiate obstacles and change direction, for responding quickly to an incident.
- Shield technique – a job-specific test simulates the static position in which you are required to hold a 6kg shield during control and restraint techniques.

The British Army

There are only two tests for entry to the British Army – sit-ups and a run. These test your stamina, strength and speed and have minimum fitness targets. They are carried out correctly and continuously.

The British Army fitness test includes the following:

- Sit-ups – 54 continuous with feet supported.
- 1.5 mile (2.4km) run in 11 minutes and 45 seconds.

The Royal Navy

You need to pass a pre-joining fitness test of a 2.4km (1.5 mile) run on a treadmill. The maximum times in which you must complete the run are between 12 minutes and 20 seconds and 16 minutes and 40 seconds, depending upon your gender and age.

Once you have joined, you are required to pass a series of fitness tests during phase one of your training:

- 2.4km runs – between 11 minutes and 13 seconds and 15 minutes and 9 seconds, depending upon your age and gender.
- Press-ups – male 23, female 17.
- Sit-ups – male 39, female 29.
- Shuttle run (5 × 55 metre) – male 59 seconds, female 72 seconds.

To pass the swimming test, you are required to jump into deep water wearing overalls, tread water for two minutes, then swim 50 metres and climb out at the deep end.

Activity

You can begin to test your own fitness in the comfort of your own home. Find some free time a few days each week, mornings are usually best, and practise a few press-ups and sit-ups. Make sure that you are using the correct technique and do as many as you can before getting tired. A week later, add two or three to your total, gradually increasing the number over the following weeks. You will be surprised at how much better you feel and, hopefully, you will continue to participate in the tests, adding new tests as you get fitter.

Improvements in performance in a fitness test

M3

Once you have performed a number of basic fitness tests, you will be able to see what components of fitness you need to work on in order to improve your chances of passing the entry fitness tests used by the uniformed public services. Choose one of the services for which you performed the fitness test – if you participated in more than one of the services' fitness tests – and assess the scores you achieved. In which of the individual tests did you give 100 per cent, therefore meaning it is not possible to achieve a higher score? In which ones did you not quite give your best effort and, therefore, could probably improve the score?

Think about it!

Predict what scores you could achieve in each component of the test and write down how you intend to reach that target. In the meantime, continue to practise the tests in your own time and try to improve all the scores, including those you thought you could not improve. After a few weeks, you should approach your fitness trainer and ask to carry out the tests again to improve your original targets. Write down your new, improved scores alongside the originals.

Grading tip!

P6 For P6, you need to identify components of fitness and testing methods of fitness.

P7 For P7, you need to perform fitness tests used by the uniformed public services.

M3 For M3, you should demonstrate improvements in performance in a fitness test used by a uniformed public service.

Participating in a personal health improvement programme for uniformed public services

P8   **M4**   **D3**

P8

Planning a personal health improvement programme

Now that you have described the benefits of exercise on the body systems, kept a food diary and performed at least one fitness test as part of this unit, it is time to plan and participate in a personal health improvement programme. This programme will give you the opportunity to develop your knowledge of various training methods and programmes used by the uniformed public services to assess and develop your fitness in preparation for entry into your chosen career.

A personal health improvement programme takes into account three main aspects: nutrition, fitness and lifestyle factors. You set yourself targets, both short term and long term, on one or more of these factors and create an action plan for further improvements in health.

Nutrition

The energy you need on a daily basis is gained from the food you eat as part of a balanced diet. The total amount of energy needed is easy to work out; it is the basal metabolic rate (BMR) plus the working energy. BMR is the energy you need to stay alive and awake, and when you are resting, while working energy is the extra energy you need to perform all other activities, such as moving, digesting food and exercise. Energy is usually measured in kilojoules (kJ) but more commonly the term calorie (cal) is used, and is therefore measured in, kilocalories (kcal). We do not all need the same amount of energy (calories) as it depends upon a number of factors, including age, lifestyle, gender and exercise.

Fitness

Fitness is about your body being able to do what you want and need it to do. How fit you are depends upon how active you are and, if you wish to join a public service, you will need to have more than just basic fitness. A way of improving your fitness is to take regular exercise and to let your body adapt to the demands you place upon it. As you exercise more, you will get better and you will enjoy it more. When you enjoy exercise and feel and notice the benefits, you will feel better in yourself.

Lifestyle factors

Lifestyle factors include your stress levels, whether you smoke cigarettes, take drugs or drink alcohol and your family history. They also include your diet and how much you exercise, as mentioned in the previous sections. You need to have a balance between your work time and your free time to lead a contented and happy life.

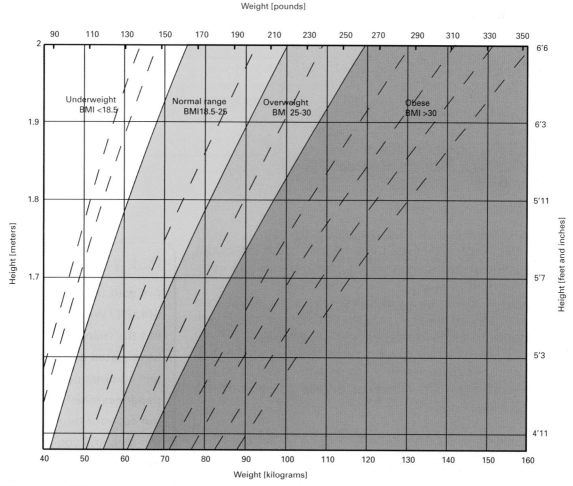

Figure 5.8 What is your BMI?

Source: http://en.wikipedia.org

To start your programme, it is necessary for you to complete a health and fitness profile – where you are now, regarding your present lifestyle. It will tell you how fit you are, give you a baseline to work from and help you to use your exercise time effectively. Firstly, you need to take the following five basic body measurements:

- height
- weight
- resting heart rate
- body mass index (BMI)
- maximum heart rate.

When you have completed your programme, take the same five basic body measurements and you may find that some of these measures have changed!

You can then test your stamina, strength and suppleness through a variety of tests, such as the Cooper 12-minute run, shuttle run, press-ups, sit-ups and the sit-and-reach test. You must score or measure your results at the beginning of the programme and at the end to determine whether your level of fitness has improved.

SMART targets

You have to work out what you want your programme to achieve and, in order to set the goals or objectives, it is necessary to have some targets to aim towards to further improve a particular aspect of your health or fitness.

> **Key term**
>
> **SMART** stands for specific, measurable, achievable, relevant and time constrained.

Your targets must be SMART:

Specific – the objectives must be specific to you.
Measurable – the objectives must be able to be measured so that you can check whether an improvement has been made.
Achievable – objectives must be flexible so that you can adjust and achieve them. If you do not achieve the objectives, then you will need to set some easier ones.
Relevant – set your objectives so that they are relevant to the personal health improvement programme and to you.
Time constrained – the objectives should be set within a reasonable time limit.

Nine principles of fitness programming – FITT and SPORT

Once the targets are in place, you need to think about the nine principles of fitness programming: frequency, intensity, time and type (FITT), and specificity, progression, overload, reversibility and tedium (SPORT) in order to put your programme together.

> **Ask yourself!**
>
> Are your targets really SMART? Will you carry out the training as you have stated or are you just completing the paper exercise? Do not set your targets too high and you will have a better chance of achieving them!

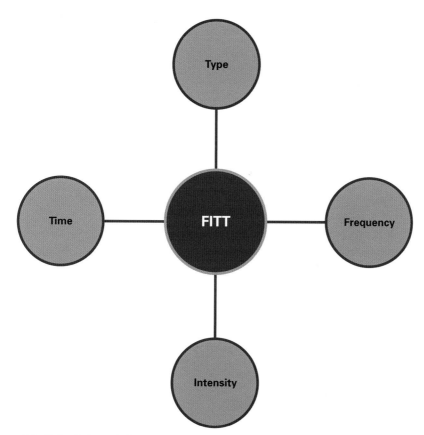

Figure 5.9 Principles of fitness programming – FITT

Frequency – how often you need to exercise each week. You should train at least three times a week for a minimum of 30 minutes and spread the sessions out so you allow yourself some rest days.

Intensity – how hard you need to work. You will only get fitter if you make your body systems work hard enough for them to adapt but you must know your limits, such as the training threshold of 80 per cent.

Figure 5.10 Keeping fit

Time – amount of time you intend to spend in each session. Training sessions should gradually last longer to make the body systems work harder.

Type – which type of activities will you include to keep it fun and interesting? For instance, try cross-training and something completely different, like swimming or cycling.

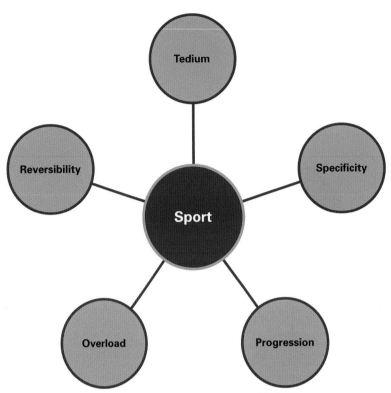

Figure 5.11 Principles of fitness programming – SPORT

Specificity – each person will need a different training programme because everyone is different and does different things. Therefore, the programme should be specific to you and only include the specific exercises and activities that you will be participating in. The programme should be set at the correct level for you and be designed so that it conditions your body to develop the correct type of fitness.

Progression – you need to ensure that you slowly and gradually increase the amount of training, exercise and activities that you carry out so that your body adapts to the changes. Your fitness levels usually increase quite quickly at the beginning of the programme but then slow down as you get a routine going, eventually, sometimes, staying at the same level for a while.

Overload – the idea of setting up a programme is to make your body work harder, so you must do one of three things: increase the number of times you participate, increase the intensity (how hard you make your body work) or increase the times that you take part. If you do not overload the programme, you will see very little improvement, but be careful not to overload it too much or you may injure yourself.

Reversibility – as your fitness levels can change so quickly, it is important not to stop training and competing as your fitness will go down and it will be so much harder to get back to where you were originally. However, if you are injured or ill, you must stop immediately and return to the start of the programme once you are fully fit.

Tedium – if the activities and the exercises are boring you will not want to take part. Try to use a variety of methods and exercises to keep the programme exciting and ensure that you will continue to participate and to improve.

In some instances the SPORT principles of Reversibility and Tedium are replaced by Relevant and Time, particularly in a more specific health improvement programme.

Activity

In order to design a programme of activities and exercises, it is necessary to know where you are starting from, so you will need to find a number of baseline test measurements against which you can check later on during the programme to see if you have made any improvements.

Try 30 seconds each of sit-ups, press-ups, squats and star jumps and record the scores. Carry out the same exercises a few days later, preferably at the same time, and compare your scores. You should have improved, if only very slightly.

These results could be the foundation for designing your personal health improvement programme.

Participating in a personal health improvement programme

M4

Once you have planned and designed your personal health improvement programme, you must get it started. It is no use on paper; you actually have to carry the plan out. With your fitness assessed, you can use the health improvement programme to monitor your fitness levels and to review your progress. You must keep constant checks on your weight management, blood pressure, body fat percentage and your heart rate to ensure there are no large fluctuations, either up or down.

Action plan for further improvement in health

D3

After participating in your personal health improvement programme for a few weeks or months, it is necessary to evaluate the progress, and any improvements made, and amend the programme as required to further increase your health and fitness. You cannot be complacent as it is all too easy to eat more than is necessary, move away from your normal diet or reduce the amount of exercise your body has got used to during the programme.

Task	Why does it need changing?	Action required	Date set	Date achieved

Table 5.2 Personal health improvement plan

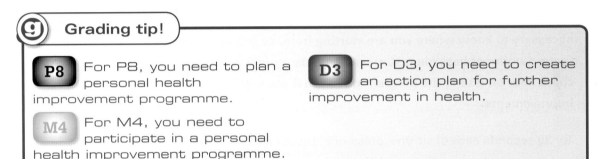

g) Grading tip!

P8 For P8, you need to plan a personal health improvement programme.

M4 For M4, you need to participate in a personal health improvement programme.

D3 For D3, you need to create an action plan for further improvement in health.

End of unit knowledge check

1. List and briefly describe the five key terms associated with a healthy lifestyle.
2. What are the immediate effects of exercise on the circulatory and respiratory systems?
3. Describe three ways in which you can benefit by taking part in exercise.
4. List and briefly describe the five main food groups.
5. What is the recommended minimum amount of exercise you should participate in each week?
6. How would you calculate your body mass index (BMI)?
7. List and describe four types of exercise methods.
8. Why is the physical fitness entrance test for the British Army relatively easy to pass?
9. Briefly describe a personal health improvement plan.
10. What do the terms 'FITT' and 'SPORT' stand for?

Grading criteria

In order to pass this unit, the evidence that the learner presents for assessment needs to demonstrate that they can meet all the learning outcomes for the unit. The criteria for a pass grade describe the level of achievement required to pass this unit.

Grading criteria		
To achieve a pass grade the evidence must show that the learner is able to:	**To achieve a merit grade the evidence must show that, in addition to the pass criteria, the learner is able to:**	**To achieve a distinction grade the evidence must show that, in addition to the pass and merit criteria, the learner is able to:**
P1 Define key terms associated with a healthy lifestyle	**M1** Explain the impact of regular exercise on body systems associated with health	**D1** Evaluate the short- and long-term effects of regular exercise on body systems associated with health
P2 Describe the effects of exercise on the body systems associated with health		
P3 Outline the benefits of exercise		
P4 Keep a personal food and lifestyle diary		
P5 Explain the effect of basic nutrition and lifestyle factors on fitness	**M2** Review the effect of basic nutrition and lifestyle factors on fitness taking account of your personal food and fitness diary	**D2** Evaluate the effect of a personal food diary suggesting areas for improvement
P6 Identify components and testing methods of fitness		
P7 Perform fitness tests used by the uniformed public services	**M3** Demonstrate improvements in performance in a fitness test used by a uniformed public service	
P8 Plan a personal health improvement programme	**M4** Participate in a personal health improvement programme	**D3** Create an action plan for further improvement in health

Introduction

This unit explores the meanings of the terms 'citizen' and 'citizenship' and how the issues surrounding our perceptions of citizenship are employed by individuals, as well as by the public services. We will investigate the United Kingdom's legal, humanitarian and political understanding of citizenship, including how modern society defines a 'good citizen' and how this benefits the public services and society.

You will gain an understanding of contemporary issues that show the potential influence of social groups and the media on the uniformed public services. You will also develop an in-depth understanding of national, international and global issues that have affected, or are likely to affect, the uniformed public services in the UK.

Learning outcomes:

By the end of this unit, you should:

1. Know what is meant by the terms citizen, citizenship, individual rights and human rights

2. Understand the relationship between individuals, society and the public services

3. Understand the importance of equal opportunities in society and the public services

4. Be able to investigate the roles of statutory and non-statutory public services to the citizens and to a changing society.

Citizenship and rights

Within the public services, the perception of citizenship is extremely important; members of these services need to display excellent skills of citizenship within their work surroundings. In this way, they will be able to demonstrate that they afford the rights and accept the responsibilities of all citizens within society.

All police recruits in England and Wales are required to attest (confirm) that they will remain true to the following declaration:

> 'I ...... (name) of ...... (town of residence) do solemnly and sincerely declare and affirm that I will well and truly serve the Queen in the office of constable with fairness, integrity, diligence and impartiality, upholding fundamental human rights and according equal respect to all people; and that I will, to the best of my skill and knowledge, discharge all the duties thereof according to law.'

The Welsh form of the oath is as follows:

> 'Rwyf i ...... o ...... yn datgan ac yn cadarnhau yn ddifrifol ac yn ddiffuant y byddaf yn gwasanaethu'r Frenhines yn dda ac yn gywir yn fy swydd o heddwas (heddferch), yn deg, yn onest, yn ddiwyd ac yn ddiduedd, gan gynnal hawliau dynol sylfaenol a chan roddi'r un parch i bob person; ac y byddaf i, hyd eithaf fy nghallu, yn achosi i'r heddwch gael ei gadw a'i ddiogelu ac yn atal pob trosedd yn erbyn pobl ac eiddio; a thra byddaf yn parhau i ddal y swydd ddywededig y byddaf i, hyd eithaf fy sgil a'm gwybodaeth, yn cyflawni'r holl ddyletswyddau sy'n gysylltiadeg â hi yn ffyddlon yn unol â'r gyfraith.'

The British armed forces have their own oath of allegiance – all members of the Army, Royal Air Force and Royal Marines are required to affirm their loyalty to the Crown.

> 'I swear by almighty God that I will be faithful and bear true allegiance to Her Majesty Queen Elizabeth II, Her heirs and successors and that I will, as in duty bound, honestly and faithfully, defend Her Majesty, Her heirs and successors in person, crown and dignity against all enemies and will observe and obey all orders of Her Majesty, Her heirs and successors and of the generals set over me.'

For those who do not believe in God, the words 'swear by almighty God' can be substituted with 'solemnly and sincerely declare and affirm'.

Key terms

A **citizen** is a person who lives in, has loyalty to and contributes to a community.

A **constable** is a citizen, locally appointed but having authority under the Crown, for the protection of life and property, the maintenance of law and order and the prevention and detection of crime.

Figure 6.1 Army recruits swearing allegiance to the Queen

If you asked ten people to describe the term 'citizenship', you would probably get many different responses. Within this unit, you will understand how the many views of citizenship have developed and why it is important to understand that every citizen within society is afforded the same protection under law.

Activity

Write a list of as many words or phrases as you can think of that identify a citizen. This should not take more than five minutes.

Now discuss your ideas with another member of your class and put the words and phrases in order of importance.

Which factor did you decide was most important – place of birth, nationality, something else?

Is an individual considered a citizen only if they pay tax to the government, or are unemployed, young and retired people also included in the definition? What about those who were born in the United Kingdom but now reside elsewhere? When does someone become a citizen? Is it at birth, when they are capable of active thought, at 16, 18 or 21 years of age, or at some other time?

Citizenship

The ways in which someone becomes a UK citizen may vary greatly, depending on individual circumstances.

Key term

Citizenship is a status that is inferred on citizens, the collective term by which people are known.

However, the definitions of citizenship in relation to political and moral issues are continually being challenged and developed.

Citizenship is more than the acquisition of particular knowledge, skills and understanding. It has to do with a vision of what it is to 'be' a citizen, with personally owned values, with hope and aspirations. The effective citizen is someone with the temperament, values, attitudes, skills, knowledge and understanding to engage meaningfully in community and wider public life. It includes the ability to own and understand values, to work together, to express an opinion, to empathise and to act on behalf of others. Citizenship is also about learning from experience, to respect others who are different, to analyse current issues and much more.

If you do not understand any of the terms that have been mentioned, it is important that you investigate them before going into this unit in more detail.

The status of citizen is used to denote the link between an individual and a state. A state is a form of political organisation with territorial boundaries, which may encompass more than one nation (as in the case of the United Kingdom, which incorporates Great Britain and Northern Ireland).

> ### Key term
>
> A **nation** may be defined as a collection of people having some kind of collective identity, recognised by themselves and others; a nation is a history of association.

In this way, an individual may hold the legal citizenship of one state but identify their status as originating from their attachment to a nation; an example of this is someone whose nationality is British but who sees themselves as English, Welsh or Scottish, denoting their country of birth.

Most often, reference to nationality is understood to be the outward-looking aspect of one's ties to a state. By contrast, citizenship is identified as the inward-looking characteristic of rights and responsibilities exercised and performed within the society of that state.

Let us look at what it means to be a British citizen. The rules are quite complex but, briefly, someone is either born British or able to acquire British citizenship. For those who already have some connection to the United Kingdom, acquiring British citizenship would involve registration; for others this would involve naturalisation.

The legal requirements of citizenship are set out by parliament and are fixed. Laws that set out the foundations of citizenship include the British Nationality Act 1981, the British Overseas Territories Act 2002 and the Nationality, Immigration and Asylum Acts 2002, 2006.

People who wish to adopt British citizenship are invited to attend a 'citizenship

> ### Activity
>
> **Working in groups of four to six, research one of the laws mentioned here and prepare a PowerPoint presentation, in which you explain to the rest of the class the main points of the Act and why it came into force.**

ceremony.' The first ceremony took place in April 2004 in London, and 19 people, including three children, took part. These citizens came to the United Kingdom from ten countries. The 19 citizens swore allegiance to the Queen, sang the national anthem and pledged to respect the UK's rights and freedoms.

Pledge for new UK citizens

'I will give my loyalty to the United Kingdom and respect its rights and freedoms. I will uphold its democratic values. I will observe its laws faithfully and fulfil my duties and obligations as a British citizen.'

Before 2004, those who successfully gained British citizenship had no opportunity to mark what was, for many, a very important day in their lives. It was decided that more should be done to emphasise the impact and value of becoming a British citizen. The main, formal purpose of the ceremony described here is for new citizens to swear their oath of allegiance and receive their certificate of naturalisation. Previously, the oath was sworn before a solicitor and the certificate was received through the post.

Figure 6.2 A citizenship ceremony

Many of the perceptions of citizens were established before widespread travel became a regular feature of many people's lives. Although a citizen resides in one country, the concept of citizenship is not restricted to that country's boundaries. With continual advances in technological fields, it is now possible to be a citizen of a much wider social world than previously. With almost 200 social networking sites available, including the familiar Facebook and Twitter, it has never been easier to share news and friendship with so many other like-minded people across the world and to become a member of 'global citizenship'.

Individual and human rights

Citizenship is, in many ways, similar to a contract; although not written down, citizenship brings with it assumptions involving rights and responsibilities. When these rights and responsibilities are not upheld, then the upset party is likely to show displeasure and demand that things are put right. Regardless of nationality or

Key terms

Individual rights are things that an individual is entitled to have or to do, based on principles of equality and impartiality.

Human rights are rights that are set out under the United Nations Universal Declaration of Human Rights 1948.

citizenship, there is the ideal that every citizen should have access to fundamental rights.

All citizens are protected by legislation; however, these laws are balanced by certain responsibilities of every citizen. You will not be expected to understand every piece of legislation referring to individual and human rights, but the next section provides an introduction to this important issue.

In 1948, the first piece of present-day legislation was introduced, the United Nations Universal Declaration of Human Rights (UDHR). This document was developed soon after, and directly from the experiences of, the Second World War. The declaration set out, for the first time, the rights to which all human beings are entitled. Within the UDHR, there are 30 articles, each dealing with a separate area, detailing the ways in which all citizens should expect to be treated. Some of the fundamental rights are set out in the box below.

United Nations Universal Declaration of Human Rights

Article 1:
'All human beings are born free and equal in dignity and rights. They are endowed with reason and conscience and should act towards one another in a spirit of brotherhood.'

Article 3:
'Everyone has the right to life, liberty and security of person.'

Article 5:
'No one shall be subjected to torture or to cruel, inhuman or degrading treatment or punishment.'

Source: United Nations Universal Declaration of Human Rights

Activity

Working in small groups, research the UDHR. Following discussion in class, produce a poster that sets out the main points of the declaration. Display the poster in your classroom.

Fifty years after the introduction of the UDHR, a piece of legislation was introduced in the United Kingdom that further enhanced the fundamental rights set out in the declaration. Whereas the UDHR focuses in many parts on the issues of life and death, the Human Rights Act also affects the rights you have in your everyday life, including what you can say and do, how you express your beliefs and your right to a fair trial.

Most rights are limited to make sure that in exercising them you do not unduly affect the rights of others. Some rights though cannot be limited by a court; an example of this is the right not to be tortured.

Whilst the Human Rights Act affords many rights to every citizen, one of the most basic responsibilities is that you have to respect other people's rights (even if you do not agree with their views).

Your human rights are numerous. They include:

- the right to life
- the right to a fair trial
- the right to respect for private and family life
- the right not to be punished for something that was not a crime when you did it
- the right not to be discriminated against
- the right to participate in free elections
- the right to liberty
- the right to freedom of expression
- the right to an education.

If any of the rights or freedoms are violated, you have a right to an effective resolution in law. This applies even if the person who breached your rights was someone in authority – for example, a police officer or a senior person in your public service.

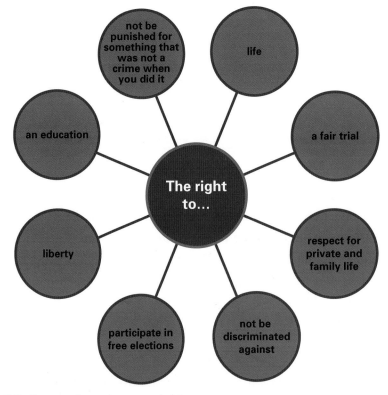

Figure 6.3 Some of our human rights

Many of these rights are not dependent upon citizenship; the rights to welfare, health care, education and employment and the duty to pay taxes are given to all those who live in the country, whether or not they have achieved citizen status. Even those who are in the country on a temporary basis can share similar rights, as long as they have been given authorisation from the authorities.

Other rights, such as the right not to be discriminated against, are given not because someone is a citizen but because it is accepted that all people ought to be treated fairly according to their needs. As more people migrate between different countries, it has been necessary for national legislation to become more flexible to allow for social integration.

Qualities of a good citizen

Go back to the first activity in this chapter (page 146) and the ways in which you described a citizen. We will now explore the ways in which these citizens display their values and skills. There are many roles that citizens can take on – these include students, volunteers and neighbours.

The public services recruit from the community and their members are subject to the laws that affect all citizens. Another major law that came into force towards the end of the 20th century was the Police and Criminal Evidence Act 1984. This Act provides the police with certain powers and also protects the public. The Act manages the ways in which the police carry out stops, how they search people and property and how people are cared for while in custody.

Activity

Using the list you made in the first activity of this chapter, define the citizens listed below. The first two have been completed for you.

- **Volunteer** – someone who freely gives their time to provide a service for others.
- **Neighbour** – a member of a social community, often enjoying face-to-face interaction.
- **Taxpayer** –
- **Voter** –
- **Service user** –

Who else would you describe as a citizen?

Key features of the Police and Criminal Evidence Act 1984 (PACE)

The Police and Criminal Evidence Act established a wide-ranging power of 'stop and search' for individuals and vehicles. The police must have 'reasonable suspicion' of finding stolen or prohibited items, the suspect must be informed of the reason for the search and the police must maintain correct written records.

The police may also enter and search premises to find evidence; once again, reasons must be made clear to the accused and written records of the search must be made. Any property that is taken as a result of this search must also be logged.

PACE made clear the powers afforded to the police to carry out an arrest. An arrest can be made only if there is a solid reason for believing the suspect has carried out an offence or if there is no time to obtain a summons to order that person to appear in court. This might involve the belief that the suspect might leave the country.

Keeping someone in custody (detention) is allowed only where it is vital that evidence is preserved. This is usually in the more serious cases, where agreeing to the suspect being bailed could pose a threat to witnesses or the victim.

When someone is held in police custody, they have a right to legal advice and to someone being told they are being detained. If they request legal advice, the rules say that they must not be interviewed before they have spoken to this person. PACE also states that where the suspect is a juvenile, or if they suffer from a mental disorder, there must be a 'responsible adult' present during the interview.

For every person who is detained, accurate records must be kept.

Regardless of what people do within society, there are certain elements that make them who they are. Those citizens who wish to join a public service need to demonstrate the qualities that are needed within the service. With this in mind, the public services are interested in individuals who possess these 'good' qualities.

One of the basic qualities that must be demonstrated by potential recruits to the uniformed public services is being able to present yourself appropriately. There is an expectation by the public that those who serve to protect them, including the police, armed forces, ambulance service and fire service, 'look the part'. Officers who appear to not take any pride in their appearance could very well have the same attitude to their work. In all public services, there are times when personnel need to work as a team. Think back to the qualities discussed in Unit 1 (Public service skills).

The way in which public service personnel deal with other people is also important; it would be a bad reflection on the service if a member of staff were rude to another person.

What type of people do public services want?

- The Royal Air Force is always ready to consider people who display a sense of adventure and enjoy working in a team.
- The Army is very keen to recruit people with interpersonal skills.

- The ambulance service requires people who work well in a team and who can carry out their role with the minimum of supervision.

Activity

Carry out research into the qualities that other public services wish to see in their workforce.

(g) Grading tip!

P1 To achieve P1, you need to provide a definition for the terms 'citizen', citizenship', 'individual rights' and 'human rights'.

P2 P2 will be awarded if you describe the qualities a good citizen needs to enter a public service.

How to upgrade to M1, M2 and D1

M1 A *description* of how individual and human rights protect citizens is needed for M1.

M2 To achieve M2, you need to *justify* why citizens joining the public services need the qualities you described for P2.

D1 To achieve D1, you need to *analyse* the ways in which citizens are protected by individual and human rights.

Individuals, society and the public services

P3

In Unit 2 (Employment in the uniformed public services), you will have investigated the role, purpose and responsibilities of a range of public services. For the P3 criterion, you need to demonstrate how these public services work with individuals and within society.

On a daily basis, you can read accounts of the ways in which citizens carry out activities that assist the communities in which they live. The qualities possessed by these individuals or groups might include perseverance (the ability to see things through), community membership (for example, Neighbourhood Watch) and being aware of the needs of others.

In Unit 20 (Volunteering in public services), you will investigate the ways in which citizens may become involved in activities that support the community and other people. This includes volunteering within public services – for example, as a police special, a member of a lifeboat crew, a soldier in the Territorial Army or a retained firefighter. Many public services look favourably on citizens who have demonstrated the skills described in this unit because this shows that they are community-minded and ready to serve the public.

During your studies for the Public Services qualification, you will receive visits from members of public services. To get the best out of these occasions, you need to make sure you are well prepared. You need to

Figure 6.4 A group of volunteers assisting the public services

understand the reason for the visit – is it to give information about their roles, purpose and responsibilities? Maybe they will 'put you through your paces' in readiness for fitness entry tests or provide assistance with interview skills. Whatever the reason for the visit, the more you put into it, the greater the benefit. You might have the opportunity to visit one of the establishments where a public service carries out its duties – for example, the local police station or fire station – or you might even get to spend some time at a camp run by the Army.

Public service personnel are also involved in other sections of the community – you might find a fire service crew offering to wash cars at a supermarket or providing smoke alarms to people in their homes. Part of the reason for these activities is to create an awareness of the ways in which the service can assist the local community and, of course, it helps to remind citizens that the service is available 24 hours a day, every day.

In the final part of this chapter, we will look at the ways in which individuals, society and the public services work together in difficult times.

 **Grading tip!**

P3 To achieve P3, you must *explain* the ways in which public services, citizens and society work together.

Equal opportunities

The beliefs and opinions that we all hold about people or groups of people, whether these are friends, colleagues or people you do not know very well, could promote good working relationships and excellent customer service. If anyone is discriminatory in any way, this could result in difficulties, including the risk of legal action or even being dismissed.

There is much confusion within society about the meaning of 'equal oppor-tunities'. Many people will say it is about treating everyone the same; in fact, the real meaning is that everyone is treated fairly *according to their needs*. This means making allowances for (for example) those who speak a language that is different from the majority of the population, those who need assistance with walking or those who belong to a particular religious group and need to pray at certain times.

The issues of equal opportunities and diversity are important to individual citizens, society and the public services that serve that society. It is necessary for every member of the public services to treat every citizen (whether they are a British citizen or not) fairly and not to be prejudiced towards them because of their sex, race, disability or any other factor. This is equally important when dealing with members of society as it is when dealing with colleagues.

Within this chapter, we will consider equal opportunities in relation to sex discrimination, race relations, disability discrimination, direct and indirect discrimination, harassment, victimisation and the rights of part-time employees.

Many companies fail to comply with equal opportunities requirements; in most cases, this is because they do not fully understand what is involved. From an employment point of view, equal opportunities means the right of all to access employment and education, to be provided a service regardless of age, sex, faith, colour, race, religion or sexuality, and to be treated fairly within the workplace.

Prejudice and stereotyping

The prejudices that we hold are often the result of our upbringing or perhaps experiences that we have had in our lives. Sometimes these prejudices concern groups of people, most of whom we may never have met. Prejudices are usually unfounded and stand in the way of making judgements based on facts.

The prejudices we hold can lead to stereotyping. Stereotyping means giving a set of attitudes to an entire group of people. This can be described as *labelling*. It can also involve not recognising that, within any social group, there are many people who have many different attitudes, behaviours and skills.

The most common forms of prejudice and stereotyping are based on race, gender, age, nationality, disability, colour, religion and sexual orientation.

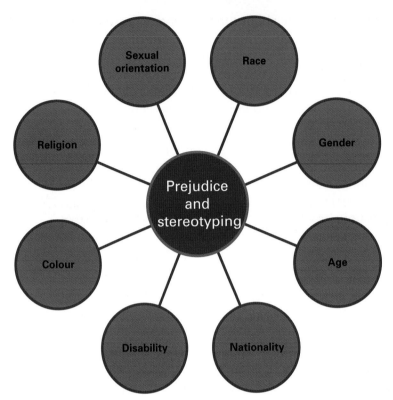

Figure 6.5 Forms of prejudice and stereotyping

Discrimination

This involves putting into action the prejudices we hold; it could affect people we work with or members of the public. There have been many cases of discrimination in the workplace that have been brought before employment tribunals. Some of the high-profile cases are outlined later in this section.

There are two types of discrimination – direct and indirect.

Direct discrimination occurs when one person is treated less favourably than another, purely on the grounds of sex, race, gender, disability or age. Direct discrimination is illegal.

Examples of direct discrimination include not offering someone a job because they are female or deliberately harassing a person because of their nationality. It does not matter if the person carrying out this act was having 'a bit of fun' or if the person affected had not previously complained about the behaviour.

Under legislation, an employer is seen to be discriminating against a disabled person if they treat the person less favourably because of their disability and this treatment cannot be justified.

Indirect discrimination means putting in place a requirement or condition that is applied to everyone but that results in a disadvantage to a particular group in society.

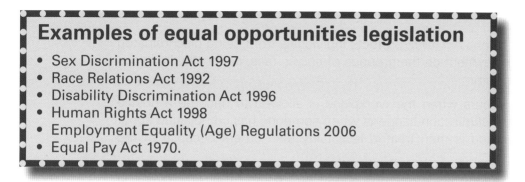

Examples of equal opportunities legislation

- Sex Discrimination Act 1997
- Race Relations Act 1992
- Disability Discrimination Act 1996
- Human Rights Act 1998
- Employment Equality (Age) Regulations 2006
- Equal Pay Act 1970.

A variety of laws exist to provide equal rights to males and females in the UK. The Sex Discrimination Act protects individuals from being discriminated against in employment and education. The Equal Pay Act aims to ensure that males and females are paid the same *for comparable work*.

Awareness of age discrimination is relatively new. The Act that protects people on these grounds became law very recently. The Employment Equality (Age) Regulations 2006 protects people aged 50 and over from being discriminated against in the workplace. Employment equality for younger workers is dealt with in another piece of legislation.

Discrimination against individuals with disabilities is also illegal in the UK. The Disability Discrimination Act 1996 forbids discrimination on the grounds of disability in employment and education. This Act also requires public bodies to promote equal opportunities for every individual regardless of ability and sets minimum standards to be provided for all passengers who use public transport.

The Disability Discrimination Act places a duty on employers to make *reasonable adjustments* for people with disabilities to help overcome the practical effects of their disability. This means that employers should attempt to remove any disadvantage caused by the disability. These conditions apply where any physical feature of the premises places a disabled employee at a considerable disadvantage. Failure to do this, without good cause, is unlawful discrimination.

Figure 6.6 It is unlawful discrimination for employers not to make reasonable adjustments for people with disabilities

Examples of reasonable adjustments might typically include:

- relocating a person with limited mobility to the ground floor or moving a disabled employee to other premises if the usual place of work is inaccessible

- buying a specially adapted keyboard for someone with arthritis in their hands or with a visual impairment
- providing special telephone equipment for an employee with a hearing impairment.

The Race Relations Act 1992 protects individuals from being discriminated against in employment on the grounds of colour, race, nationality, religious beliefs or ethnicity.

Harassment occurs when the workplace is allowed to become a hostile environment. Victimisation happens when someone has complained about discrimination and is then treated less fairly than others because of the complaint.

The Race Relations Act protects the religious rights of all employees in the UK. Though there is no list of religions or beliefs that are included in UK legislation, most of the widely recognised religions and also less well-known beliefs are acknowledged and protected.

Case study

Sex discrimination
Investment banker Julie Bower took her company to court in 2002, claiming that her male counterparts were given much bigger bonuses. She won her case and received £1.5 million in compensation.

Age discrimination
In 2007, 66-year-old Ann Southcott became the first person to win an age discrimination case at an employment tribunal. She was dismissed from her clerical job at a hospital in the south-west of England the day before the Employment Equality (Age) Regulations came into force. Instead of receiving one month's pay for every year she had worked there, she received just 11 days' pay. She won her case and was reinstated with back pay.

Race discrimination
At the end of 2008, Balbinder Chagger won a record £2.8 million in a race discrimination case against a high street bank, from which he was made redundant. He claimed that he had been held back because of his race and was made redundant in 2006. The record payment took account of his future loss of earnings from his former £100,000 a year post.

Religious discrimination
In 2003, a bus cleaner was the first person to win a religious discrimination case under new equality legislation. Mohammed Sajwal Khan asked his employer for extended leave to go on a religious pilgrimage. His manager told him this request had been granted, but when he returned from his six-week trip, he was suspended. The tribunal found in his favour.

These cases show that discrimination can happen to anyone, whatever their job, status or salary and the large payouts show that discrimination is taken seriously by the courts.

All employers in the UK, including public services, have an obligation to ensure that they remain within the laws that govern equal opportunities; in the examples given on the previous page, you can see what happens when they get it wrong.

Equal opportunities policies

Taking account of equal opportunities in the workplace is designed to remove bias and prejudice and to ensure that organisations promote best practice. Equal opportunity, from an employment point of view, means the right of everyone to access employment regardless of age, sex, colour, religion, creed, race or sexuality and the right to be treated fairly within the workplace.

There are many benefits for an organisation that has in place an equal opportunities policy. It encourages senior management to review employment practices and the way in which they relate to customers. It also offers a structure where staff can work equally and identifies who has responsibility for equal opportunity matters within the organisation.

On occasions, public services have been accused of flouting discrimination laws. In the report on the well-publicised case of the murder of Stephen Lawrence, the Metropolitan Police were accused of 'institutional racism'. This was an accusation that remained with the force for a long time afterwards.

The Army is another public service that regularly receives criticism about the way it conducts its activities within the organisation. In Unit 1 (Public service skills), you will have read about the claim of bullying within this service. Once again, when accusations are made against a public service, the damage can last for a long time.

The public services need to demonstrate that they are acting not only within the letter of the law but also within the spirit of the law and are fostering an understanding and appreciation of equality and diversity within its own ranks.

This needs to be clear in everything they do, from recruiting staff, in training programmes and in opportunities for promotion. They must also ensure that their actions in dealing with members of the public are fair.

Here is Staffordshire County Council's commitment to equality:

'We believe that every employee has the right to be treated as an individual. As a result, we value and celebrate people's differences. To make sure that all our employees know about and understand equal opportunities, we will offer appropriate training and individual personal development.'
Source: www.staffordshire.gov.uk © Crown copyright material is reproduced with the permission of the Controller of HMSO and the Queen's Printer for Scotland.

Even when steps are taken to ensure that laws are observed, it might not be possible to please every individual on all occasions. When you consider that in many of the major cities in the UK, there could be citizens from more than 200 countries, with their associated cultures, religions and languages, it is unlikely that public service employees would be able to communicate effectively with everyone. On such occasions, the public services rely on individuals from the community who can provide assistance in communication or advice on acceptable behaviours.

Many public services present information in many languages. This includes organisations in Wales providing information in English and Welsh. In cities where there is a large population of certain nationalities, public buildings (e.g. hospitals) publish leaflets and posters and display signs in a number of languages that can be understood by citizens who do not read English.

> ### Key terms
>
> **Equality** means giving every person a fair chance, according to their needs.
> **Diversity** means recognising people's different characteristics and making sure they are considered so that they can get maximum benefit from their uniqueness.

 Grading tip!

P4 To achieve P4, you need to explain why equal opportunities are important in society and the public services.

P5 For P5, you need to refer to legislation to illustrate how equal opportunities are enforced in the UK.

How to upgrade to M3 and D2

M3 For M3, you need to compare how two public services use legislation to address equal opportunities.

D2 To achieve D2, you need to evaluate the approaches used by public services to support society by addressing the main issues of equal opportunities.

Public service roles and effect on society

In Unit 2 (Employment in the uniformed public services), we investigated the role, purpose and responsibilities of public services. In this unit, we will consider the roles of the statutory and non-statutory services and consider how these roles affect the lives of citizens within our society. You should also remember that all uniformed public services employ a number of personnel who are not in the front-line of that service. An example of these employees is the people in the police service who put together the files that are needed in court. In some services, the staff involved in the training department could also be civilians. The article below is taken from Cornwall County Council's website.

'Not everyone who works for the fire and rescue service is involved in firefighting. Cornwall Fire and Rescue Service employs a number of non-uniformed personnel at various locations:

- Headquarters in Truro
- The training centre at RAF Portreath
- Engineering workshops and stores at Cambourne
- Divisional offices in Falmouth, St Austell and Bodmin.

The non-uniformed personnel provide essential back-up administration and technical services to the front-line firefighters who depend upon this contribution to maximise their efficiency. That in turn affects the safety of the general public.'

Source: www.cornwall.gov.uk © Crown copyright material is reproduced with the permission of the Controller of HMSO and the Queen's Printer for Scotland.

A real-life example of individuals, society and public services working together

In November 2009, the safety of many citizens was put at risk when days of torrential rain and winds resulted in devastating floods in the county of Cumbria in northern England. Many people were very afraid as water gushed through their homes and businesses. A number of cars and other vehicles were swept away by the force of the flood and deposited a distance from where they had been parked by their owners.

Many residents had to be rescued from their homes as the waters continued to rise. One man recalled, 'It (the water) got up to the first landing on the stairs and then I thought, "Well, I can't get out." I got rescued out of here on Friday afternoon with the mountain rescue and lifeboat. It was pretty scary.'

The Environment Agency stated that rainfall in Cumbria reached record levels with one site (Seawaite Farm) recording 314.4mm (over 12 inches) in 24 hours, a UK record for 24-hour rainfall; the previous maximum rainfall in 24 hours was 279mm (at Martinstown, Dorset), in July 1955.

After the initial shock and relief that they had not been physically harmed, some residents returned to their homes to face the sheer scale of the damage. Furniture, carpets and other belongings too damaged to save were put onto pavements and into skips for removal. As the waters receded, shopkeepers and residents began the task of

Figure 6.7 Victims of the Cumbrian floods

sweeping mud from their properties and trying to remove water that had been left behind.

One business owner, whose family had run the company for over 70 years, lost almost all her stock as well as computers and the records they contained. But, like others in the town, she realised that there was no time to feel sorry for herself and she just had to get on with the task of clearing up.

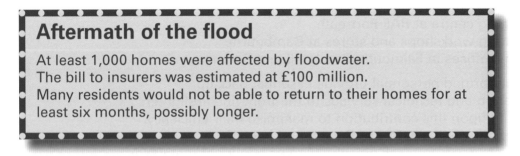

Aftermath of the flood

At least 1,000 homes were affected by floodwater.
The bill to insurers was estimated at £100 million.
Many residents would not be able to return to their homes for at least six months, possibly longer.

Policeman loses his life

A police constable with 25 years' service, Bill Barker, was swept away by the floodwaters while trying to save the lives of motorists by directing them from Northside Bridge, spanning a swollen river in Workington. He was described by the Prime Minister as a very heroic, very brave man. Assistant Chief Constable Jerry Graham said, 'He was directing motorists off the bridge, saving lives, when the tragic incident occurred.'

How would this community get back to normal?

Exactly a week after the floods arrived, a huge effort from local communities and a wide range of agencies (including public services and voluntary agencies) were involved in helping those affected in the county return to something that reflected normality.

In many parts of Cumbria, people were unable to return to their homes, and damage to roads and bridges caused great disruption to those who needed to travel – in some cases, a journey that would normally take just ten minutes required a round trip of many miles and took about 45 minutes. Some children were unable to get to school because, although they could see it from their homes, the bridge had been washed away and they could not get there.

Flood support centres were established in Keswick, Cockermouth, Workington and Ulverston by a range of public sector agencies. Mobile centres in Keswick and Workington provided support to communities cut off by the floods. A daily newsletter offering advice and information was also distributed via the flood support centres. Guarantees of support were given by the government that they would help meet the cost of repairing the damaged infrastructure.

Fund raises £1 million

Within just ten days, an amazing amount of money was donated to help the victims of the flooding in Cumbria. Although over 1,300 people were affected, among the first to benefit from the generosity of others was a man whose spectacles had been lost in the floodwaters and a couple who needed to buy replacement clothes for their baby.

One individual involved in helping those affected by the devastating events of the flooding was Heather Shepherd. Her own home near Shrewsbury had been flooded nearly ten years before. At the time of the Cumbrian floods, Heather was the coordinator for the National Flood Forum, which provides support and advice for victims of flooding. She acknowledged that the first weeks were early days for people who were unable to return to their homes. As she had needed to live in a caravan for over a year, Heather could understand the emotions that the residents of Cockermouth and other areas of Cumbria were experiencing. She described the experience of suffering a flood as being the nearest to dealing with a death in the family.

A local resident spent many days wheeling a trolley through the streets that had been the worst hit, handing out hot drinks and food, on behalf of church groups in Cumbria.

The contribution by public service organisations

It soon became clear that of 1,800 bridges in the county many might be affected by the floods, so structural checks were a high priority. Many of these bridges were closed because they were either damaged beyond repair or their safety could not be guaranteed.

Shortly after the floods hit the county, the Army began work on constructing a new temporary footbridge crossing the River Derwent in Workington. Following the collapse of the previous bridge, communities had become isolated. Network Rail built a temporary rail station just north of the River Derwent to improve links on both sides of the river. Extra bus services were provided for both schoolchildren and the public.

The health service needed to ensure that there was adequate provision for those residents who needed assistance. This included opening a pharmacy at a former job centre and GP surgeries relocating near Cockermouth Community Hospital.

Mobile banking facilities and food deliveries needed to be arranged for a large number of families. Those residents who had secured temporary accommodation found that they were unable to take their pets with them, so the RSPCA was involved in operating a scheme whereby these animals could be cared for on a temporary basis.

The leader of Cumbria County Council commented on the amount of effort that had been made by people working together to assist in the rebuilding of the community. Although he acknowledged that there was still a lot to do, he paid tribute to the 'community spirit' that everyone had demonstrated.

After just seven days, the Army had completed its task of building a footbridge over the River Derwent. On 7th December 2009, the Barker Crossing (named after the police officer who lost his life) was opened. Schoolchildren were the first to cross the bridge, at just after eight o'clock. The work was coordinated by the Army, with help from the Royal Engineers, Royal Logistic Corps, Royal Signals and Royal Military Police.

Major Nigel Hindmarsh said that he was very proud of what his men had achieved in so short a time. He also praised the local community for their support in what they were trying to achieve. Captain Caroline Graham-Brown helped to design the new crossing.

However, the road connection between north and south Workington was not expected to be complete until the summer of 2010.

This brief look back at the effects of flooding in Cumbria serves to provide an example of how individuals, society and public services can come together to provide a win–win situation for all concerned.

There are many examples of ways in which the public services and individuals have worked together to support society; these include the ways in which members of the non-statutory services give their time and expertise to help those who find themselves in need of assistance.

In Unit 2 (Employment in the uniformed public services), you will find examples of many non-statutory public services without whom society would not benefit to the extent that it does today. This is especially true when you consider the ways in which society is changing; the ways in which family make-up has altered over the last 50 years, changes in the level of crime in our neighbourhoods and the latest economic crises mean that we rely more heavily on these 'additional' services than we ever have in the past.

 Grading tip!

P6 To achieve P6, you need to *explain* the ways in which public services have supported society.

P7 P7 requires you to *demonstrate* the different ways in which public services have affected society.

How to upgrade to M4 and D2

M4 An *analysis* of the different ways in which public services have supported society is needed for M4.

D2 To achieve D2, you need to *evaluate* the approaches used by public services to support society, by addressing the main issues of equal opportunities.

End of unit knowledge check

1. Explain what makes a 'good' citizen.
2. Give two examples of how someone might become a British citizen.
3. Why is the Universal Declaration of Human Rights important?
4. Name four different acts associated with equal opportunities.
5. Name three public services that provide opportunities for volunteers.

Grading criteria

In order to pass this unit, the evidence that the learner presents for assessment needs to demonstrate that they can meet all the learning outcomes for the unit. The criteria for a pass grade describe the level of achievement required to pass this unit.

Grading criteria		
To achieve a pass grade the evidence must show that the learner is able to:	To achieve a merit grade the evidence must show that, in addition to the pass criteria, the learner is able to:	To achieve a distinction grade the evidence must show that, in addition to the pass and merit criteria, the learner is able to:
P1 Define the terms 'citizen', 'citizenship', 'individual rights', and 'human rights'		
P2 Describe the qualities a good citizen requires to enter a public service	**M1** Describe how citizens are protected by their individual and human rights	**D1** Analyse how citizens are protected by their individual and human rights
P3 Explain how public services, citizens and society work together		
P4 Explain why equal opportunities are important in society and the public services	**M2** Justify the requirements of good citizenship that are needed to enter a public service	
P5 Illustrate how equal opportunities are enforced in the UK with reference to appropriate legislation	**M3** Compare how two public services use legislation to address equal opportunities	**D2** Evaluate the approaches used by public services to support society by addressing the main issues of equal opportunities.
P6 Explain the different ways in which public services have supported society	**M4** Analyse the different ways in which public services have supported society	
P7 Demonstrate the different ways in which public services have affected society		

Unit 7
Health and safety in the public service workplace

Introduction

Health and safety is vital in our everyday lives, whether we are at home, out socialising, studying or at work. There are many laws (legislation) that provide rules for how employers and employees should ensure they carry out their health and safety responsibilities. In this unit, we will consider these laws in relation to public service situations and explore the roles of organisations and their employees.

We will also investigate the services offered by employers in relation to health, safety and welfare, as well as how and why it is important to carry out risk assessments in the workplace.

Throughout this unit, you will find 'key terms': these are basic occupational health and safety definitions and will be useful to you in understanding the legislation.

Learning outcomes:

By the end of this unit, you should:

1. Understand the role of public service employees in maintaining good health at work

2. Understand how public service employers can provide services to help maintain the health of their workforce

3. Know sources of help to ensure good health when working in a public service environment

4. Know legal and procedural aspects of health and safety at work.

Activity

Working with a partner, write down as many examples as you can think of where health and safety issues are important in public service situations.

Use a table to list your examples, such as Table 7.1 below.

Public service	Situation
Fire service	Attending incident of a burning building
Ambulance service	Tending to a casualty who is bleeding

Table 7.1 Public service situations in which health and safety is vital

You will need to refer to your completed table later in the unit, so make sure it is stored safely.

Key terms

Health, in the context of employment, means the protection of bodies and minds of people from illness resulting from the materials, processes or procedures used in the workplace.
Safety means the protection of people from physical injury.
Welfare, in the context of employment, means the provision of facilities to maintain the health and well-being of individuals at the workplace.

Health and Safety at Work Act 1974

This Act is the main piece of health and safety legislation in England and Wales. It is an enabling act, which means that other laws (regulations) may be added to it when needed, without the need to pass another Act of Parliament. Before this act came into force, there were separate laws for each industry, which meant that many workers were unprotected; contractors and members of the public were not included in previous laws. The Health and Safety at Work (HSW) Act sets out general duties for both employer and employee. The main duties are set out below.

Employers' responsibilities include:

- so far as it is reasonably practicable, ensuring employees' health, safety and welfare at work

- consulting employees on matters relating to health and safety at work
- carrying out risk assessments
- implementing measures identified in risk assessments
- reporting certain injuries, diseases and dangerous occurrences.

Employees' responsibilities include:

- taking reasonable care for their own health and safety and that of others
- cooperating with their employer on health and safety
- correctly using work items provided by their employer
- not interfering with, or misusing, anything provided for their health, safety and welfare.

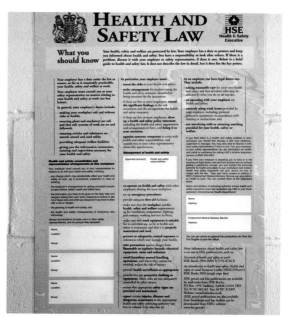

Figure 7.1 Health and Safety Law poster

You will find information on some of the other major health and safety laws later in this unit.

Every workplace should display a Health and Safety Law poster and appoint a person responsible for health and safety.

The role of employees in maintaining good health

Everyone has a responsibility to maintain (as far as possible) their own health at work. This includes ensuring you enjoy a suitable diet, undertake sensible exercise and get enough rest. These are the things that you can directly control; however, despite your best efforts, there will be times when your health will not be at peak level. This could include contracting a virus, a bout of sickness or an infection. In the event that you do become unwell, it is expected that you should deal with the illness in a sensible manner, so that you do not affect anyone else in the workplace and you return to work as soon as is practical.

As well as organising your personal life to ensure a good mix of rest, diet and exercise, it is essential that, as far as possible, you also manage these aspects while at work. This is often easier said than done – you might already have a part-time job, which means you need your meal earlier or later than the rest of your family, or maybe you agree to go with another student to play tennis after college, so you miss your bus and have to walk home. These are examples of occasional problems that might be a nuisance; when these instances become regular, maybe resulting in you not having time to take regular breaks, they could lead to serious health issues.

As well as looking after your own and others' health and safety, you are required to play your part in reducing potential hazards and risks in the workplace and, where you find these hazards and risks, reporting them to the appropriate person.

Within some organisations, including many of the public services, you will be required to wear suitable clothing. This is designed to provide the wearer with proper protection from foreseeable harm in the course of their normal duties. In some services, different clothing may be required depending on the particular circumstance.

Consider the regular uniform worn by police officers and then look back to Figure 1.1 in Unit 1 (page 4). Why do you think these officers have replaced their trousers and jackets with overalls? Why are they wearing helmets and visors? What do they have in their hands? You should be able to answer these questions fully by carrying out the following activity.

When people are required to wear specific clothing, or to use particular tools, to carry out an aspect of their work, it is known as *personal protective equipment*. The Personal Protective Equipment at Work Regulations 1992 set out conditions for the ways in which this equipment should be maintained to ensure it is fit for purpose. Personal protective equipment includes safety helmets, gloves, eye protection and high-visibility wear, as well as many more items.

Key terms

A **hazard** is the potential of a substance, activity or process to cause harm.

A **risk** is the likelihood of that substance, activity or process to cause harm.

A risk can be reduced and a hazard controlled by good management.

Activity

Select a public service of your choice and research the uniforms worn by its workforce. You might already be aware that uniforms can change in line with promotion, particularly in relation to the symbol that is worn on the shoulders to denote the rank of the wearer. Look more closely and you will realise that, in some services, the nature of the task determines the uniform that should be worn.

See if you can determine the materials used in the manufacture of these 'alternative' uniforms and the relevance of this to health and safety issues.

Key term

Personal protective equipment (PPE) means all equipment (including clothing) intended to be worn or held by a person at work and which protects him or her against one or more risks to his or her health or safety.

Activity

In preparation for assessment of P1, keep a record of anything that you or another person does that helps to maintain the health, safety and welfare of people in the workplace. This might include spotting a potential health and safety issue *and reporting it*, disposing of waste materials, administering first aid or mopping up spillages.

(g) Grading tip!

P1 To achieve P1, you need to explain how employees can maintain good health in the workplace.

How to upgrade to M1

M1 M1 requires an analysis of the ways that employees can maintain good health in a public service workplace.

How employers maintain health of employees

P2   M2

The second learning outcome is concerned with the ways the employer provides services to ensure the health, safety and welfare of their employees. To achieve M2, will need to make sure you relate your evidence to a public service workplace.

However careful we are in undertaking work or leisure activities, there will be times when incidents occur that require the attention of a person trained to respond to an emergency situation that has resulted in injury. The Health and Safety (First Aid) Regulations 1981 set out employers' duties to provide adequate first aid facilities. Information on the number of first aiders and the level of training required is available on the Health and Safety Executive website (www.hse.gov.uk).

Key term

First aid is the treatment:
- for the purposes of preserving life and minimising the consequences of injury and illness until medical help is obtained
- of minor injuries that would otherwise receive no treatment or that do not need treatment by a medical practitioner or nurse.

It is important that employees know how and where to access the services of a trained first aider. After all, any situation where an individual requires treatment should be considered an emergency and an immediate response is vital.

Remember that both employer and employee have certain legal responsibilities. Some of these are shown in Table 7.2 on page 173.

Sometimes an injury will occur as a result of an accident. All workplaces are required by law to keep a record of all accidents or 'near misses'. An entry in an accident book should record the location, date and time of the incident, what happened, who was involved, any injuries incurred and the action that was taken. It is important that all accidents are recorded in case of future legal allegations.

Key terms

An **accident** is any unplanned event that results in injury or ill-health, or damage or loss to property, plant, materials or the environment.
A **near miss** is any incident that could have resulted in an accident.

Research has shown that for every ten near-miss events at a location in the workplace, a minor accident will occur. Therefore, it is important that a record is kept of these occurrences so that measures can be put in place to prevent an accident.

Reporting of Injuries, Diseases and Dangerous Occurrences Regulations (RIDDOR) 1995

This legislation is concerned with injuries, some diseases and dangerous occurrences. All these incidents *must* be recorded and may be reported to the Health and Safety Executive (HSE). In the event of a serious accident, the HSE will investigate. Incidents that must be reported under RIDDOR include:

- the death or major injury of an employee on the premises

Responsibilities	Employer	Employee
Risk assessment (examination of what may cause harm to people)	To examine the workplace and identify what may cause harm, to whom and how to minimise the risk. To inform employees of risk assessment.	To follow risk assessment procedures and to notify employer of any changes.
Monitoring of working practices	To put measures in place to monitor workplace and practices.	To follow working practices and to inform employer of any changes.
Storing equipment	To provide guidance on how to store equipment and materials and the means to carry this out.	To follow policies and procedures and to store equipment and materials appropriately.
Dealing with hazardous and non-hazardous materials	To provide risk assessments, policies and procedures on how to use these materials. To train workers how to use them.	To follow policies and procedures. To clear up spillages according to risk assessments.
Manual handling	To assess the risks and reduce the need for manual handling. To train workers in manual handling.	To follow manual handling procedures and to report any faults with equipment.
Reporting health and safety issues	To report major accidents to the Health and Safety Executive.	To report any issues to employer or representative.
Completing health and safety and security records	To keep all records, such as risk assessments, up to date.	To keep all records up to date and confidential. These may include accident books.

Table 7.2 Examples of responsibilities in relation to health and safety

- an injury (to anyone) that requires immediate hospital treatment
- an injury that results in the employee being off work for three days or more
- 'reportable' diseases
- dangerous occurrences, including incidents that did not result in a reportable injury.

Examples of a dangerous occurrence include the failure of any equipment

> ### Key term
>
> A **dangerous occurrence** is a near miss that could have led to serious injury or loss of life.

that carries passengers – for example, a big wheel at a funfair or an electrical short circuit. These incidents are always reportable under RIDDOR and will almost certainly lead to an investigation into the cause. Measures will also need to be put in place to prevent a recurrence of the incident.

In 1969, F.E. Bird collected a large volume of accident data and produced an 'accident triangle' (Figure 7.2).

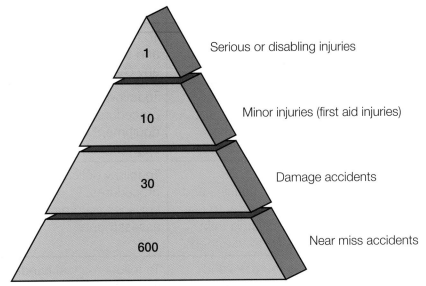

Figure 7.2 F.E. Bird's accident triangle

From this diagram, you can see that damage and near-miss accidents occur much more regularly than accidents resulting in injury. F.E. Bird's full study showed that most accidents are predictable and could therefore be avoided. One way of avoiding accidents is to carry out an assessment of risk associated with any planned activity.

Risk assessment

A risk assessment is an exploration of what might cause harm to people or cause damage to property. It is a legal requirement to carry out a risk assessment before embarking upon many activities, including some of the things you will be doing on you course!

The HSE provides a five-step guide to risk assessment. The following process should identify many potential hazards, enabling the person carrying out the activity to plan accordingly. The law does not expect an employer to remove all risk but they must protect all people as far as is practicable.

For many people, carrying out a risk assessment for the first time is a daunting experience but, by following some straightforward guidance, it can be completed relatively easily.

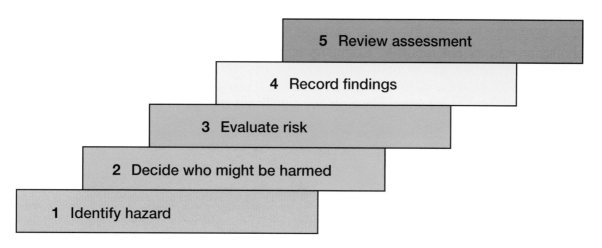

Figure 7.3 Five steps to risk assessment

Source: www.hse.gov.uk

Step 1 – Identify hazards

Take a walk around the workplace and look for anything that might reasonably cause harm. It is a good idea to ask others using the workplace if they have seen anything that you might have missed. Guidance sheets on equipment and products should be followed. Do not forget that some ill-health problems occur over a period of time; an example of this is hearing damage or hearing loss so be aware of sound levels too.

Step 2 – Decide who might be harmed

You need to be particularly alert to people who might be especially vulnerable – for example, young workers, pregnant women or people with disabilities. The 'people' are not just those who are employed in the workplace; it includes visitors, contractors, cleaners and others who are not there full-time.

Step 3 – Evaluate the risks

Once you have found any potential problems, you need to decide what to do about them. First, you will look at what is being done already – is this sufficient? Once again, the law requires you to do everything practicable to protect people from harm. This step can be divided into two parts; first, ask yourself, 'Can the risk be eliminated?' and, if this is not possible, you need to ask yourself, 'How can the risk be managed?' so that harm is unlikely.

Step 4 – Record your findings

Although very small companies do not need to do this, all public service organisations are required to write down their risk assessment findings. This will help on future occasions, so that there is a record of any particular problems that have not been properly dealt with. It will also assist employees in being aware of potential dangers to their health or safety.

Step 5 – Review the assessment

Few workplaces stay the same over a long period of time, so this process should be carried out regularly. Examples of changes in the workplace include the introduction of new equipment or changes to procedures, which would mean new hazards might be present. It is a good idea to keep risk assessment in mind when planning any significant change to working practices.

Case study

College lecturer hurt in fall on wet ramp
A college lecturer who suffered injuries to his wrist and shoulder after slipping on a wheelchair ramp received a 'substantial sum' in compensation. The lecturer fell on the ramp while entering a temporary classroom. The classroom was fitted with a wooden access ramp, which was wet following rain. The shoulder injury required intensive physiotherapy and caused prolonged pain. Employers have to ensure that access routes in the workplace do not become slippery. If the ramp could not be kept dry, it should have had a surface that was slip-resistant in the wet. The college said, 'Since the accident, we have introduced much more robust health and safety procedures to ensure that something like this can never happen again.'

Initiatives to keep employees healthy

In addition to their legal responsibilities, many employers provide services to help keep employees healthy and that may even prevent them becoming unwell. As part of your work in Unit 2 (Employment in the uniformed public services), you will have explored 'conditions of service' for one public service (P5). Some of the public services provide 'extras' for their personnel, over and above what is legally required. These might include membership of a private health scheme at a reduced rate, regular medical check-ups and, where required, early referral to occupational health experts.

As in other sectors, members of the public services might become vulnerable to illnesses such as stress or addiction. If those affected are able to access relevant support networks at an early stage, there is a good chance that the symptoms of the illness may be successfully treated.

Examples of initiatives that may be available include healthy eating campaigns, where canteen staff provide meals and snacks that are nutritionally balanced, helping to prevent ill-health through poor diet. Many public service organisations have gymnasium facilities on site or are able to offer their employees a reduced rate membership at private gyms. Another example is a grant or loan to buy a bicycle to travel between home and work – this has the double benefit of improving the health of the rider and also contributing less to the pollution caused by the number of motor vehicles on the roads.

Ride 2 work schemes

Under this government initiative, the employer enters into a contract with a provider and pays for the bike, helmet, lights and reflective clothing. The employee then pays back this cost to the employer over a period of 12 months. The payments are deducted from the employee's salary, which means that they pay less tax and National Insurance.

Activity

Research your chosen public service and find out what services it provides to ensure the health and well-being of its employees.

Grading tip!

P2 To achieve P2, you need to summarise (provide the main points) how the employer helps to maintain the health of its workforce.

How to upgrade to M2

M2 M2 requires an assessment of the services provided by an employer in the public services. This means you need to give a detailed account of what is available and then judge the worth of services provided.

Sources of help to ensure good health

P3

In Unit 4 (Career planning for the public services), you will have researched the entry requirements for various public services and found that this often involves pre-appointment medicals and specific activities to test your fitness. In many public service organisations, there is a requirement for employees to undergo regular medical check-ups throughout their career. In this section, we will consider the ways in which you and your employer can ensure you maintain the high level of health and fitness you had when you initially completed those gruelling tasks. After all, you will probably expect to remain in the service for many years and the employer will have spent a lot of effort and money in training you to become a valued member of their organisation.

Taking good care of employees depends on having access to people with the right specialist knowledge, who are able to deliver suitable services where they are needed. These services might be available within the organisation itself or outside services may be used.

Occupational health service

Many employers will, at some time, use occupational health services. Many large organisations, including some public services, will employ occupational health specialists, while others will refer an employee to a professional.

Occupational health practitioners focus on the relationship between health and work. For some people, a health issue will affect their ability to work or the type of work they can do will be limited by the health issue. In other cases, the work itself may affect people's health. An occupational health specialist might work with a single employee, a group or even the entire workforce, depending on the specific issue. Occupational health aims to ensure that people can be as effective as possible in their work and that their health is protected.

As part of a preventative approach, occupational health professionals might be employed to carry out health surveillance on employees. This is a targeted medical check to ensure that employees remain in good health and are not being harmed by their work. As part of an awareness of the problems that could occur over time (e.g. hearing damage or loss), occupational health professionals may also conduct regular hearing checks. Any changes would be identified at an early stage and appropriate action could be taken. They may also consider the activity that the employee is to carry out and evaluate the risk of stress-related illness from this.

Occupational health professionals can provide benefits to individuals and organisations by carrying out a number of specific services, as outlined below:

- advising on compliance with health and safety law
- identifying where aspects of the job affect the health of the employee
- dealing with work issues (e.g. the 'sickness culture')
- identifying symptoms of stress at an early stage
- recognising a 'cluster of illness' in the same organisation
- ensuring people are fit to do the job they are employed to do
- assisting individuals to return to work
- reducing the cost of sickness absence
- advising organisations on the management of sickness absence
- assisting management to keep up to date with health and safety policies.

Many employees within the public services are required to spend at least some time using a computer. Under law, every employer is required to undertake a Display Screen Equipment (DSE) assessment; this is an analysis of the computer operator's workstation. The purpose of the process is to assess any risks that may be present and reduce those risks, if necessary. Some organisations train their own staff to carry out these assessments and others buy in the service.

Stress at work

Work is generally good for people, if it is well designed, but it can also be a great source of pressure. Pressure can be positive and a motivating factor; it can help us achieve our goals and perform better. Stress is a natural reaction when this pressure becomes excessive.

> ### Key term
>
> **Stress** is the adverse reaction people have to excessive pressures or other types of demands placed upon them.

Stress is not an illness – indeed, many people perform better when they are subjected to a certain amount of stress. However, if the stress becomes excessive and/or prolonged, mental and physical illness may develop.

Stress at work is a major issue but it can be prevented or managed effectively. Work-related stress arises when work demands of various types and combinations exceed the person's capacity and capability to cope. You can think of this as 'bad work'. It is a significant cause of illness and disease and is known to be linked with high levels of sickness absence, staff turnover and other indicators of organisational underperformance, including human error.

For some organisations, the way to deal with work-related stress is to diagnose, treat and rehabilitate people who experience it. The result of this could be that the individual or individuals who are suffering from the stress will be able to carry on in their employment, maybe in a different role or, in some cases, the individual may need to leave the employment.

> ### Think about it!
>
> How would you know if you were at risk of suffering from stress at work?

Stress produces a range of signs and symptoms. Some of the most widely recognised signs are given in Table 7.3 on page 180.

Behavioural signs	Physical symptoms	Mental problems	Emotional signs
Difficulty sleeping	Tiredness	Indecision	Irritability, anger
Change in eating habits	Indigestion, nausea, headaches	Lack of concentration	Anxiety
Dependency on alcohol or drugs	Aching muscles	Loss of memory	Hypersensitivity
Sexual problems	Palpitations	Low self-esteem	Feeling drained, listless

Table 7.3 Signs and symptoms of stress

Anyone can suffer from work-related stress, no matter what work they do. Any employer who fails to act upon this and ignores their responsibilities under health and safety legislation could find themselves in serious trouble.

Manual handling

Another area of work that affects public service personnel is lifting and using equipment. Examples of this include members of the armed forces carrying kit bags and fire officers using ladders, cutting equipment and hoses.

The Manual Handling Operations Regulations 1992 aim to reduce the risk of injury from lifting or moving people or objects. These regulations were amended in 2002. The main principle of this law is that, wherever possible, you should avoid lifting altogether. Where this is not possible, it is important that the risk of injury is assessed. As with other health and safety legislation, this law sets out responsibilities for both employer and employee, as outlined in the box below.

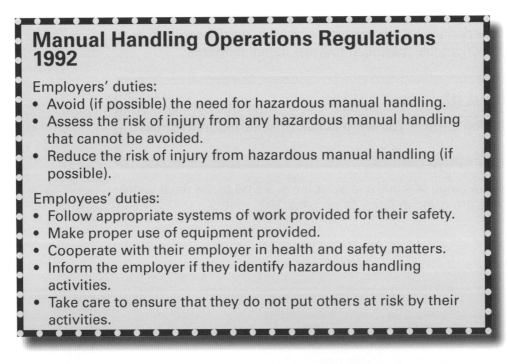

Manual Handling Operations Regulations 1992

Employers' duties:
- Avoid (if possible) the need for hazardous manual handling.
- Assess the risk of injury from any hazardous manual handling that cannot be avoided.
- Reduce the risk of injury from hazardous manual handling (if possible).

Employees' duties:
- Follow appropriate systems of work provided for their safety.
- Make proper use of equipment provided.
- Cooperate with their employer in health and safety matters.
- Inform the employer if they identify hazardous handling activities.
- Take care to ensure that they do not put others at risk by their activities.

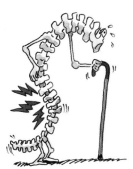

Figure 7.4 More than one million people in Great Britain suffer from musculoskeletal disorders

Think about it!

More than a third of injuries reported to the HSE and local authorities each year are caused by manual handling.

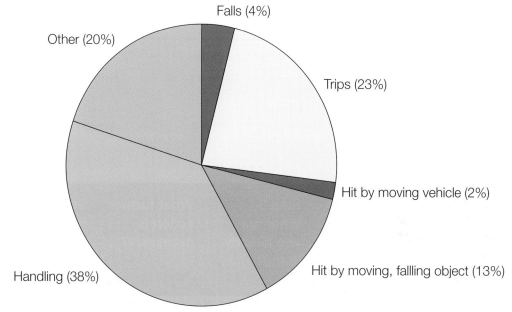

Falls (4%)

Other (20%)

Trips (23%)

Hit by moving vehicle (2%)

Hit by moving, fallling object (13%)

Handling (38%)

Figure 7.5 Type of accident reported to HSE 2001/2002

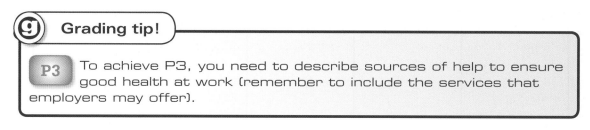

Grading tip!

P3 To achieve P3, you need to describe sources of help to ensure good health at work (remember to include the services that employers may offer).

Legal aspects of health and safety at work

P4 P5 P6 M3 M4

This final section of this unit covers all the legal aspects of health and safety. You have already been introduced to many of the major pieces of legislation that exist to ensure a safe working environment. In this section, we will investigate some others.

You will use the knowledge you have gained to carry out a risk assessment, consider procedures for emergency situations and explore the role of the Health and Safety Executive. Finally, you will consider the consequences of failing to act in accordance with legislation and the penalty that could attract.

Activity

Using the five steps to risk assessment described earlier (page 175), carry out a review of the risks in your workplace. Record your results in a table (for example, see Table 7.4 below).

Table 7.4 Example of a risk assessment

Company name:

Date of risk assessment:

Step 1 What are the hazards?	Step 2 Who might be harmed and how?	Step 3 What are you already doing?	What further action is necessary?	Step 4 How will you put the assessment into action?

Step 5 Review date:

Fire awareness

Three elements are necessary for fire to exist; these are fuel, heat and oxygen.

Remove one of the elements and the fire will be extinguished. This can be done by:

- cooling the fire to remove the heat
- starving the fire of fuel
- smothering the fire by limiting the oxygen supply.

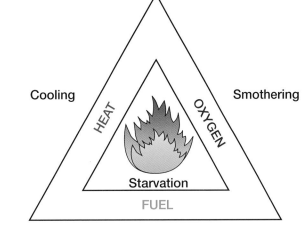

Figure 7.6 The fire triangle

Classification of fire

Fire can be classified in a number of ways, depending on the type of fuel that is present (see Figure 7.7).

CLASS A – Textiles – Wood, paper, cloth etc.

CLASS B – Liquids – Miscible with water – Petroleum, oil, paint etc.
Non-miscible with water – Alcohol.

CLASS C – Gases – Hydrogen, LPG, i.e. propane or butane, oxygen etc.

CLASS D – Metals – Magnesium, aluminium, titanium

Figure 7.7 Classes of fire

Fire extinguishers

Figure 7.8a Water extinguisher; red body; suitable for use on Class A fires

Figure 7.8b Foam extinguisher; cream label; suitable for Class A and Class B fires

Figure 7.8c Powder extinguisher; blue label; safe for any fire, but best for Class C fire

Figure 7.8d Carbon dioxide (CO2) extinguisher; red body with black label; safe on all fires but best on Class B and Class C fires

Activity

Carry out research into the ways in which each of the fire extinguishers shown in Figures 7.8a–d deals with fire. (Look back at the fire triangle in Figure 7.6 for clues.)

There are many laws that govern the ways in which health and safety issues should be dealt with in the workplace. Let us now look at some of these.

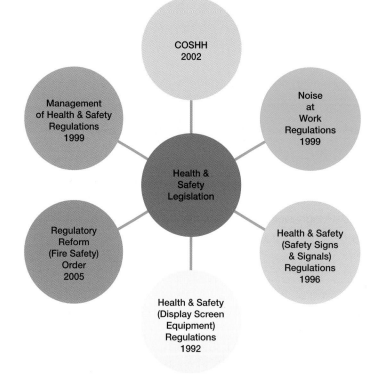

Figure 7.9 Health and safety legislation

The Regulatory Reform (Fire Safety) Order 2005

This law came into effect in October 2006 and replaced more than 70 pieces of fire safety law.

Control of Substances Hazardous to Health Regulations (COSHH) 2002

These regulations are concerned with using, storing and disposing of substances. Employers are obliged to assess the risk that hazardous substances could present and, where risk is identified, they must take reasonable precautions to ensure the risk is as low as possible. A simple example of this law in action is ensuring that cleaning materials (e.g. bleach and polish) are labelled and stored in a suitable place.

Some products display hazard signs, providing additional warning (Figure 7.10).

Extremely or Highly Flammable

Harmful or Irritant

Corrosive

Figure 7.10 Hazard signs

Food Safety Act 1990

All employees have to eat and this law covers the ways in which food should be handled, stored, cooked and served.

The Management of Health and Safety at Work Regulations 1999

The Management of Health and Safety at Work Regulations set out broad general duties that apply to most work activities. They make clear the general requirements of employers that are made under the Health and Safety at Work Act. The aim is to encourage a systematic approach to managing health and safety.

Managers are required to assess the risks to health and safety posed by all work activities. Important findings of the risk assessment need to be recorded. Managers should then put in place the required health and safety measures that were identified in the risk assessment. These measures form the health and safety management system for the workplace and should cover policy, organising, planning, monitoring, auditing and reviewing.

Procedures must be put in place to deal with emergencies and other serious or imminent dangers. Employees must be informed of major risks and receive training in how these may be reduced. People who do not work on the premises all the time – for example, temporary and part-time staff – should also be made aware of these risks.

Summary of managers' duties

- Ensure that equipment is suitable for its intended use.
- Take into account the working environment, conditions and hazards.
- Ensure that equipment is used only for its intended purpose.
- Ensure equipment is regularly maintained and is in good working order.
- Give adequate instruction and training.

Health and Safety (Safety Signs and Signals) Regulations 1996

Safety signs are one method of control. There are five different types of signs.

1. **Safe condition** – rectangular or square on a green background.
2. **Fire equipment** – rectangular or square on a red background.
3. **Prohibition** – round with a red border and diagonal cross on a white background.
4. **Warning** – triangular with a yellow background and black border.
5. **Mandatory** – round with a blue background.

Activity

What is the meaning of each of the signs in Figure 7.11?

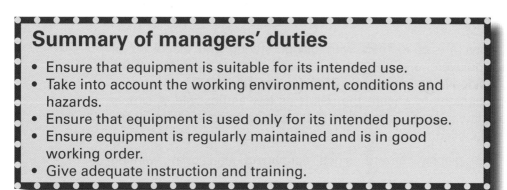

Figure 7.11 Safety signs

Noise at Work Regulations 1989 (revised 2005)

These regulations were introduced following increasing concern over the incidences of occupational deafness. Under the terms of this legislation, the employer is required to assess noise levels and keep records. The employer must also reduce identified risk from noise exposure, preferably by reducing the noise or by providing hearing protection. Employees must also be provided with information and suitable training.

The main purpose of the regulations is to control noise levels. This involves design of machinery and equipment and also ensuring that protective equipment is worn and health surveillance of employees is carried out. Noise can lead to ear damage on a temporary or permanent basis.

Health and safety policies

If there are five or more employees in a workplace, there must be a written health and safety policy in place. This policy should set out the organisation's objectives in relation to health and safety and the arrangements that exist for managing health and safety in the organisation. However, good health and safety practice means that there should not only be a policy but it should also be managed in a way that benefits the organisation, its employees, clients and the local community.

There is no requirement to have policies on every aspect of an organisation's business. However, there are legal requirements to have written policies on certain things such as disciplinary and grievance procedures and health and safety. In those areas where having a policy is not a legal requirement, it is still good practice to have one, so that employees understand what is expected of them and what they can expect to get in return. Policies also help to create a culture where issues are dealt with fairly and consistently.

The Health and Safety Executive

The Health and Safety Executive (HSE) is the body set up under the Health and Safety at Work Act 1974 to support the government's aims and current targets for health and safety at work. Its main aim is to secure the health, safety and welfare of people at work and protect others from risks to health and safety from work activity. Its main legal duties are to set necessary standards for health and safety performance, implement those standards and carry out research and publish the results. It also provides an information and advisory service.

The HSE's mission is:

'The prevention of death, injury and ill-health to those at work and those affected by work activities.'

The HSE has the power to enter an area at any time without giving any notice and, if they feel it necessary, close a company down until measures are taken to improve the safety of the workplace. Failure to comply with health and safety policies and procedures, especially if it results in serious injury or, in the worst-case scenario, death, will lead to a prosecution.

Key facts for 2008/09

- 1.2 million people who worked during the last year were suffering from an illness (long-standing as well as new cases) they believed was caused or made worse by their current or past work (551,000 of these were new cases).
- 131,895 injuries to employees were reported under RIDDOR.
- 246,000 reportable injuries occurred.
- 29.3 million working days were lost due to work-related ill-health (4.7 million of these were due to workplace injury).
- 1,245 offences were prosecuted by HSE.
- 329 offences were prosecuted by local authorities.
- 180 people were killed at work.

Source: www.hse.gov.uk © Crown copyright material is reproduced with the permission of the Controller of HMSO and the Queen's Printer for Scotland.

When things go wrong!

Penalties

Magistrates' courts – for health and safety offences under sections 2 to 6 of the Health and Safety at Work Act, employers and others (self-employed, manufacturers and suppliers) may be fined up to £20,000. For all other breaches of the Health and Safety at Work Act and breaches of health and safety regulations made under the act, the maximum fine is £5,000. So the maximum fine that may be given to an employee is £5,000. For failure to comply with an enforcement notice or a court order, anybody may be fined up to £20,000 or imprisoned for up to six months.

Crown Court – fines are unlimited in the Crown Court for all health and safety offences and the possible imprisonment is up to two years for failure to comply with an enforcement notice or a court order.

The courts also have the power to disqualify directors who are convicted of health and safety offences for up to 5 years (magistrates' court) or 15 years (Crown Court). Although imprisonment is a possible penalty for breaches of health and safety, between 1996 and 2005, only five people received a custodial sentence.

Case study

Firms fined over Hatfield crash

Two firms have been fined a total of £13.5 million for breaching health and safety regulations over the Hatfield train crash in 2000, in which four people died. The crash, involving the London to Leeds express train, also left 102 people injured.

Network Rail, formerly Railtrack, was fined £3.5 million – the highest ever for a rail firm on health and safety grounds. Maintenance firm Balfour Beatty was fined £10 million. Each firm was also ordered to pay £300,000 in costs.

The Old Bailey trial, which lasted eight months, heard that the 117mph derailment was caused by a crack in one section of the track. It heard that the rail had been identified as being in need of repair almost two years previously, but a backlog of essential work had been allowed to accumulate.

Balfour Beatty apologised for its role in the crash. Garry Fellows, who was seriously injured in the crash, said he hoped the money would be spent on improving the railways.

Fining the firms, the judge was particularly critical of the construction giant and its inspection regime, saying it simply was not effective. Mr Justice Mackay said, in his 30 years in the legal profession, he regarded the company's failure as the 'worst example of sustained industrial negligence in a high-risk industry he had ever seen'.

Grading tip!

P4 To achieve P4, you need to outline the role of the Health and Safety Executive (who they are and what they do).

P5 For P5, you must give examples of how legislation affects health and safety in the workplace.

P6 P6 requires a description of the procedures involved in health and safety in the workplace (make sure you include risk assessment, emergency and evacuation procedures and the use of any equipment).

How to upgrade to M3, M4 and D1

M3 For M3, you need to select a public service and explain how that organisation (and its employees) might be held responsible for failing to act in a given situation.

M4 **D1** M4 follows on from P6 – here, you need to explain the procedures.

Finally, to achieve D1, you need to draw upon all the information you have gathered from this unit and *evaluate* the roles of the employers and employees in public services in maintaining health and safety at work.

End of unit knowledge check

1. List five ways in which public service employees can ensure they are in a fit state to carry out their duties.
2. Describe the services provided by public service organisations to keep their workforce as fit as possible.
3. What does the HSE do?
4. Name at least five pieces of legislation relating to health and safety.

Grading criteria

In order to pass this unit, the evidence that the learner presents for assessment needs to demonstrate that they can meet all the learning outcomes for the unit. The assessment criteria for a pass grade describe the level of achievement required to pass this unit.

Grading criteria

To achieve a pass grade the evidence must show that the learner is able to:	To achieve a merit grade the evidence must show that, in addition to the pass criteria, the learner is able to:	To achieve a distinction grade the evidence must show that, in addition to the pass and merit criteria, the learner is able to:
P1 Explain how employees can maintain good health in the workplace	**M1** Analyse ways employees can maintain good health in a public service workplace	**D1** Evaluate the roles of public service employers and employees in maintaining health and safety at work
P2 Summarise services that can be provided by employers to help maintain the health of the workforce	**M2** Assess services provided by a named public service employer to help maintain the health of their workforce	
P3 Describe sources of help to ensure good health at work and the services they offer		
P4 Outline the role of the Health and Safety Executive	**M3** Explain particular health and safety issues which may impact on a named public service and its personnel and the consequences of failing to act	
P5 Outline the legal aspects of health and safety at work		
P6 Describe the procedural aspects of health and safety in the workplace including risk assessment, emergency and evacuation procedures and the use of equipment	**M4** Explain the procedural aspects of health and safety in a named public service workplace	

Unit 9
Sport and recreation in the public services

Introduction

Sport and recreation play important roles in the uniformed public services. Participation in sport and recreation is also growing at an increasing rate due to the greater awareness of the health benefits associated with exercise and fitness. Exercise is physical activity done mainly to improve your health and fitness but it will also benefit you physically, mentally and socially.

In this unit, we will look at the variety of sporting and recreational activities available and their importance in many of the uniformed public services. You can then research which activities each public service provides, especially in the career path of your choice, and decide if they are the ones you show an interest in at present.

You will be asked to plan a sporting or recreational activity for your peers so it is vital to know the people, the facility and the equipment required for the delivery. A session plan and risk assessment will need to be completed before you actually run the session. In addition, you will be made aware of the very important safety issues that need to be considered before and during the activity. To complete this part of the unit, you will be asked to evaluate the session with the help of your participants and anyone else who witnessed your performance.

While studying this unit, and upon completion, you are expected to be able to take part regularly in sport and recreational activities, as well as follow exercise and fitness regimes in preparation for entry to the public services. For this reason, you will design your own personal programme of sport and recreational activities for your personal use.

Learning outcomes:

By the end of this unit, you should:

1. Know the importance of sport and recreation to the public services

2. Understand the safety issues to be considered when organising sport and recreational activities

3. Be able to plan a sport activity used in the public services

4. Be able to participate regularly in public services sport and recreational activities.

Importance of sport and recreation to the public services

There are many, many benefits of playing sport and participating in physical recreation and, though there are a few concerns such as injury and mental fatigue, on the whole the benefits outweigh the concerns. Firstly, you need to define the difference between sports and recreation.

You probably have your own definitions that you would like to write down.

For the benefit of this unit, we will be looking at only sport and physical recreation, rather than passive recreation or leisure. Sport and physical recreation are the ones that the uniformed and non uniformed public services prefer their staff to participate in, due to the fact that they provide more benefits to individuals and to the public services themselves.

Key terms

Sports are competitive and have rules. The aim is always to win.
Physical recreation is not as competitive, as you are mainly competing against yourself, so you can set your own rules. It is generally something you do because you want to.
Passive recreation is sometimes referred to as leisure; it is done for pleasure and can, at times, be sedentary.

Activity

List as many sport and physical recreational activities as possible in a table (e.g. see Table 9.1 below). Indicate whether you participate as part of a team or as an individual and then place them into one of the following categories:

- Invasion sports
- Court sports
- Striking/fielding sports
- Water sports
- Target sports
- Martial arts
- Field sports

Sport or recreational activity	Team or individual	Category

Table 9.1 Sport and physical recreation

Different sports and recreational activities used by the public services

P1

All the uniformed and non-uniformed public services offer a variety of sport and recreational activities to their staff. The armed forces in particular offer a tremendous range of summer and winter sports for all levels of competitor, from the very beginner up to the 'elite' standard; some members of the armed forces even won medals in the recent Beijing Olympics. The 'blue light' services tend to offer more year-round sports and not so many of the adventurous activities.

Figure 9.1 The armed forces offer a large range of sports

Royal Air Force

The Royal Air Force has set up a specific body to administer all sport and recreational activities within their service called the RAF Sports Board. They also have a dedicated page on their website where personnel can find out all the information they require regarding the sports and recreational activities, competitions, leagues, tours and facilities available (www.raf.mod.uk).

'The RAF Sports Board recognised sports are:
- Team sports: basketball, football, hockey, netball, rugby union.
- Racket and field sports: badminton, cricket, golf, tennis.
- Athletics: athletics, triathlon.
- Combat, target and equitation sports: boxing, clay pigeon shooting, equitation, polo, judo, martial arts.
- Water sports: sea angling, rowing, sailing, surfing, swimming, water skiing, wakeboarding.

- Air sports: gliding and soaring, sports parachute.
- Winter and adventure sports: alpine championships, biathlon, mountaineering, power kiting.'
      Source: www.raf.mod.uk © Crown copyright material is reproduced with the permission of the Controller of HMSO and the Queen's Printer for Scotland.

The British Army

Sport is an important part of Army life. All soldiers who are keen to pursue a sporting interest can do so, whatever their ability or disability. The best athletes can compete internally and also at a Combined Service level against the Royal Air Force, the Royal Navy and civilian teams. 'Elite' athletes are given encouragement and assistance to compete at the highest level possible.

'The Army Sport Control Board (ASCB) is the regulatory body for all sport played in the Army. Based in Aldershot Garrison at the Army Centre of Sporting Excellence, the ASCB authorises and monitors over 150 tours and visits to over 30 countries in an average year. The facilities include hockey and cricket pavilions; sports hall and fitness centre; swimming centre; golf club; gymnasium; rugby stadium; football and athletics stadium and a tennis centre.'
      Source: www.army.mod.uk © Crown copyright material is reproduced with the permission of the Controller of HMSO and the Queen's Printer for Scotland.

Figure 9.2 A public service in sporting action

The Fire Service

The Fire Service Sport and Athletic Association (FSSAA) have a vision to encourage all forms of sport and athletics, both indoor and outdoor, for the benefit of serving and retired members of the fire and rescue services.

'(The FSSAA) promotes, organises and does all things necessary to provide, establish and support competition, championships and events of a like nature.'

'The FSSAA oversees a wide spectrum of different sporting

activities in a number of sections: athletics, badminton, bowling, clay target shooting, cricket, cycling, football, golf, rugby, sailing, squash, swimming, table tennis, triathlon, volleyball, walking and mountaineering.'

Source: www.fssaa.co.uk

The FSSAA will be supporting the World Firefighter Games to be held in Daegu, Korea in 2010.

HM Prison Service

'The Prison Service Sports Association (PSSA) is committed to promoting sport, leisure and recreation for its members, in an environment that encourages participation by all abilities and interest levels. With numerous Governing Bodies of Sport you are able to take part in a variety of sporting activities at all levels. There is a list of 25 sports provided by the PSSA for men and women.'

Source: www.pssa.org.uk

Ask yourself!

What sport or recreational activities do you presently participate in and which ones would you like to try? Research all the uniformed and non-uniformed public services, including the ones mentioned above, and find out what sport and recreational activities they offer their personnel and decide if they are the ones that you are most interested in.

P2

Importance and benefits to the public services

All the public services place great emphasis on their employees taking part in sport and physical recreation, not only for the many benefits to the individuals but also as a benefit to themselves. There are many factors that come from participating in activities that will benefit your employer.

As an individual, and as part of a team, you will be able to work longer and get more done in less time, which in turn increases productivity. In most cases, you will have less time off for illness, not be as stressed and be much more willing to carry out training and development to improve yourself.

'Sport in the RAF provides an inducement to physical fitness, and contributes to military effectiveness by encouraging personal qualities such as courage, resilience, esprit de corps and has a significant effect on morale. Sport is an integral part of the RAF ethos, and the fulfilment of the sporting expectations and activities of RAF personnel remains a significant retention and recruitment factor.'

Source: www.raf.mod.uk © Crown copyright material is reproduced with the permission of the Controller of HMSO and the Queen's Printer for Scotland.

Figure 9.3 Action from the RAF

The significant retention and recruitment factor leads to a reduction of recruitment costs which, in turn, enhances profits, while staff retention develops efficient and motivated staff who have better chances of promotion.

'There are some misconceptions that sport interferes with service to the public and it is assumed by many that the only purpose of physical fitness in the police service is to reduce absence through growing sickness levels. However, sport and physical recreation increases the efficiency of the police service as a whole and stimulates the work of a police officer, in addition to a spirit of comradeship amongst the force and the country's forces.'

Source: www.policesportuk.com

The reasons for the public services, especially the uniformed public services, using sport and recreational activities are numerous. Employees who are fit and healthy are more likely to attend work each day, have less time off sick and be more loyal to the employers who provide sport and recreational activities. Recruitment of staff is considerably lessened by loyal employees and retention remains high, which helps to keep morale high and this leads to a more disciplined and motivated workforce.

> **Activity**
>
> Choose a particular public service that you are interested in and research the sporting and recreational activities that they offer their employees. Give reasons why you think that they chose those particular activities and what benefits they would bring to the service.

Recruitment and retention

Recruitment costs of new employees are extremely high. To save on costs, the armed forces have their own careers advice centres where potential recruits can walk in and discuss a career in any of the services. From there, a number of interviews are arranged where you sit a range of tests to find out if you are suitable for a position in the armed forces. These tests include a computer-generated 'touch screen' assessment of your English and mathematical skills, a full medical and a fitness test with armed forces personnel. If this were carried out by a private company, the costs would be phenomenal.

The popularity of careers in other uniformed public services, such as the police and fire service, means that recruitment is carried out quite differently. Each county recruits new employees slightly differently from another, but the basic entrance requirements are the same and recruitment is carried out internally to save on costs.

Once suitable people have been recruited, it is equally important to keep them. Once in position, new members of staff undergo very expensive and time-consuming training. Retention of staff eliminates the need to recruit and train further recruits.

Staff loyalty

When you join the uniformed public services, you immediately become a part of a team – no-one works alone in the public services! And you will remain with that team for a considerable time. This enables you and your colleagues to get to know each other very well and you will start to look out for each other. A bond of trust begins to form and the motivation to do a good job at all times helps to keep morale high amongst the team. Strict discipline within the team keeps the motivation high and this helps the operational effectiveness of the service.

Provision of sport and recreational activities

The uniformed public services provide excellent opportunities for all staff to participate in sport and recreational activities. People who regularly participate in physical activities tend to keep themselves fit and healthy, eat a sensible diet and have less time off work due to illness. They find it easier to fight off the usual bugs, such as flu, and therefore this reduces the need for time off and for another member of staff to provide cover for their shift. The facilities for sport and recreation are usually provided free of charge, which encourages the contented workforce to be loyal to the service.

In some cases, the high cost of providing sport and recreational facilities for staff has become too high and more and more forces now have arrangements with local sports or leisure centres and the private providers to offer special rates or introductory offers for their members. This type of arrangement also applies to the family of the individual.

Social cohesion within the uniformed public services

The uniformed public services benefit enormously from having personnel who join at an early age and stay with them until retirement, as would any organisation. To have someone spend their entire working career in one service is great testament to that individual and that service. In fact, it is not just the individual but the family as well and the community within which the family socialises. Friendship within the services community creates a strong bond and a social cohesion, which is difficult to replicate in normal life. The opportunity to meet individuals with similar social structures helps to reinforce a community identity and the comradeship that comes from participation in sports and recreational activities is one of the biggest factors of this success.

> **ⓖ Grading tip!**
>
> **P1** For P1, you need to identify different sports and recreational activities used by the public services.
>
> **P2** For P2, you need to describe the importance of sports and recreational activities to the public services.

Safety issues when organising sport and recreational activities

P3 **P4**

Safety has to be the most important factor when planning or participating in any sporting or recreational activity. It is the job of the activity leader to enforce the rules of the game, to encourage safe and fair play and to understand the injury risks. Therefore, each activity requires a risk assessment and a session plan to be completed before it can take place in order to reduce or minimise the chances of injuries and accidents.

Key terms

A **hazard** is the potential of a substance, activity or process to cause harm.
A **risk** is the likelihood of a substance, activity or process to cause harm.

A risk assessment helps prevent accidents by looking for any potential hazards that may occur within the facility or playing area, for the participants and staff or with the equipment used. You need to consider what could go wrong, what the risks are and how likely it is to happen and then put actions into place to ensure that the chances of accidents are minimised.

Activity

In pairs, complete a risk assessment for a badminton session that you may wish to run for your colleagues on the course at your centre (see Table 9.2).

Figure 9.4 Badminton session

What are the hazards?	Who might be harmed and how?	What are you already doing?	What further action is necessary?	Action by whom?	When?	Done
Slips and trips	Staff and participants	Good housekeeping	Keep floor clear and dry	All staff		

Table 9.2 Risk assessment for a badminton session

Safety issues to take into consideration when organising activities

P3

There are a number of safety considerations for you to take into account before organising any sport or recreational activity.

Indoor facility or playing area

The floors, doors, windows and walls of an indoor facility must be checked thoroughly before the activity takes place, even if a risk assessment has been previously completed. If there is any doubt whatsoever that a hazard is evident, then the activity cannot proceed until it has been eliminated. Outside playing areas should be checked as thoroughly as possible before the start of the activity and equipment must be in correct working order.

Correct clothing and equipment

You should wear the correct clothing for the activity and you must ensure that the participants are dressed correctly too. You should also know how the safety equipment fits and how to use it as some activities may require you to wear protective clothing (e.g. helmet, shin pads, padding, gloves).

Jewellery

No jewellery of any kind should be worn when participating in any activity. This includes bracelets, rings, earrings and necklaces. They must be removed and placed in a safe and secure place until the end of the activity

Figure 9.5 Using the correct safety clothing for sport

First aid provision

If you are not a trained first aider, then you must know who is and where you can find them in case of an emergency. It may be the member of staff on duty or the person observing you. If not, you will need a direct telephone line or radio to be able to summon someone immediately. A first aid kit must be on display within the indoor facility or located at the side of the playing area if outside and should be checked to see if it is fully stocked and in date. First aid equipment should be checked to see that it works correctly. All information regarding first aid will be located in the first aid policy and procedures held at your centre.

Staff

Staff from your centre or those when visiting other centres must have the correct and current qualifications when on duty and they must be aware of their roles and responsibilities before, during and after the activity.

Outdoor activities

If you are planning to organise an activity away from your centre into the great outdoors, there are many more safety issues to consider well in advance of your trip. A reconnaissance of the area must have been made prior to the visit to ensure it is suitable; participants may need to have consent forms completed by parents – if under 18 years of age – before setting out; everyone must have suitable clothing and footwear; a weather forecast needs to be checked and monitored; and it may be necessary to have an extra member of staff on duty.

Assignment tip

You may be asked to complete a risk assessment for an activity of your choice, taking into account the facility, the participants and the equipment that may be used. As there are a number of different types of risk assessment for different purposes, you need to choose the correct one.

Rather than trying to guess which the best one is, ask for a blank one that staff are required to fill in at your centre when they are required to complete a risk assessment for an activity, as it will contain all the necessary requirements. Also ask to see an example of one that they have already completed so that you have a guide for filling it in correctly. Once you have filled the risk assessment in, request feedback before handing it in with your assignment.

Taking part in sport or recreational activities is generally very good for you but there are possible dangers and you need to make sure that playing will be as safe as possible. Before you take part in any type of activity, it is natural for you to run through your mind if there are any possible dangers or hazards and how you can make sure that they will not occur – this is a form of risk assessment but you do not write it down!

Each sport or recreational activity requires specific safety measures to be taken into account. The Governing Bodies of Sport lay down strict guidelines, procedures and rules to follow to reduce the accidents and injuries that may occur while you are taking part. The boxes below contain examples of one indoor and one outdoor safety checklist that may be used alongside a risk assessment in preparation for planning a sport and recreational activity.

Circuit training – indoor safety checklist

- Risk assessment of the facility, activity and equipment.
- Set out the circuit, ensuring that there is enough space between each station.
- Use mats for exercises where the participants are lying on the floor.
- Have an upper-body exercise followed by a lower-body exercise.
- Check all equipment is safe to use beforehand.
- Ensure all participants are fit to take part before you start.
- Explain safety procedures for the facility.
- Demonstrate each exercise at each station, showing the correct, safe technique.
- Carry out a thorough warm-up.
- Allow participants to rest if fatigued or injured.
- One station needs to be a rest stop.
- Keep constant vigilance on all participants – non-participants can act as spotters at a station.
- Carry out a cool-down.

Football – outdoor safety checklist

- Risk assessment of the activity, participants and equipment completed.
- Check the playing area is safe immediately before starting the game – pitch, goalposts, nets, corner flags, etc.
- Ensure you have a first aid kit on the pitch side.
- Ensure all participants are wearing shin guards and correct footwear.
- Individuals to remove all jewellery and throw away chewing gum.
- Remind players of the FA fair play regulations and abide by the referee's decisions.
- Only the captain to approach and speak to the referee.
- Substitute any players playing in an unsafe or aggressive manner during the game.
- All spectators and equipment should be at least one metre from the pitch perimeter.
- Put all equipment away immediately after the game.

Figure 9.6 Armed forces participating in circuit training session

Activity

With a partner, make a list of the safety considerations for an activity of your choice. Then choose an entirely different sport or recreational activity and make a list for that one too. Which one was the easiest to complete? Why was this? Consider these points if you are asked to plan and lead a sport or recreational activity at your centre.

Figure 9.7 One example of an outdoor activity is a football match

Responsibilities of different people involved in sport and recreational activities

Depending upon where the sport or recreational activity is taking place and what the activity is, there will be a number of people involved who need to be informed of what is happening, when it will be taking place and who will be participating.

Individual's responsibility

As a participant in any sport or recreational activity, you are responsible for ensuring that you are dressed correctly, with the correct clothing and footwear, arrive on time and are in the right frame of mind to take part and give 100 per cent. You need to listen to all the safety advice, the rules and any other instructions. You are obliged to look after yourself and everyone else under health and safety law and take reasonable care while competing with fair play in mind. If you are ill or injured, inform the leader of the session and be prepared to help out as an official or to carry out observations. You must always follow the directions of the staff.

If participating outside, you must be prepared for inclement weather and ensure you have enough warm and rainproof clothing to keep out the elements. It may be necessary to attend meetings or briefings in advance of the activity.

Responsibility of public service staff

The leader of the sport and recreational activity must consider all the health and safety issues that may arise and minimise them. Risk assessments of the facility and equipment should have been completed prior to the activity and adequate first aid provision should be in place. Members of staff need to be dressed correctly and arrive early in order to prepare. They need to brief the participants fully beforehand on the health and safety procedures, such as fire, first aid and safety, as well as have medical information on the participants.

Staff should have current and relevant qualifications, ensure fair play, follow the rules and stop any aggressive behaviour. If staff are taking you out of the centre, then all the necessary paperwork should have been completed in advance (i.e. consent forms, emergency equipment checks, contingency plans, etc.).

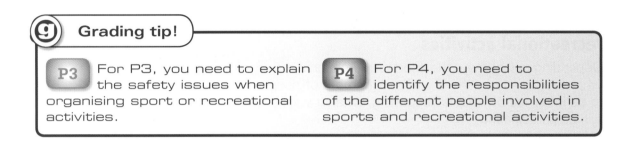

Plan a sport or recreation activity used in the public services

P5 **M1** **D1**

In order to understand the importance of correct organisation and the safety issues to be considered for every activity that takes place, you will be asked to plan and, possibly, run your own activity, either individually or, if you are not yet up to the challenge, with a colleague. You will therefore be required to complete a session plan for the activity of your choice. This will be required, along with your risk assessment completed previously, prior to the activity so that it can be checked by a leader to confirm that it is adequate for the activity.

A session plan will require you to look closely at all the details of the activity and ensure that it goes accordingly. You will need to check the facility, think about the equipment you will need, how much space you have and the safety factors (as mentioned previously). The best sessions are not just put together at the last moment; they have to be carefully planned. The activity needs to be fun, interesting and useful for you and for those taking part – if you are not enjoying it, then neither are they!

Plan an activity

P5

Every practical sport or recreational session will start with a warm-up and finish with a cool-down; these are vital to the session. However, if you decide to organise an outdoor adventurous activity, then you will have to look at other particular planning considerations, such as a route card, consent forms, transport, etc. These are looked at in more detail in Unit 15 (Expedition skills in the public services).

Warm-up

A warm-up prepares both your body and your mind for the activity that is to take place immediately afterwards. Your body moves from its non-active state to one of being ready for physical exercise, while

Key term

A **warm-up** prepares your body and mind for exercise.

your mind prepares to focus on what you are about to do so that you can concentrate and participate safely.

The warm-up usually lasts for 15 per cent of the planned activity and consists of three main parts.

1. Raising your pulse rate – fast walking, jogging, stepping side to side, rolling your shoulders, swinging your arms.
2. Loosening your joints – circling your hips, raising your knees, bending to each side, twisting from the waist, circling your ankles.
3. Safe stretching – slow and well-balanced stretches should be carried out standing, sitting or lying: neck stretch, chest stretch, shoulders, front, back and inside of thigh, calf. *Do not* bounce the stretches; stretch slowly and hold for a few seconds each.

Figure 9.8 Warming up in preparation for an activity

Cool-down

Your body needs to return to its natural resting state after physical exercise so a cool-down is essential. You need to reduce your body temperature and slow down your pulse rate. Your breathing rate should be returned to as normal as possible and you will automatically remove waste products, such as lactic acid, from your muscles.

> **Key term**
>
> A **cool-down** relaxes the body and mind after exercise.

A cool-down could consist of five minutes of gentle aerobic exercise, such as walking or jogging, and then five minutes of gentle static stretching, gently easing into the stretch and holding for a few seconds – including shoulder stretches, side bends, thigh stretches and calf stretches.

Main content

You can now consider what to put into the main content of the session, which is the largest section of the plan. The skills and techniques should be demonstrated and practised first, leading to the full game at the end. All the equipment that will be required should be noted on the plan and in position before the activity starts. You will need to liaise with the appropriate people for a date, time and venue to run your own sport or recreational activity. It will be necessary to consult with the group beforehand on the type of activity they would like to participate in and then complete the session plan for the event. Table 9.3 shows a typical session plan pro-forma.

Name:	Date:	
Venue		
Number of participants		
Equipment required		
Health and safety issues		
Goals or aims		
WARM-UP		Timings
MAIN CONTENT		
COOL-DOWN		
Aims of the next session		

Table 9.3 A typical session plan pro-forma

You can, of course, design your own session plan but remember to include all the required headings, a warm-up and a cool-down.

Activity

Your activity leader is to run a 30-minute circuit training session. You have been asked to devise a five-minute warm-up sequence and a three-minute cool-down sequence, which you could use before and after the activity. Write down the requirements of the warm-up and the cool-down, taking into consideration the stations that may be used during the activity.

Lead a sport or recreational activity

M1

Planning a sport or recreational activity correctly will enable you to achieve a pass grade for this outcome. However, if you wish to aim higher and improve your grade to a merit, then you will be required to put your plan into action!

Before the session

If you are leading the activity by yourself or with a partner, you need to double-check all the details and arrangements just prior to the session taking place.

- Read through the risk assessment and session plan.
- Arrive early for the session.
- Be dressed correctly and have personal equipment, such as a whistle and a stopwatch.
- Count all the participants and enquire if any are injured or ill and cannot take part.
- Ensure they are all dressed correctly for the activity, including personal safety equipment.
- Participants should remove jewellery and must not be chewing.
- Introduce yourself, and your partner if necessary.
- Explain the aims of the session.
- Run through the safety procedures.
- Reiterate the rules, if necessary.

During the session

- Regularly check the session plan and timings; adjust if required.
- Ensure fair play and stop aggressive behaviour – play to the rules.
- Be fair but strict; do not let them begin to take charge.
- Use the whistle and stop the activity if there any concerns.

After the session

- At the end of the cool-down, ask the participants for verbal feedback. Write it down on the back of the session plan. Perhaps award marks out of ten.
- Put all the equipment away.
- Ask observers and leader for any feedback.
- Ensure no-one is left and, if necessary, lock the doors.
- Later, when everyone has had time to think about the activity, ask the staff and participants for written feedback or copies of observation records so that you can complete a full evaluation.

Evaluate your sport or recreational activity

D1

Once the activity has finished, you will be expected to evaluate the session by asking the competitors what they thought and by looking back yourself and deciding what were the good points and what you need to do better next time. Collect, analyse and review information about the session by self-reflection and the verbal and written feedback from other people at the activity.

Consider the following:

- Was the activity effective?
- Did it achieve its objectives?

- Are there any development needs?
- Are there any action points to put into a plan for next time?
- Set future targets.

SMART targets

In order to set yourself targets for the future, you must ensure that they are SMART, or even SMARTER! These set out what is going to happen, who is going to do it, when it is going to be done by and how the achievement will be measured.

> **Key term**
>
> SMARTER = specific, measurable, achievable, realistic, time constrained, exciting and recorded.

Specific – the objectives must be specific to the activity that you are planning.
Measurable – set times, distances or scores to enable the activity to be measured.
Achievable – make the objectives flexible so that you can change them if necessary (lower them if they are too high and vice versa).
Realistic – the objectives should be challenging but within the group's capability.
Time constrained – set dates and times of completion.
Exciting – make it fun to ensure the participants will want to take part.
Recorded – keep written feedback and ask for verbal feedback from the group and anyone else who saw your organisation and running of the activity

Self-evaluation

Table 9.4 is just one example of a typical self-evaluation pro-forma that you could use after your activity.

Name:	Signature: Date: Witness name: Witness signature:
Were the goals/aims appropriate?	
Were the activities appropriate?	
Did the participants enjoy the session?	
Were the arrangements and organisation satisfactory?	
Were any changes necessary during the session?	
Verbal or written feedback?	
Action points and targets for the next session	

Table 9.4 Self-evaluation pro-forma

Evaluation from the participants and others

You need to collect the verbal and written feedback from the person in charge of the activity. This may be an observation record, giving you advice on your leadership strengths and areas for improvement in preparation for a future session that you may plan and lead. Participants should have given you verbal feedback immediately after the session and, after reflection, written comments on the activity and how they thought you led the session.

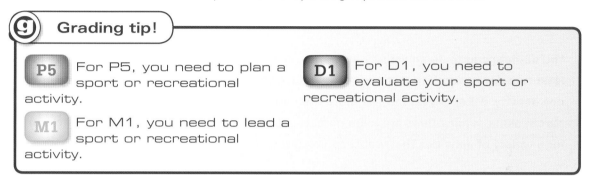

Grading tip!

P5 For P5, you need to plan a sport or recreational activity.

M1 For M1, you need to lead a sport or recreational activity.

D1 For D1, you need to evaluate your sport or recreational activity.

Participate in public services sport and recreational activities

P6 **P7** **M2**

Participate regularly in sport and recreational activities in different venues

P6

You may already play a sport or participate in physical recreation on a regular basis. You might also have a regular routine for carrying out fitness exercises or attending the local gym. If so, you should log the days and times you participate and the number of hours for each occasion. This will enable you to devise a programme of activities that you plan to take part in over the next few weeks or months and the different venues that you use.

If you do not have a regular routine of sport or recreational activities, then you really should consider doing so. You could devise an exercise programme in an attempt to start exercising regularly with the long-term aim of participating in sport or recreational activities on a regular basis in order to improve your health and fitness.

Activity

Draw up an action plan for what activities you would like to participate in regularly and at which venues, thinking about activities you would like to try for the first time. Make enquiries about activities available in your local area. You will be amazed what goes on out there!

Talk it through with a friend, leader or parent to get advice.

You do not need to do an activity every day. In fact, it is recommended that you have at least two days a week to rest and recuperate. Some days, you may only participate in one activity; other days it may be more than one. There are activities that you can take part in alone, while others are team games and require you to be with others. Try to aim for a variety of activities that will keep you interested and fit.

Review your part in the participation of sport and recreational activities

M2

After your programme is up and running and you are into a regular routine, a review of your progress is advisable. Is the programme effective? Could you make some changes, however large or small? Do you feel any benefit from the programme to date? Do you enjoy taking part?

Use the SMART or SMARTER targets mentioned earlier (page 210) to set yourself some new goals or aims. Use a variety of the components of sport, such as strength, speed and stamina, in your programme if you are not already doing so. Take into account some of the training principles mentioned in Unit 5 (Improving health and fitness for entry to the uniformed public services):

- Progression – increase the amount of participation.
- Overload – work harder than the previous session.
- Reversibility – if you are injured or do not participate, review the whole programme, probably going back to the beginning. Do not try to start again where you left off as it may cause further injury or fatigue as your body has to adapt to the changes made by regular participation.

Figure 9.9 Regular participation in sport and recreation

Personal benefits of regular participation in sport and recreational activities

Participating in sport and recreation is the activity that most people enjoy as it tends to offer a challenge, is exciting and is also very good for your health, which, in turn, is excellent for your physical and mental well-being. It will also benefit you, as an individual, in other ways. It may:

- Improve your communication skills – by listening and speaking to the coach, your team members and your parents, you learn to use your voice correctly and use the right tone and pitch.
- Improve your skills and techniques – by practising regularly, and correctly, you will soon learn to master the basic skills required to show development in your chosen activity.
- Help you to learn tactics, rules, regulations and scoring systems – playing a sport regularly will improve your knowledge of the game and help you understand the official rules and how to score.
- Make you aware of and understand the roles of officials – without officials, no-one plays sport! Qualify as an official in your chosen sport to understand how difficult their job really is.
- Make you more socially active – your social skills will develop and it will teach you how to interact with people. Sport and recreation builds confidence and gives you a sense of pride and accomplishment. It can improve your teamwork and cooperation and will improve your image. It could even lead to you getting a job and earning money.
- Teach you how to use the correct protective or safety equipment and clothing – the rules of some sports require you to wear the correct protective equipment in order to stay safe and some participants wear their own protective clothing to help prevent serious injury.
- Improve your self-esteem – sport makes you feel good about yourself; it creates a positive image, develops sportsmanship and builds a competitive spirit. It will give you some challenges and goals to aim for as well as increase your self-confidence.
- Improve your health, fitness and well-being – sport increases the efficiency of the main body systems by strengthening your bones and muscles; sport also lowers blood pressure and helps you fight illness much more easily. You are less likely to be overweight, to take drugs or smoke and it relieves stress and reduces depression. It can improve your body shape, muscle tone and posture, as well as increase your strength, endurance and flexibility.

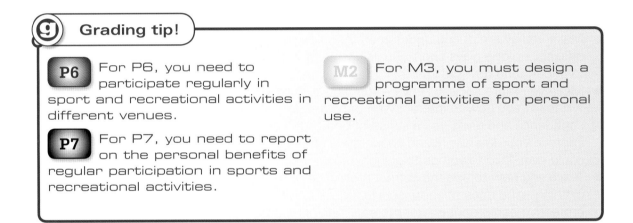

Assignment tip

Look at all the benefits mentioned, and any others you can think of, and explain them in detail. For instance, when describing an improvement in skills and techniques, mention the particular skills and techniques in which you have improved, and how you can tell, plus those that you still need to master. If you say that your fitness has increased, prove it by explaining the particular parts of your fitness that show improvement (e.g. lower resting heart rate, increase in the number of sit-ups or press-ups you can do).

Grading tip!

P6 For P6, you need to participate regularly in sport and recreational activities in different venues.

P7 For P7, you need to report on the personal benefits of regular participation in sports and recreational activities.

M2 For M3, you must design a programme of sport and recreational activities for personal use.

So, sport and physical recreation increases your overall fitness and quality of life. Don't just sit there and read about it – get out and do it!

End of unit knowledge check

1. List and describe the different sports and recreational activities used in the public services.
2. Describe the importance of these activities to the public services.
3. List three benefits of sport and recreational activities to the public services.
4. Describe the safety issues that need to be taken into consideration when leading an indoor activity.
5. What are the roles and responsibilities of a leader of the activity?
6. How long should a warm-up last and what should it consist of?
7. What should the activity leader consider after the cool-down?
8. SMART is a 'mnemonic' (a method for remembering something). What does it stand for?
9. List some of the personal benefits gained from regular participation in sport or recreational activities.
10. List the headings on a risk assessment.

Grading criteria

In order to pass this unit, the evidence that the learner presents for assessment needs to demonstrate that they can meet all the learning outcomes for the unit. The assessment criteria for a pass grade describe the level of achievement required to pass this unit.

Grading criteria		
To achieve a pass grade the evidence must show that the learner is able to:	To achieve a merit grade the evidence must show that, in addition to the pass criteria, the learner is able to:	To achieve a distinction grade the evidence must show that, in addition to the pass and merit criteria, the learner is able to:
P1 Identify different sports and recreational activities used by the public services		
P2 Describe the importance of sports and recreational activities to the public services		
P3 Explain the safety issues when organising sport or recreational activities		
P4 Identify the responsibilities of the different people involved in sports and recreational activities		
P5 Plan a sport or recreational activity	**M1** Lead a sport or recreational activity	**D1** Evaluate your sport or recreational activity
P6 Participate regularly in sport and recreational activities in different venues	**M2** Review your part in the participation of sport and recreational activities in different venues	
P7 Report on the personal benefits of regular participation in sports and recreational activities		

Introduction

In this unit, we will look at the definition of crime, explore types of crimes and consider how crime impacts upon society. The impact of crime may be felt by individuals, businesses, local communities, public services and the wider environment. The ways in which society deals with crimes will also be investigated, along with the role played by public services. We will also consider the victims of crime and how they may be supported in coping with their ordeal.

The systems employed for reporting and recording crimes will also be examined, along with the ways in which local areas are attempting to reduce crime through a variety of initiatives. Finally in this unit, we will examine the management of offenders.

Learning outcomes:

By the end of this unit, you should:

1. Understand the impact of criminal behaviour

2. Be able to investigate a local crime reduction initiative

3. Understand the methods used to report and record crime

4. Know the options available to effectively manage offenders.

What is crime?

Before we look at the issues surrounding criminal behaviour, we need to have a good understanding of the term 'crime' itself. In this section, we will look at what crime is and why it is unacceptable. We will also briefly examine some particular crimes that affect individuals and the wider community.

Some crimes – for example, murder – have always been regarded as wrong; however, some other 'wrongs' are viewed by individuals in different ways, as in the first case study below.

Some of the relatively low level (*summary*) crimes, which are heard only at a magistrates' court, are often referred to as *offences* and include theft where property of little value has been stolen, assaults that involve little or no visible injury and minor traffic offences.

More serious (*indictable*) crimes are sent directly to the Crown Court for trial. These crimes include fraud, murder and crimes of a sexual nature.

There are many laws that set out the requirements of a crime. For example, theft is covered by the Theft Act 1968; this act also covers other types of criminal behaviour.

> ## Key terms
>
> **Crime** is a violation of the law, a wicked or forbidden act.
> Crimes under the Theft Act 1968:
> **Theft** is the taking of property that belongs to another person.
> **Burglary** involves entering a building where you should not be and stealing property. A crime is also considered burglary if you intend to assault someone or damage property in the building you have entered.
> **Robbery** is theft when using (or threatening to use) force in order to steal.

Who is affected by crime?

The individual

Some crimes, including theft of personal property, assault or damage to property belonging to an individual, usually affect only the owner of the property or the person who has been assaulted.

Crimes vary greatly in their severity and this is reflected in the penalties associated with them. For every crime that is committed, there will be a victim or victims. Some people believe that some of the less serious crimes do not involve anyone else and that there is no real victim. Read the three case studies below and see what you think.

Case study 1

An office worker uses a pencil, highlighter pen or other small item, puts it in their pocket or bag and forgets about it. Some time later, this person finds the item and uses it for their own purpose. When that person takes the conscious decision to use the item as their own and not return it to their workplace, they have stolen it (committed a theft).

Figure 12.1 A victimless crime?

This case study may seem like a very minor example of theft but, if multiplied by all the staff in a company, on a weekly basis, this would result in a considerable loss to that company. In this case, the victim of the crime is the company that owned the property that was stolen. This company will suffer financially because the property will need to be replaced.

The community

On some occasions, the effects of a crime are experienced by more than the direct victim alone. An example of this is when harm is inflicted upon a child – at the very least, the family of the child will feel the effect of this crime.

Case study 2

In September 2009, Vanessa George, a nursery worker from the south-west of England, pleaded guilty to sexual assaults on children in her care. Throughout her trial, and even when she was sentenced, George refused to name the children whom she had abused. This meant that the families of all the children attending the nursery did not know if their child had been subject to the abuse. In this way, the actions of one person had an effect on an entire section of the community.

The state

Occasionally, such a horrendous crime occurs that it has an effect upon the whole of society, far removed geographically from where the crime happened.

Case study 3

On 22nd August 2007, 11-year-old Rhys Jones from Liverpool was returning home from football practice when he was hit in the neck by a bullet, resulting in his death. Very soon after the killing, police arrested four teenagers; these were all later released on bail. More than 300 officers were involved in the hunt for Rhys's killer and, by April 2008, 11 people aged 17 to 25 had been questioned. In December 2008, 18-year-old Sean Mercer was convicted of murder and sentenced to life imprisonment.

Activity

Draw a table (e.g. see Table 12.1) and enter in the first column things that you consider to be crimes. In the second column, provide an example of these crimes and in the final column explain the effect these crimes have on individuals or other victims. An example is given to get you started.

Crime	Example	Effect of the crime
Theft	Shoplifting	Costs rise to cover losses; this is passed on to customers.

Table 12.1 Crimes and their effects

Public services, victims and society

Public services

When a crime is committed, most people think that what happens afterwards is determined by the police. While it is true that the police will usually be the first public service involved in investigating a crime, they will work in cooperation with a number of other agencies. These agencies might include the ambulance and hospital service, where someone may have been injured and need medical attention. If the offender is a member of the armed forces, the service in which he or she was employed will also be involved. This is because elements of military law will need to be enforced, either instead of or in addition to the criminal law of England and Wales.

When the police receive notification that a crime has occurred, they have a responsibility to investigate that crime. The purpose of this investigation is to find out exactly what happened and who was responsible. They will need to find evidence to prove these points. The duties of the police include taking statements from witnesses and arresting those they believe are responsible for committing the crime.

Once the police have finished their investigations, they refer the case to the Crown Prosecution Service (CPS). The CPS then makes a decision as to whether the suspect or suspects should face charges. If the CPS decides this should be the case, then they determine what those charges should be.

In order to arrive at a decision, the CPS reads all the papers in the file and examines the evidence provided by the police. The main point the CPS needs to consider when deciding if a charge should be made is whether there is enough evidence for the suspect to be convicted if the case goes to court. If the CPS does not believe there is a good chance that the magistrates or jury will find the suspect guilty, they must end the process at this stage. They must always ensure the decisions are taken in the interest of justice being carried out.

When the CPS has decided that a conviction is likely, they make a decision as to what charge will be brought. The police then put this charge to the suspect and, unless the suspect is thought to be dangerous or might not appear in court, he or she will be bailed to appear at court on a later date.

Activity

Go back to Table 12.1 on crimes and their effects, which you completed earlier. Now discuss with a partner which public services might be involved when each crime has been committed.

Victims

Victims of crime are those people who are affected by the criminal act. Everyone reacts differently to crime and this reaction will depend upon many factors. Some of the things that influence the way we react to a situation relate to the incident itself; some relate to the individual and the experiences they have encountered previously. The effects will also stay with individuals for different lengths of time – some people will be able to get on with their lives straight away, while for others it may take weeks, months or even longer. Some people never fully recover from the ways in which the crime has affected them.

Responses to being a victim of crime also differ greatly. The majority of victims feel angry, upset or afraid immediately after the crime, but often these feelings diminish over time.

Victims often have great difficulty coming to terms with the effects that a crime has had on them. Historically, there was no support for these people, but over recent years the situation has improved, with support and assistance now provided to victims of crime.

Many people who become victims of crime suffer physically or they might relive the event for a long time afterwards. It is at this time that advice and support is essential if the victim is to recover from the experience.

Victims of crime are entitled to free, confidential advice from a charity called Victim Support. This is an independent national charity and staff and volunteers are trained to provide emotional support and practical assistance. Victim Support aims to get in touch with the victim within four days of them reporting a crime; if the victim agrees, the police provide Victim Support with their details.

What does Victim Support do?

Victim Support offers advice on victims' rights and also gives information about police and court procedures. It provides advice on how to seek compensation and complete insurance claims and, if necessary, it can direct victims to other types of help, such as counselling.

Anyone affected by crime can contact Victim Support for help, regardless of whether they reported the crime to the police or when the crime happened.

Right to privacy

On occasions, if it would help with their investigation, the police may release details of a crime to the media. They will normally seek permission from the victim before doing this. One reason for this action is that media coverage might uncover more evidence, such as an eyewitness coming forward. However, in the case of sexual assault or rape, it is a criminal offence for *anyone* to publish the name or photograph of the victim, or any other details that may identify them. As you will have read in Unit 6 (Citizenship, the individual and society), a victim's right to privacy and the media's right to freedom of expression are both set out in the Human Rights Act 1998.

Society

As discussed earlier, crimes may result in a single victim or a number of victims. The reasons for this may be the severity of the crime itself or the attention it has received from the media, such as newspapers or television reports.

When a crime has been committed, there are many ways in which the public services, victims and society can work together towards an acceptable outcome. One of these measures is the use of the *restorative justice* scheme.

Restorative justice brings victims, offenders and communities together to decide on a response to a particular crime. It is about putting victims' needs at the centre of the criminal justice system and finding positive solutions to crime by encouraging offenders to face up to their actions.

This approach can be used for a wide variety of crimes, ranging from incidents described as *anti-social behaviour*, such as graffiti or name-calling, to serious crimes, such as robbery or burglary. For restorative justice to be used, the offender must have admitted responsibility for the crime and the effect it has had on their victim.

The ways in which offenders and victims might be brought together include:

- direct mediation – where victim, offender, facilitator and possibly supporters for each party meet face-to-face
- indirect mediation – where victim and offender communicate through letters
- conferencing – involving supporters for both victim and offender.

A victim might ask for a restorative justice outcome to make the offender realise how their life has been affected by the crime. Through this process, they might discover some information that will help them to put the experience behind them. It might be possible for the victim to forgive the offender through this approach.

There are benefits to the use of this approach, including the victim being able to make choices, the victim receiving an explanation of why they were targeted and making the offender take responsibility for their actions.

Evidence gathered from those involved in the restorative justice approach suggests that dealing with the aftermath of crime in this way can reduce post-traumatic stress disorder (PTSD) in victims. In some cases, offenders have been so moved by the experience of confronting their victim that they have changed their ways and moved away from committing crime.

Examples of possible outcomes of restorative justice include making offenders remove graffiti or repair property they have damaged, or asking them to write a letter of apology to their victim.

In certain circumstances, victims of crime may be eligible to receive a sum of money – this is known as *compensation*. The Criminal Injuries Compensation Authority (CICA), a non-government body, is responsible for the scheme in England, Wales and Scotland, making financial awards to recognise the injuries (physical and mental) that have been caused by a crime of violence. In certain circumstances, the CICA may include in this award a sum to compensate for loss of earnings or other special expenses, if these losses were as a result of the violent crime. In the case where someone has been killed by an act of violence, their next of kin (who is also a victim) may be awarded compensation in respect of loss of earnings of the deceased person.

There is a scale of the level of compensation that can be awarded to a victim of crime. This scale includes over 400 injuries and each injury may attract an award of between £1,000 and £25,000. Additional sums may be added where there has also been financial loss – for example, if someone is unable to work or if the applicant was dependent upon someone who has been murdered. The crime should have been reported to the police, unless there was a valid reason not to do so, and the claim must be made within two years of the crime that resulted in the injury.

At the beginning of 2010, government ministers announced that they were considering adding an extra penalty for motorists who commit minor offences in order to fund a victim compensation fund (see box).

Drivers face fine surcharge for victims' fund

2nd January 2010

'Motorists found guilty of speeding and other driving offences will face an extra £15 added to their fine to fund a victim compensation fund, it has been revealed.

The surcharge – used to finance support services for crime victims – is already added to fines for those convicted of crime in the courts. But now ministers want to extend the levy to on-the-spot fines and fixed penalty notices in England and Wales.

This would include motorists caught speeding, using a mobile phone while driving, not wearing a seatbelt, or given a parking ticket.

Justice minister Claire Ward said in a parliamentary answer: "The victim surcharge was introduced on 1 April 2007 and has been applied initially only to fines imposed in magistrates' and Crown courts, at a rate of £15. We intend to add the surcharge to other disposals as soon as it becomes feasible to do so."'

Source: www.news.sky.com

g Grading tip!

P1 To achieve P1, you need to explain the role of public services in assisting and supporting victims of crime.

P2 For P2, you need to describe the impact of crime on society.

Crime reduction and crime prevention initiatives

Following the publication of the Crime and Disorder Act in 1998, every borough in England established a Crime and Disorder Reduction Partnership (CDRP). The purpose of the CDRP is to monitor crime and disorder in the area and set up a strategy to reduce it. The results of these strategies are published regularly.

Crime reduction initiatives

Crime reduction initiatives target specific types of offenders, including repeat and prolific offenders and those who have been released from custody and might need assistance to lead a decent lifestyle away from crime. A proportion of crime is committed by people who are dependent on drugs and other stimulants; for this reason, many of the initiatives involve working with those who are addicted to drugs and other substances. These programmes might include treatment for the addicts in the hope that, when they are 'clean', they will cease to carry out crimes to pay for more drugs.

Figure 12.2 Examples of crime reduction and prevention initiatives

The organisations that deliver crime reduction initiatives rely on support from volunteers to be able to deliver their services. Read Sarah's story in the case study below.

Case study

'Sarah' is a volunteer with a crime reduction initiative in London: 'I had a positive experience of volunteering for the crime reduction initiative when I worked on a drug testing and treatment project in London. I began by answering the telephone and, as I became more confident and gained new skills, I undertook training so I was involved in group work. I found the whole experience of helping individuals turn their lives around very rewarding and intend to continue in this role.'

Activity

Working in pairs, select one of the organisations/teams listed below and find out how they are involved in crime reduction initiatives.

- Police community support officers
- Neighbourhood Watch
- Community wardens
- Community beat officers
- Church groups
- Community Action teams
- Youth offending teams
- National Probation Service

Safer Stations Scheme

In parts of England and Wales, trains were not being used to their full extent. When questioned, people indicated that this was because they were afraid that they might become victims of crime if they used these often isolated stations, and they thought of them as places where criminals gather. The Department for Transport wanted research to be carried out so that people would feel safer to use the trains again.

The Safer Stations Scheme was undertaken in 2005–2006. Its aim was to identify measures that could address the issues of crime and fear of crime at the stations. Eight stations were involved in this scheme. The following problems were identified:

- The problems that were identified were seen as being part of the culture of the neighbourhood, not just on the railway.
- The problems of anti-social behaviour displayed by adults and young people were partly associated with alcohol misuse.

- Half of the stations had been used for drug dealing, or dealers used the railway to get about.
- Young people were found to trespass on the track – this was seen as partly because there was no controlled access to the station and trains.
- Many people would not use the railway after dark because of the behaviour; members of staff were also worried for their own safety.
- A common problem at all stations was that of people travelling without paying the fare – this is dealt with by the British Transport Police (BTP) as anti-social behaviour.

One of the first areas to be addressed was the need to improve the appearance of stations. This was achieved at very little cost by using the services of volunteers who were involved in the initiative. This was seen as an essential first step to positively changing the perception of the whole area.

It was decided that a partnership approach that involved the local community and businesses was needed because the problems that affect railway stations will often be similar to those in the community. A close working partnership between the crime and disorder reduction group, BTP and those who provide the transport was seen as crucial. Increased security on stations and trains was identified as necessary and this required cooperation between staff, BTP and private security officers. It was also decided that individuals within the various organisations needed to be identified and that they would take the lead in ensuring that all recommendations were dealt with and a coordinated approach to tackling the identified problems was undertaken.

At the end of this initiative, it was found that the eight stations were being used far more than previously. Travellers reported that many of the types of behaviour that had led to them to not use the service had been greatly reduced and that they no longer felt threatened when using the trains.

This is an example of how a partnership approach to reducing crime in a community has been successful. To achieve the P3 criterion, you need to investigate an initiative *in your local area*. You might consider approaching the police, local authority or voluntary group that is involved in such a scheme. Remember to take plenty of notes, so you will have something to look back at when you are writing up your assignment.

Crimestoppers

Another partner in the fight against crime is Crimestoppers. This is an independent charity that offers a route for people to give information about a crime without revealing their own identity. Anyone with information that could help the police with their investigations can call 0800 555 111 (free). Callers will not be asked for their name, they will not be asked to provide a statement or go to court to give evidence and the call cannot be traced or recorded.

Crimestoppers is an effective partnership between the police, the community and the media. It was formed in 1988 in response to the fear people felt if they went to the police with information about crimes. In many cases, they were afraid that they too would become a victim if they told the police what they knew. As a result of breaking the 'wall of silence' in this safe way, more crimes have been prevented and solved.

The charity relies on the support of about 600 volunteers to deal with calls and provide advice on community safety. The charity's promise of anonymity for callers has never been broken.

Anti-social behaviour

One term often used to describe the ways in which individuals or groups go about their daily lives is 'anti-social behaviour'. This type of activity is extremely upsetting for individuals and it can cause them great distress. Very occasionally, the effects of this type of activity can have devastating effects, as in the case of a mother and daughter in Leicestershire (see case study).

Figure 12.3 Crimestoppers poster

Case study

Fiona Pilkington and her family had suffered many months of harassment, including damage to property, name-calling and threats, by a group of 16 youths. She reported these incidents to the local police, but the incidents did not stop.

In desperation, and with her daughter Francesca at her side, on 23rd October 2007, Mrs Pilkington drove her car to a lay-by and set it alight. Both mother and daughter perished in the blaze.

At the inquest into the deaths, the police superintendent said that police officers were allowed only to issue warnings to young troublemakers (unless their behaviour was judged to be serious) and he agreed that the criminal justice system was set up 'to avoid sending juveniles to prison'. He also added that low-level anti-social behaviour is mainly the responsibility of the council.

Activity

Working in pairs, jot down as many examples of activities as you can of that could be described as anti-social. What is it about the activity that you believe makes it unacceptable to most people?

Key term

Anti-social behaviour is any aggressive, intimidating or destructive activity that damages or destroys another person's quality of life.

Your examples from the above activity might include rowdy or noisy behaviour, fly-tipping, begging, drinking on the street and setting off fireworks late at night.

Anti-social behaviour does not just upset individuals in the community; it can prevent areas developing into places people want to be and can create 'no-go' areas where crime can easily escalate.

There are ways in which this type of behaviour can be discouraged and hopefully stopped before it goes too far. These include police visits and warning letters – often this is enough for the offenders to stop what they are doing. If not, further ways of tackling the problem might include contracts and agreements, involving juveniles and families, parenting orders, anti-social behaviour orders (ASBO), arrests and custodial sentences.

An acceptable behaviour contract (ABC) is a method that can be used and is designed to allow the individual to recognise their behaviour and how it affects others. ABC is usually put in place for young people but it can also be used for adults. It usually lasts for six months but can be renewed if needed.

Anti-social behaviour orders (ASBOs) are orders issued by the court that forbid certain threatening or intimidating actions. This might include preventing someone from spending time with a group of friends or visiting certain areas. ASBOs are in place for at least two years and can be longer. If someone breaks the conditions of an ASBO, they have committed a criminal offence and could be fined or sent to prison.

Crime prevention initiatives

Neighbourhood Watch

One way in which communities can get together to help each other stay safe and keep crime down is by forming a Neighbourhood Watch scheme. These schemes involve groups of volunteers, working in partnership with the police and the local council, who provide advice on personal safety and home and business security. A high priority for Neighbourhood Watch is protecting elderly and vulnerable people, to try to ensure they do not become targets for criminals.

Neighbourhood Watch also gathers information that can assist the police in tackling local problems and, because they are working in close partnership with the police and local council, they are able to warn local residents when there is a particular crime problem in their area.

Safer Neighbourhoods

The Safer Neighbourhoods scheme is a crime-prevention initiative employed in many police areas across the country. This involves local people working with local police and other partners to identify and deal with issues of concern in their own neighbourhood.

A Safer Neighbourhoods team comprises one sergeant, two constables and three police community support officers (PCSOs). The team members are trained to communicate with members of the community and other partners to help tackle and solve problems affecting individual citizens, groups and businesses.

By allocating the same officers to the Safer Neighbourhoods strategy, the local population gets to know them and they are in a better position to be able to contact a suitable person when they need assistance. In most cases, these schemes have been found to improve problems associated with anti-social behaviour, graffiti and abandoned cars.

Figure 12.4 Safer Neighbourhoods team members

Safer School Partnerships

This is a formal agreement drawn up between a school (or schools) and police to work together to keep young people safe. It is also intended to reduce crime and improve behaviour in schools and in the community.

Case study

In 2007, a Safer School Partnership began at Morpeth School in London. The school had over 1,500 pupils and the primary schools in the area were also included in the partnership. A police constable was based in the school. She worked closely with staff and pupils to build up an understanding of how she would work and the aims of the scheme. As a result of this 'hands-on' approach, the relationships between the police, pupils and staff grew and the police constable based at the school gained the trust and confidence of all those involved. This, in turn, led to a sharp decrease in the number of bullying incidents, and pupils, staff, parents and other people in the community were more likely to approach the police with any concerns they had about unwanted behaviour and other problems.

Is your school or college part of a Safer School Partnership?

Other crime prevention measures

As well as official schemes that operate around the country, there are many ways in which individuals and businesses can take measures to prevent crimes and to reduce the risk of them becoming victims of crime. These might include, for example, making sure that all doors and windows are locked, especially (but not only) when premises are left unoccupied.

Think about it!

When you are sitting in the garden, or upstairs studying, would you really know if someone was letting themselves in by the front door?

Activity

Discuss with a friend what you do in a typical day – this might include using your bank card at an ATM or walking home alone after a night out.

Can you identify any times when you might be vulnerable to those who would wish to commit an offence at your expense?

Make a list of the things you find and discuss ways in which you might take sensible precautions to minimise your risk in the future.

There are many products available to mark property – for example, you could use a special pen that contains ink that can be read only under ultraviolet light. If you are unlucky enough to have property stolen, this method of marking can result in the property being returned to you, the rightful owner.

Figure 12.5 CCTV cameras

Closed-circuit television (CCTV) is used in many areas, especially shopping precincts and around entertainment venues. The purpose of CCTV is to protect the area, property and those who use the facilities.

CCTV images can sometimes be used as evidence in court to prove that someone was in a particular place or that they committed a crime. It can also act as a deterrent; someone who might be thinking of committing a crime might not do so in an area where CCTV is installed.

Some people feel that CCTV cameras are an invasion of their privacy. If anyone believes that they have been captured on camera, they can request to see the images. Some companies charge a fee for this service and a copy of any footage must be provided within 40 days. The CCTV recording may be edited to make sure that you cannot see any other personal data that does not relate to you.

Whatever individuals might think of CCTV systems, it is important to remember that the main reason for their use is to make our communities, towns, cities and roads safer places.

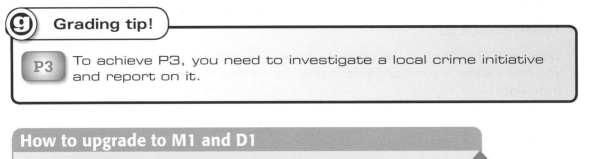

Grading tip!

P3 To achieve P3, you need to investigate a local crime initiative and report on it.

How to upgrade to M1 and D1

M1 **D1** M1 requires an *analysis* of your chosen local crime initiative. You will be awarded D1 if you are able to *evaluate* how the initiative has reached the people it targeted and how it has resulted in a reduction of crime levels.

Reporting and recording crime

P4 **M2** **D2**

Crimes are recorded using different sources of information. One source of data on crime is police records. Police-recorded crime figures can provide a reliable picture of crimes that are reported to them and are useful for analysing local crime patterns. However, these figures might not provide an accurate picture of all crimes that occur because many crimes that happen are not reported to the police at all. On occasions, the police will also decide not to record a crime that has been reported to them. The ways in which police record crimes is set out by the Home Office Counting Rules and the National Crime Recording Standard (NCRS).

The reason the NCRS was introduced in 2002 was to ensure that all police forces across England and Wales were consistent in how they recorded crimes. By the end of 2004, there had been a marked improvement on previous systems.

Crime recording follows three stages: *reporting* is when someone reports to the police that a crime has happened. At this stage, it should be recorded as a 'crime-related incident' and the police decide whether to record it as a crime. The second stage is *recording*. When the decision has been made to record the incident as a crime, the police need to decide how many offences and what type of offences to record. The final part of the process concerns *detection* of the crime. This involves collecting evidence that demonstrates who was responsible for committing the crime.

Since the NCRS was adopted, there has been a steady reduction in the number of crimes recorded by police forces in England and Wales. The total number of police-recorded crimes has fallen from almost six million to a little over four million per year during this time. In the case of fraud and forgery, the numbers have halved, from just over 331,000 in 2002–03 to

155,000 in 2008–09. For full details of these figures, visit the Home Office website (www.homeoffice.gov.uk).

An alternative to police records of crime figures is the British Crime Survey (BCS). This includes crimes that are not reported to the police. It asks people about their experience of crime and it also provides information on the ways in which the public might be concerned about levels of crime. This extra information about crime is used to determine the government's response to these issues.

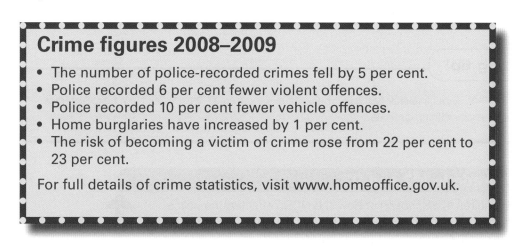

Crime figures 2008–2009

- The number of police-recorded crimes fell by 5 per cent.
- Police recorded 6 per cent fewer violent offences.
- Police recorded 10 per cent fewer vehicle offences.
- Home burglaries have increased by 1 per cent.
- The risk of becoming a victim of crime rose from 22 per cent to 23 per cent.

For full details of crime statistics, visit www.homeoffice.gov.uk.

The crime figures recorded by the police and those on the British Crime Survey (BCS) vary for a number of reasons. Here are some examples of these variations, using figures for 2008–2009.

- Violent crime – BCS figures remain stable; police figures show a 6 per cent decrease.
- Burglary – BCS figures show no change; police figures show a 1 per cent increase in home burglaries and a 2 per cent decrease in other types of burglaries.
- Vehicle offences – BCS figures show no change; police figures show a 10 per cent fall in vehicle crime and damage.
- Robberies – BCS figures remain stable; police figures show a 5 per cent drop.

Do you think that crime is going up or down? About half the people who were questioned in a survey believe they live in a lower-than-average crime risk area; almost 40 per cent think their area is typical risk area and the rest believe they are at a greater risk of crime. When asked about the level of crime nationally, three-quarters of the same people thought that crime was increasing across the whole of the UK. This figure was about the same for all types of crime.

Think about it!

Why do you think some people might be afraid they will become a victim of crime?

What type of crimes do you think people most fear?

Do you think men and women have the same fears?

Grading tip!

P4 For P4, you need to identify the process involved in reporting and recording crime.

How to upgrade to M2 and D2

M2 M2 requires a *description* of how the NCRS affected the police service nationally and the effect this has had on crime statistics.

D2 To achieve D2, you need to provide an *evaluation* of the impact of national crime recording on the reduction of crime.

Crime scene investigation

Traditionally, crime scenes were investigated by detectives, but in 1968 the Metropolitan Police introduced the first scene-of-crime officers (SOCOs) to carry out this specialised task. This meant that the detectives were then able to concentrate on gathering evidence and using this information to find the offender. Around the country, other police forces began employing these specialists, with teams of SOCOs developing in most areas.

Figure 12.6 Crime scene investigators at work

Scene-of-crime officers, also known as crime scene investigators (CSIs), examine the scenes where offences such as burglary, criminal damage or murder have occurred. They are trained to look for traces of any material that may be used as evidence to assist in the detection of the crime. This includes photographing the scene and ensuring that any materials removed are not contaminated in any way.

Duties of a scene-of-crime officer

Duties of a SOCO include:

- preserving the scene of a crime to prevent contamination
- photographing accidents and injuries
- taking samples for DNA testing
- presenting exhibits in a court case.

Although SOCOs are employed by the police, their role is a civilian one. They usually work a 40-hour week, but could be called upon at any time of the day or night to attend a crime scene. After all, criminals do not restrict their activities between the hours of 9am and 5pm!

As well as the regional forces, SOCOs are also employed in the British Transport Police and the Ministry of Defence Police. While each force sets its own entry requirements for SOCOs, it is becoming more usual to expect applicants to already have a degree in a relevant science subject. It is expected that SOCOs will update their knowledge and continue their training while they are employed in their role. There is opportunity for progression within the crime scene investigation department. Those who possess particular skills could be promoted to a managerial post, so they would be responsible for all those who attend the crime scene or they may be able to apply to become forensic scientists.

The nature of a crime scene means that the SOCO will usually have only one chance to capture evidence, such as fibres, blood or other bodily traces, or fingerprints. Sometimes the scenes can be extremely distressing, especially in the case of murders, rapes or arsons where someone has been burned or killed. As you studied in Unit 7 (Health and safety in the public service workplace), there is help available for those whose health is affected by the work they carry out. This could be from an occupational health officer or a counsellor.

Some offenders will commit just one crime in their lifetime, while others make it a career. It is essential that, wherever possible, evidence that will link the crimes carried out by the same person is collected and that the link is established early on in the investigation. Sometimes, the scene of the crime will not produce suitable forensic evidence to be able to certify that an individual was present. In these cases, collection of other information is needed.

Activity

In Unit 1 (Public service skills), you investigated the skills and qualities needed by public service personnel. Carry out some research into the work of a SOCO and compile a table to show what skills a SOCO needs, and explain why.

This might include examining the *modus operandi* (the way in which the crime was committed). If a number of burglaries were committed where it is shown that entry was gained by smashing a window with a hammer, then it is possible that the crimes might be connected and might have been committed by the same person.

Another useful weapon for investigators is the practice known as *offender profiling*. This is used when investigators do not know who the offender might be. They will consider the crime itself and whether there is a likelihood of links to other crimes, and then try to establish the personality of a person who might be responsible for committing such crimes.

⬤ Case study

Towards the end of the 19th century, a doctor, Thomas Bond, attempted to profile the personality of Jack the Ripper. Bond had been an assistant at the post-mortem of Mary Kelly, one of the Ripper's victims. In his notes, written after the post-mortem, Bond wrote about the sexual nature of the murder and that the killer had appeared to be in a rage.

The profile suggested that, of seven murders that had been committed in the area, five had been carried out by the same person and that this person was physically strong, composed and daring. The unknown offender would be harmless in appearance, possibly middle-aged and smartly dressed. He would be a loner, without a permanent job and mentally unstable. Bond also believed that the offender had no medical knowledge and could not be a surgeon or a butcher. Later on, Bond believed that this same person was responsible for the death of a sixth woman.

ⓖ Grading tip!

P5   To achieve P5, you need to describe the role of the crime scene investigation unit.

How to upgrade to M3

M3   For M3, you need to *explain* how crime scenes can be linked and offenders profiled.

National Intelligence Model

P6

Traditionally, police activity involved trying to solve crimes by looking for clues after the crimes had occurred. More recently, however, the focus has changed to being proactive and targeting criminals known to the police and whom the police believe to be active in carrying out offences. The information that the police use in this approach is gathered through a process known as *intelligence*, based on gathering information from many reliable sources.

With advances in technology and the ease with which people can travel over large distances, it became apparent that intelligence held on known criminals by one police force could prove useful to other forces in the United Kingdom, so the National Intelligence Model was devised.

This model has been tested by officers, researchers and others from a number of police forces and other agencies. As the model was to be employed across the whole of the UK, it was seen as vital that the same standards were put in place by each agency that used it. The result being that it is now possible to review information and decisions made on that information and also those agencies involved in law enforcement are better able to work together.

The model was intended to tackle crime in three specific areas: crimes that affect businesses, crimes that occur over several areas and serious crimes carried out by organised gangs. These serious and organised crimes could very well be committed nationally or internationally.

(g) Grading tip!

P6 To achieve P6, you need to explain how the National Intelligence Model and intelligence-led policing has led to new policing strategies.

Management of offenders

P7

Most people would agree that the public needs to be protected from offenders. As we discovered earlier in this chapter, the lives of many of those who fall victim to crime are changed forever and the ways in which some people behave prevents others from carrying on with their daily lives in the way they would choose.

If found guilty of a crime, some offenders will serve a term in prison or other institution. However, the time will come when some of these criminals will be released and they could very well return to the area where they committed their crimes. Some offenders will receive non-custodial sentences and remain in the community.

The National Offender Management System (NOMS) was brought into place in an attempt to deal with all offenders while they serve their sentences, and the goal is that they will be less likely to repeat the criminal behaviour. The system is designed to support offenders and to restore their place in society.

Agencies involved in the NOMS are from the public, private and voluntary sectors. They deliver services that help to reach those offenders from sections of the community that traditionally do not engage with others and are locally based. There are nine areas in England and one in Wales. Some of the factors that provide a challenge for the NOMS include the education, employment history, possible substance misuse and family make-up of the offenders.

Many sections of the legal system work together in an attempt to manage offenders. These include the Crown Prosecution Service (CPS), whose role is to prosecute criminal cases in England and Wales. The CPS works closely with the police, the courts, the Home Office and other agencies. They must ensure at all times that the service they provide is seen to be fair and that their actions will help to reduce crime and the fear that some people have that they could become victims of crime.

In 2001, the National Probation Service was set up to work with offenders in an attempt to reduce the numbers who re-offend and, in so doing, protect the public.

There are many ways in which offenders can be dealt with in an attempt to encourage young or first-time offenders to see the errors of their ways and turn away from a life of crime. We will look at some examples of these now.

Reprimands and final warnings replace the cautions that were previously given to offenders under 18 years of age. Depending on the crime that has been committed, young offenders might receive a reprimand for a first offence. This is then followed up with a final warning. If the crime is very serious, they will be given a final warning immediately, or they could be prosecuted. The final warning is given in the presence of the young person and their parent or other responsible adult, and they are referred to the youth offending team (YOT) and a programme to manage the offender is put in place.

Another measure implemented to prevent young offenders committing further crimes is the reparation order. The YOT meets with the victim before the offender is dealt with and their responses influence the sentence that is given in court. This might include the examples provided earlier in the section on restorative justice and offenders could have the opportunity to apologise for their actions or do something practical to put right the damage they had caused.

An action plan order is a fixed-term method of dealing with offenders. It lasts just three months and is concentrated on addressing the behaviour that led to the crime that has been committed. The action plan order is carried out as a community sentence and is used for the more serious crimes.

Partnership approaches to managing offenders exist, most notably the partnerships between the police, prison and probation service, which focus on managing offenders throughout the whole of their sentence. This approach allows the organisations to share information and provide support mechanisms that will help the offenders to move away from crime and restore their place in the community.

The court system

The courts of England and Wales are structured in a hierarchy in much the same way as the chain of command in public services. The magistrates' courts, which deal with summary offences, sit at the bottom of the hierarchy and the Supreme Court, the highest court in England and Wales, is at the top.

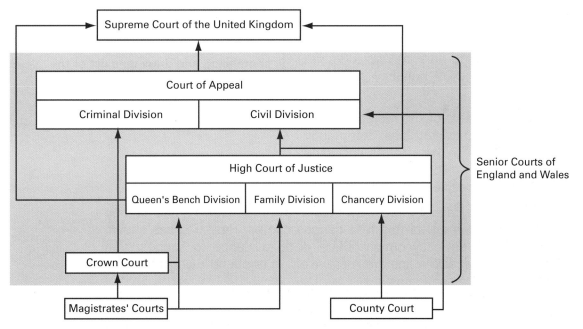

Figure 12.8 Courts of England and Wales

Courts have a number of available options when they need to impose a punishment on those found guilty of a criminal offence. These fall into four main categories: discharges, fines, community sentences and custody (prison).

Certain crimes carry an automatic prison sentence but, in many instances, a sentence served in the community is more suitable. In addition to punishing the offender, community sentences often force the offender to consider the reasons they committed the crime.

The sentence given by a court depends on the seriousness of the crime. Before deciding on the most suitable punishment, the court may ask probation staff to prepare a report on the offender. Judges or magistrates will take this report into account when they deliver the sentence. The offender's past is also likely to have an effect on the sentence – a first-time offender will be unlikely to receive the same sentence as someone who has a history of offending.

On average about eight per cent of people convicted of a crime receive a discharge – this might be an *absolute discharge*, in the case of a very minor offence or when the court decides that the experience of being found guilty is sufficient. Alternatively, the offender might receive a *conditional discharge*; although no actual punishment has been given at this time, if the offender commits another crime within a certain period, they can be punished for the original crime as well as the new one.

Some people see this as the offender 'getting away with it' but they still get a criminal record.

Thirteen per cent of convicted people receive a community sentence. Community sentences come in many forms, including carrying out compulsory (unpaid) work, curfew orders or not being allowed to take part in specified activities.

Almost three-quarters of those convicted of a crime receive a fine as their punishment; these will be the less serious crimes. Research has shown that this is not an 'easy option'. There is no evidence to suggest that offenders who receive a fine are more likely to re-offend than those who receive alternative sentences.

A very small percentage of offenders – just seven in every hundred – are given a prison sentence, and two-thirds of these sentences are for less than one year.

Key terms

Absolute discharge means that no further action is taken against an offender. **Conditional discharge** means the offender receives no immediate punishment, but may do at a later date if another crime is committed.

Activity

Carry out research into community sentencing and draw up a list of the many options available to the courts when using this punishment.

Grading tip!

P7 P7 requires a description of the different ways in which the legal system manages offenders.

End of unit knowledge check

1. List four ways in which the public services support victims of crime.
2. Explain why police crime figures differ from the British Crime Survey.
3. Provide a job description for a crime scene investigator.
4. Describe the differences between the criminal courts.

Grading criteria

In order to pass this unit, the evidence that the learner presents for assessment needs to demonstrate that they can meet all the learning outcomes for the unit. The assessment criteria for a pass grade describe the level of achievement required to pass this unit.

Grading criteria		
To achieve a pass grade the evidence must show that the learner is able to:	To achieve a merit grade the evidence must show that, in addition to the pass criteria, the learner is able to:	To achieve a distinction grade the evidence must show that, in addition to the pass and merit criteria, the learner is able to:
P1 Explain the role of public services in assisting and supporting victims of crime		**D1** Evaluate a local crime reduction initiative showing how it has reached relevant groups in the community and reduced the fear of crime
P2 Describe the impact of crime on society		
P3 Investigate a local crime reduction initiative	**M1** Analyse a local crime reduction initiative	
P4 Identify the process involved to report and record crime	**M2** Describe how the National Crime Recording Standards impacted nationally upon the police service and the effect on crime statistics	
P5 Describe the role of the crime scene investigation	**M3** Explain how crime scenes can be linked and offenders profiled	**D2** Evaluate the impact of national crime recording on crime reduction
P6 Explain how the National Intelligence Model and intelligence-led policing has led to new policing strategies		
P7 Describe the different ways the legal system manages offenders		

Unit 15
Expedition skills in the public services

Introduction

The uniformed public services have always used expedition training to develop the qualities and attributes of their personnel. In this unit you will gain an insight into the reasons for participating in an expedition and look at the skills required to plan, take part in and evaluate at least one expedition with your peers.

You will gain a greater understanding of your needs and values when leading or taking part in an overnight expedition and this will enable you to develop your own knowledge and understanding of the personal and group equipment required for such an adventure.

All expeditions require first-class planning, which is vital to the organisation of a successful, safe and enjoyable experience. You are also expected to take into account present-day environmental issues and the impact your expedition will have on the countryside, as well as current government legislation.

Any experience gained from the Duke of Edinburgh's Award, cadet groups or the Scout and Guide Associations will allow you to improve and expand on your knowledge, improve your skills and techniques and put leadership qualities to the test.

Figure 15.1 On an expedition

Learning outcomes:

By the end of this unit, you should:

1. Know the correct equipment required for an expedition

2. Understand the planning necessary for an expedition

3. Be able to participate in an expedition

4. Be able to review an expedition.

Correct equipment required for an expedition

For every expedition, you will need the correct equipment and clothing. Whether it is a two-hour stroll or a week-long venture up in the mountains, you must ensure that you are prepared for the worst. People have been found wandering on Ben Nevis in the summertime suffering from hypothermia, dressed in t-shirt, shorts and trainers! The weather can alter dramatically and very quickly anywhere in Great Britain so you must always expect the worst weather possible and take too much rather than not enough. Remember, there is no such thing as atrocious weather, just inadequate equipment.

The group must carry all the equipment and food to be used during the expedition and all individuals must always carry their own personal kit (see page 247).

Clothing, footwear and equipment should be suitable for the activity and the environment in which it is to be used and generally conform to current accepted standards. The equipment must be capable of resisting the worst weather anticipated since, in the event of a serious deterioration in conditions, safety may well depend on it being able to withstand the prevailing conditions.

There is no single fabric available that will maintain the body at a constant temperature while protecting you against the elements, so a layering system uses a number of different fabric types to transfer any moisture away from the body and at the same time keeping out the wind and rain.

Ask yourself!

Do you need to buy all new clothing for the expedition?

It is not always necessary to buy equipment or even windproof or waterproof clothing for your expedition. Many people have the required essentials in their loft, shed or garage after trying out camping, having a bad experience and vowing never to do it again! Mention to your parents, family and friends that you are going camping and they may have some equipment or waterproof clothing you could borrow. Do not forget, you may also vow never to go again after this expedition, so there is no point in spending money on things you will never use again! Also enquire at your local cadet force, school, college or scout hut for equipment you could borrow.

Personal clothing (layering system)

Thermals or cotton underwear; socks; shirt; trousers; fleece; sweatshirt; windproof jacket; waterproof jacket and trousers; hat and gloves; walking boots or shoes; gaiters.

Figure 15.2 Personal clothing

The base layer should be made of a high wicking fabric that allows perspiration to evaporate. It is generally synthetic, machine washable, easy care and fast drying with an antibacterial finish to prevent odours. This layer will keep the body warm and comfortable.

The mid layer will trap air, keep the body warm and allow the perspiration vapour from the base layer to pass through. The most common material for this is a fleece as it is light, warm and very breathable. Fleeces tend to be washable, easy care and fast drying. Two thin layers are better and more versatile than one thick layer.

The shell layer needs to be wind and rain repellent but breathable to allow perspiration vapour to escape. The jacket must be an accurate fit against the mid layer because if it is too tight, it will restrict your movement and if it is loose, it will mean condensation can form on the inside. Waterproof and windproof clothing come in a variety of materials that have a variation of breathability, durability and handling.

Activity

Draw up your own kit list of items you think you will need for an expedition. You may be surprised at how long the list is!

EXPEDITION

Expedition Kit List

These are the items you will need when undertaking a DofE Expedition for any Level of Award. This is to be used as a GUIDE only. Quantities of some items depends on level and duration of expedition. Click on the links below for details of DofE Recommended Kit, or visit www.dofe.org/expedition DofE participants and Leaders can get a great discount off expedition equipment at Cotswold Outdoor, the Recommended Retailer of Expedition Kit to the DofE. Find out more from www.DofE.org/go/cotswold

TO WEAR WALKING

- 1 x **Pair Walking Boots** (broken in)
- 1 x **Pair Walking Socks** e.g. Bridgedale - Endurance Trekker, Women's Endurance Trekker or a similar item.
- 2 x **Pair Sock Liners** (optional) e.g. Bridgedale - Coolmax, Women's Coolmax or a similar item.
- 1 x **Thermal top or T-shirt**
- 1 x **Shirt**
- 1 x **Sweater** (woollen or fleece)
- 1 x **Walking Trousers** (warm, NOT jeans)
-

PERSONAL KIT (TO CARRY)

- 1 x **Large Rucksack** (approximately 55-65 litre capacity) e.g. Vango - Contour, Fitzroy, Sherpa or a similar item.
- 1 x **Rucksack Liner** (or 2 x plastic bags) e.g. Sea to Summit - Ultra Sil Pack Liner, Ultra Sil Dry Sack or a similar item.
- 1 x **Sleeping Mat** e.g. Vango - Adventure, Premium, Trek, Ultralite or a similar item.
- 1 x **Sleeping Bag** e.g. Vango - Nitestar, Summit, Ultralite or a similar item.
- 1 x **Waterproof Bag** for storing your Sleeping Bag e.g. Sea to Summit - Ultra Sil Dry Sack or a similar item.
- 1 x **Sleeping Bag Liner** (optional) e.g. Sea to Summit - Premium Silk Liner, 100% Cotton Liner or a similar item.
- 1 x **Survival Bag** e.g. Adventure Medical Kits - Emergency Bivvy, Emergency Blanket or a similar item.
- **Small quantity of money** (optional)
- 1 x **Notebook & pen/pencil**
- 1 x **Torch** e.g. hand-held torches from Maglite - LED 3xAA Maglite, Incandescent 2xAA Maglite, Holster Incandescent 2xAA Combo Pack Maglite or a similar item. Alternatively, a Head Torch if preferred.
- 1 x **Personal First Aid Kit**
- 1 x **Watch**
- 1 x **Whistle**
- **Maps**
- **Spare Batteries for Torch**
- 1 x **Emergency Food Rations** (NOT to be eaten until the end!)
- 1 x **Water Bottle** (1 - 2 Litres) e.g. Sigg Traveller Bottle (1.0 lt.
- 1 x **Knife, Fork, Spoon**
- 1 x **Small pocket knife/pocket tool** e.g. DofE Pocket Tool by Victorinox.
- 1 x **Plate/Bowl**
- 1 x **Mug**
- 1 x **Box of Matches** (sealed in a dry container or bag)
- 1 x **Small Wash Kit**
- 1 x **Small Towel** e.g. Sea to Summit - Dry Lite Travel Towel or a similar item.
- 1 x **Cagoule/Coat** (must be waterproof and windproof)
- 3 x **Pairs Underwear**

- 2 x **T-shirts**
- 1 x **pair Walking Socks** e.g. Bridgedale - Endurance Trekker, Women's Endurance Trekker or a similar item.
- 2 x **pair Sock Liners** (optional) e.g. Bridgedale - Coolmax, Women's Coolmax or a similar item.
- 1 x **Shirt** (woollen, cotton or fleece)
- 1 x **Spare Sweater** (woollen or fleece)
- 1 x **Spare Walking Trousers** (warm, NOT jeans)
- 1 x **Pair of Trainers** (optional)
- 1 x **Hat** (warm)
- 1 x **Pair Gloves** (woollen)
- 1 x **Pair Shorts** (if appropriate)
- 1 x **Sunhat**
- **Suncream** (if appropriate)
- 1 x **Thermal Long Johns** (optional)
- 1 x **Pair Gaiters** (optional)
- 1 x **Waterproof Over-trousers**

GROUP KIT (to carry between the team)

- 1-2 x **Tents** e.g. Vango - Hurricane, Ultralite, Typhoon, Spectre, Banshee, Equinox, Tempest, Tornado or a similar item.
- 2-3 x **Camping Stoves**
- **Camping Stove Fuel**
- 2-3 x **Cooking Pots**
- 2 x **Scourers**
- **Maps** (1:50 000 / 1:25 000)
- 1 x **Compass** e.g. Recta - Starter, Romer, Elite or a similar item.
- **Map Cases** e.g. Sea to Summit - Waterproof Map Cases or a similar item.
- 1 x **Camera** (optional)
- 2 x **Tea Towels**
- **Food** (small and lightweight)
- 5 x **Plastic Bags** (for rubbish etc.)

ADDITIONAL OPTIONAL KIT (for you to consider)

- **Storm Shelter** e.g. Vango - Storm Shelter or similar item.
- **Waterproofing For Kit** e.g. Granger's - G-Wax Tin, G-Max Proofer with Conditioner, G-Max Cleaner, 30 Degree C Cleaner, 30 Degree C Proofer, 30 Degree C 2 in 1 Cleaner/Proofer, 30 Degree C Down Cleaner or similar items.
- **Rucksack Protector** e.g. Pacsafe - Pacsafe 85 or similar item.
- **Secure Money Pouch** e.g. Pacsafe - Pouchsafe 100 or similar item.
- **Survival Pack** e.g. Adventure Medical Kits - Pocket Survival Pack or similar item.
- **Stuff Sack** e.g. Sea to Summit - Ultra Light Stuff Sack or similar item.
- **Food Box** e.g. Sigg - Aluminium Food Box or similar item.

Figure 15.3 A typical kit list

Personal equipment

Watch; backpack; map; compass; whistle; emergency foil blanket; bivouac bag; torch; mirror; energy-giving food and emergency rations; cutlery; thermal cup or mug; plate/bowl; matches; water bottle; sun cream; insect repellent.

(For an overnight expedition, you will also need the following: sleeping mat; sleeping bag; spare clothes; food to cook; towel; toiletries.)

Group equipment

Route card; map case; tent; stove; fuel; matches or lighter; cooking pots; food; soap pads; washing-up liquid; tea towel; water container; trowel; plastic bags; first aid kit; survival bags; flares.

The use of safety equipment

P2 M1

Before going out on an expedition, it is good practice to set up and demonstrate the use of the safety equipment so that you are sure how to use it correctly and safely and that it will work when needed.

Cooking on stoves requires correct safety procedures and precautions to be observed when using them and when handling the fuels that they run off. There are a number of different types of stove to use while on an expedition and different types of fuel, so it is a good idea to try as many as you can and find out which ones you are most comfortable with and which you can easily get the fuel for. Always use stoves in a well-ventilated area and change fuel away from naked flames. Using dehydrated foods is the most economical, efficient and clean way of cooking under camp conditions.

'Trangia' storm-proof stoves can be set up anywhere, are simple to clean, require no special maintenance and have no ignition devices. Whatever the weather, the methylated-spirits burner lights quite easily and assembling the stove is quick and easy. The hooks are folded upwards to use a frying pan and down when using the cooking utensils. Five centilitres of spirits will boil one litre of water in 12 minutes. Beware of the transparent naked flame when removing the cooking utensils and when trying to extinguish the flame after use. Keep the spirits in a leak-proof container and, if you spill any fuel, move the stove away and do not try to light the burner until you have thoroughly washed yourself.

Gas or butane canister stoves are very compact, light and dependable, though you must ensure they are placed on even, solid ground. The canisters can be bought at all retailers and are relatively inexpensive. Always assemble, fill and use the stove out of doors and away from any source of ignition or other people. Do not refill when alight or still hot. Do not carry it around when alight and turn off the stove immediately should a fuel leak occur.

Great care must always be followed when using cooking stoves.

You will also need to practice using a whistle, mirror and torch in case of emergency while out on expedition, in preparation for attracting attention any time of the day or night. Check that the first aid kit is correctly stocked and in date and who will be carrying it. Learn how to set up the group survival bag in case of a storm or heavy rain and, if possible, learn to set up the tent before venturing out into an unknown environment to ensure there are enough pegs, poles and ropes to secure your accommodation.

Purpose and function of expedition equipment

D1

Expedition equipment can be found in a variety of styles, materials and prices. The most expensive is not always the best, so it is necessary to shop around to get the right equipment for yourself, whether it be from a shop, a catalogue or online.

Tents

Before buying a tent, you need to take into account a few basic factors. How many people will be sleeping in the tent? Will you be carrying the tent around? If so, weight will be important. What time of the year will you be using the tent – summer or winter? What will the probable weather conditions be – hot, windy, wet? Will the tent be used in lowland areas or on mountains?

There are a number of different styles of tents – single hoop, tunnel, dome or geodistic – so it is important to check out the various sizes, materials and styles before paying for one. Some tents are pitched with the inner first; some set up the outer first; others just pop up when you open them. You need to see if it is waterproof with a breathable inner tent, whether it has a sewn-in groundsheet and ventilators or mosquito netting, and what types of poles are used to hold it up (are they alloy, fibreglass or shock cord?) The lighter tents tend to be the most expensive. Ideally, you need one with a porch so you have somewhere to store items or to do the cooking.

It is a good idea to visit a camping exhibition or large retailer to get a view of all the tents on display and the range of prices before deciding on which one is best for you and your future exploits. A good tent that is well-maintained can last a lifetime.

Sleeping bags

As with tents, sleeping bags come in a variety of styles and materials, so you need to choose carefully. Do not just go for the cheapest, as a good purchase will last for many, many years. Firstly, decide upon the filling of the sleeping bag – do you prefer synthetic or down?

Synthetic sleeping bags have fibres that give high durability, can pack down into very small sizes and have a quick recovery from compression. They also have the ability to insulate you when they are damp.

Down is taken from duck or goose feathers so may cause allergies. However, down sleeping bags last much longer than synthetic bags, have better warmth-to-weight ratio and compress to a very small size. However, there are a real problem if they get wet as it takes a long time and the right conditions to get them dry.

Then you need to decide upon the construction of the sleeping bag: a single layer, an offset double layer, a box wall or trapezoid? Each one has its merits and generally the more expensive, the better it will be at keeping out the draughts and the easier it will be to get into. You will need a shaped foot, a neck collar and preferably a hood to keep you warm. Ensure it has a good, sturdy zip that works from inside and outside and can withstand the conditions you are likely to encounter. Sleeping bags generally come in temperature ratings of 1, 2, 3 or 4. The higher the tog rating of the sleeping bag, the better it will be at dealing with the colder temperatures.

Sleeping mats

You will require a sleeping mat to insulate you from the cold, wet ground even if you have a sewn-in groundsheet – unless you have a camp bed! The choice is either a roll-type mat made of a synthetic insulating material or a very thin air mattress which you inflate, therefore taking up much less room in your backpack. The self-inflating camping mats keep you warm and are quite comfortable. You open the small valve to suck air into the mat. A few breaths of air will make the mat firm enough to sleep on. The closed-cell type mats take up more space but require no inflation and are very comfortable and provide excellent insulation.

Backpacks

There are literally thousands of different types of backpacks on the market and, if you are purchasing one, then you need to make sure you get the right one for your needs as, once again, the right choice will last forever if well-maintained. The first decision is to get the right size and they generally come in measurements of litres.

- Up to 25 litres is a day sack for general walking.
- 25–35 litres is useful for winter day walking as you will require extra clothing and equipment, or for multi-functional use.
- 35–45 litres is ideal for winter walking and climbing or weekend walking when you will be carrying a tent, stove, food and sleeping equipment.

- 55–75+ litres are usually for serious backpacking of a few days and those used by the military.

Each specialist outdoor company has their own back system attached to their backpack in order to optimise the load distribution on your back, hips and shoulders, which is fully adjustable for different sizes. Check that yours has a comfortable padded hip belt and padded adjustable harnesses and is made from tough, heavy-duty fabrics. Separate base compartments are useful, as are large side pockets and an extendable lid with pockets. Some backpacks also come with accessory attachment points.

Walking boots (shoes)

Probably the most important piece of expedition equipment you will need – any foot problems and you are going nowhere! Boots are made from a variety of materials, synthetic and leather, and in a number of styles, depending on what you will be using them for. Will you need them for multi-activities and light hiking or for hill walking and backpacking? Ensure you try them on in the shop and with two pairs of socks to stop rubbing on your feet. Once you have bought your boots, use them as much as possible before the expedition to 'bed' them in. Do not go on a long walk in new boots!

Again, if you choose the right boots or shoes, with the correct care and maintenance, they will last you many years. You should carefully check the ankle collar, the boot lining, the foot bed and the sole to ensure you have the right footwear for the right conditions.

Figure 15.4 There are many different types and sizes of backpacks on the market

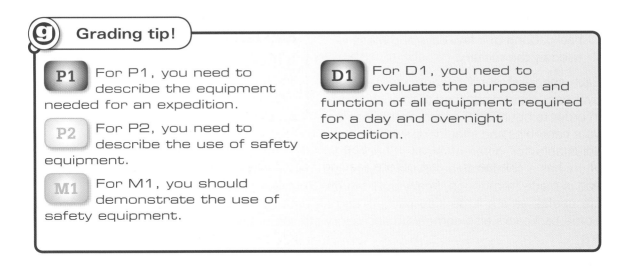

Grading tip!

P1 For P1, you need to describe the equipment needed for an expedition.

P2 For P2, you need to describe the use of safety equipment.

M1 For M1, you should demonstrate the use of safety equipment.

D1 For D1, you need to evaluate the purpose and function of all equipment required for a day and overnight expedition.

Planning for an expedition

P3 **M2** **D2**

Expeditions involve joint planning and preparation by all members of the group and should have a clearly defined purpose. The first step is to have an initial briefing to decide on the type and length of expedition. This will help the participants to consider the options available and clarify the commitment required by all members of the group. A short practice journey is advisable before making the final decision.

Planning an expedition

P3

The purpose, aims and objectives of the expedition should relate to the interests and abilities of those taking part and should not be devised just to fulfil the requirements of the unit or the qualification. You may wish to test yourself on a physically demanding journey, see the countryside in a more relaxed manner or find a way of bonding your group outside the normal environment of your centre.

If travelling on foot, the routes should make as little use of roads as possible and avoid villages. Cycling expeditions should involve minor roads, lanes, tracks, bridleways and disused railway tracks. Cycling on footpaths is illegal unless there are marked cycle ways. Expeditions involving water should use safe waterways, such as inland waters, lochs, estuaries or sheltered coastal waters.

Figure 15.5 A typical 1:25000 map for expeditions

First, decide where the expedition will take place and find the map that relates to the area. All route finding should be based on the 'Explorer' 1:25000 scale maps as they make instruction and learning easier, with precise footpaths, tracks, lanes and field boundaries. A compass should then be studied to take precise bearings for the route card. Identify and avoid any hazards while taking environmental issues into account, such as not trespassing on private land. The route card can now be completed.

You need to take into account your destination, how you will get there and the costs involved. Ensure everyone is available for the day(s) planned for the expedition and they have all the necessary equipment prior to leaving. A risk assessment of the route should be completed by someone in authority who will be travelling with you well before the intended trip.

Participants under the age of 18 will be required to have their parents sign a consent form agreeing to the expedition, and a long-range weather forecast of the area should be checked a week before setting out. This forecast should be updated the day before leaving and, if there are any doubts regarding the conditions, the trip should be cancelled.

Safety and environmental considerations for an expedition

M2

Safety issues

Safety of all participants is paramount. It is important that everyone should be aware of the possible hazards and of the need for a disciplined approach where matters of safety are concerned.

When you are changing gas cartridges or filling stoves, it must be done out in the open, not inside the tent, and away from a naked flame. Cooking should be carried out inside a tent only if the weather conditions are not suitable for outdoor cooking. Make sure there is plenty of ventilation.

Know how to use the cooking utensils before venturing out in the open. You should:

- stir pans while holding the handle
- be aware of the translucent flame
- put hot pots and pans on the ground.

Following these points will reduce the risk of scalding accidents.

Try not to start a fire outside unless you are highly confident in setting one up, keeping it going and being able to extinguish it properly after use or if it gets out of control.

Ensure that you have checked the weather forecast correctly prior to setting out. The weather conditions can change dramatically and very quickly, even more so the higher you climb. Forecasts are now very easily obtained via radio, television and most notably the internet.

Know the effects, causes and treatment for the two extremes of weather conditions – extreme cold and heat. During the cold, make sure you are well wrapped up and drink warm liquids, while on hot days, drink plenty of cold water and allow your body to breathe and perspire.

Do not carry too much in your backpack and wear the correct clothing and footwear. By following this advice, you should find the expedition enjoyable rather than a chore, with the thought that all the safety issues have been taken into account.

Think about it!

Safety is the most important part of any expedition. Leaders of expeditions must be correctly qualified and be fully responsible for people they take out on outdoor adventures. Providers must meet nationally accepted standards of good practice to receive a licence from the Adventure Activities Licensing Authority (AALA).

Research why the AALA was first set up to understand the reasons for all the safety precautions that need to be taken before you can venture out on your expedition.

Environmental issues

There are many contributory factors as to why the environment is in a fragile state presently. A huge population growth, more leisure time, increased car usage, better roads, a higher standard of living and the growth of outdoor activities are amongst them. All these factors are having a detrimental effect on the countryside so, in order not to spoil it for future generations, it is vital that we all take the following issues seriously.

Refer to recent maps or guidebooks as they change regularly. Keep to footpaths, bridleways, byways and trails, normally referred to as "rights of way", to prevent erosion. Contact visitor information centres and always tell someone where you are going and with whom.

Get to know the signs and symbols to show paths and open countryside. Read and follow the Countryside Code. This has been updated and simplified from the previous Country Code so that it is easier to remember and it will enable you to get the best out of the countryside by helping to maintain it now and for the future.

Follow paths across land that has crops growing on it and follow instructions on signs. Do not climb over walls, hedges or fences and do not disturb ruins and historic sites. Do not damage, destroy or remove features like rocks, plants and trees. Do not block gateways, driveways or entry and exit points.

Key term

The **Countryside Code** is a set of guidelines designed to help us all to respect, protect and enjoy our countryside. The five rules of the code are as follows:

- Be safe, plan ahead and follow any signs.
- Leave gates and property as you find them.
- Protect plants and animals and take your litter home.
- Keep dogs under close control.
- Consider other people.

Figure 15.6 Environmental issues in the countryside

Activity

Research outdoor legislation such as the Countryside and Rights of Way Act 2000 (CROW) and understand the rights of access across all areas of Great Britain.

Evaluating the planning of an expedition

D2

Once all the planning for the expedition is finalised, it is good practice to look back at all that has been done, by everyone involved, and see what went well and what could have been done better. This will help when eventually evaluating the expedition once completed, as in grading criterion D3. There are many ways of evaluating or reviewing tasks that have been completed, including peer evaluation, questionnaires and self-evaluation.

Peers can be interviewed or given a short questionnaire to complete. These are very useful because you are receiving information from others on the expedition who are on a level with yourself, so you should get some good, honest feedback. Did all the planning go smoothly? Did everyone play their part in the planning or was it left to just a few to do all the work? Has everyone got the necessary clothing, footwear and equipment for the expedition? Does everyone know their roles and responsibilities prior to, during and after the expedition?

If you prefer not to get into a question-and-answer debate, devise a small questionnaire that can be filled in by everyone involved with their feedback about the planning of the expedition. Once an analysis has been carried out of the answers, you can use the questionnaires as evidence of your work for D2.

Finally, it is time for some self-evaluation. Be brutally honest in your account of the planning process as the weaknesses you show will become the areas for improvement that you will need to make whenever you are asked to complete a similar task in the future. Do not consider it as criticism but as a developmental factor for yourself. It will help you to identify any future training requirement or learning of a skill in which you are not too competent at the present time. Did you do all you could have in the planning process? Do you feel your contribution to the planning was positive and well received? What would you do differently next time?

  Grading tip!

P3 For P3, you need to explain the planning needed for an expedition.

M2 For M2, you must explain in detail safety and environmental considerations for an expedition.

D2 For D2, you should evaluate the planning of an expedition.

Participating in an expedition

P4   P5   M3

P4

Expedition route card

The route card is a vital part of any expedition. To be able to complete one successfully is a skill that you should master and that should be worked on by all members of the team. Using the correct map, check the scale and distances to travel, note all the conventional signs, the gradients marked by contours, give a description of the route and mark the grid reference of two points on the map.

Practical map skills

- Set the map.
- Locate position on the map.
- Determine direction of travel.
- Check direction of footpaths.
- Identify features in the countryside.
- Mark the route on the map using a highlighter pen if laminated or pencil if on paper.
- Mark checkpoints at natural points on the route – approximately every 2km.

How to complete your route card

- Fill in the top part of the route card – who you are, dates, times, etc.
- Fill in the grid references for the start, leg 1 and leg 2.
- Write a description of your route as you will walk it between the two points – mention buildings, rivers, woods, etc.
- Fill in the grid references and description for the other legs on the route card.
- When that is complete for the whole route, fill in the distance and height gained sections of the route card.
- Complete the times for each leg – assuming 4km can be completed per hour, plus one hour for every 600 metres climbed.
- Fill in the times for rest stops – usually ten minutes in each hour with one longer stop at the halfway point.
- Complete the estimated times of arrival at each checkpoint.
- Check the detail and photocopy enough for each tent group, with one to be left at the centre and one to be left at your start point or campsite.

EXPEDITION ROUTE CARD (use one per day)

Leg	PLACE WITH GRID REF	General direction or bearing	Distance in km	Height climbed in m	Time allowed for journeying	Time allowed for exploring, rests or meals	Total time for leg	Estimated Time of Arrival	Brief details of route to be followed or planned activity. (Enter full details of activity on reverse)	Escape/Notes
(a)	START (b)	(c)	(d)	(e)	(f)	(g)	(h)	(i)	(j)	(k)
1	TO									
2	TO									
3	TO									
4	TO									
5	TO									
6	TO									
7	TO									
8	TO									
	Totals:									

Aim of expedition:

Day of the week: Date: /   /

Day of venture: (1st, 2nd etc.)

Names of team members:

Name of DofE Group:

Address:

Tel No:

Email:

Setting out time:

Supervisor's name, location and Tel No:

Expedition Route Card

Figure 15.7 Typical route card

P5

Roles and responsibilities on the expedition

Each member of the group will have roles and responsibilities to carry out while on route, regardless of their experience or knowledge. The main responsibility of everyone on the expedition is to take care of their own, and everyone else's, safety.

Roles include:

- making the expedition a success and enjoyable
- helping anyone who is struggling or finding it difficult
- helping with navigation
- being part of the team and working together
- ensuring you have all the correct clothing, footwear and equipment for yourself
- arriving on time and at the right place
- listening to the leader at all times and following instructions
- helping with all chores, such as washing up and cleaning
- setting up and taking down tent if required.

Responsibilities include:

- ensuring you have no drugs, alcohol or dangerous objects in your possession
- not carrying too much in your backpack – you may have to carry it a long way
- following the Countryside Code at all times
- being careful when cooking on the stoves
- keeping the campsite tidy, keeping noise to a minimum and obeying camp staff rules
- getting plenty of sleep in preparation for the following day.

Key terms

A **role** means the behaviour or duty expected of an individual or institution. **Responsibility** a duty, obligation or liability for which someone is accountable.

Activity

Within your tent or cooking group, list all the roles and responsibilities required on an expedition and then share them out amongst the individuals. That way, everyone will know what they are supposed to do and when it needs to be done.

M3

Benefits of expeditions to the public services

Expeditions require individuals to show leadership, communication skills, teamwork, problem-solving and cooperation – the perfect requirements for entry to the uniformed public services. All the public services, most particularly the armed forces, use expeditions on a regular basis to test recruits on their physical, mental and emotional strengths.

Public service work includes working with each other, with the public and in some cases with the enemy, so it is important that you have the necessary skills to be effective and efficient in your job. You need to be mentally strong, be confident and have a high self-esteem for everyday duties in different environments and situations. You have to be able to communicate verbally, on a computer, using a telephone and in writing, as well as being able to listen intently to others, sometimes in a foreign tongue.

Being physically fit is also a huge benefit to the public services. All the services require you to pass a fitness test for entry and some even put you through a vigorous and tough training programme once you have joined, so if you are already fit it will not feel as daunting and be as hard as it may be for others who have just entered the profession. Of course, it is not just a case of being a good runner, cyclist or swimmer; you need strength, suppleness, coordination, balance and agility – in other words, 'all-round' fitness not specific fitness.

The ability to carry all your necessities on your back for a day or more, as you do for an expedition, is also of great benefit. Skills used in camping are highly regarded by the public services, such as:

- being able to use a map and compass
- completing a route card
- camp craft
- navigation by day and night
- safety and environmental awareness.

These are all important factors to write on your CV in preparation for entry to the public service of your choice.

If you are unfortunate and unable to gain entry to your chosen public service, do not worry; your expedition skills will not have been wasted because what are benefits to the public services are benefits to you and any other future employer.

Think about it!

'An expedition aims to provide an enjoyable, challenging and rewarding development for a person. By participating you develop:

- self-belief and self-confidence
- the ability to plan and use time effectively
- a sense of identity
- independence – of thought and action
- the ability to learn from and give to others
- new relationships and a sense of responsibility
- an awareness of your potential
- new talents and abilities
- skills including problem-solving, presentation and communication
- an understanding of strengths and areas for improvement
- the ability to lead and work as part of a team.'
  Source: The Duke of Edinburgh's Award handbook and www.theaward.org

An expedition, by definition, is a physically demanding challenge for a given distance but is also helpful for the development of individuals, of teamwork and of the social interaction of the group. Together you have to plan and execute a given task, which requires attention to detail and organisational ability. You then respond to the challenge of the expedition with planned and unforeseen circumstances and develop self-reliance by carrying out the expedition, for most of the time unaccompanied. These skills are invaluable in the uniformed public services. It will give you time to enjoy and appreciate the countryside and make you aware of the growing environmental awareness by having a minimum impact on your chosen route.

Figure 15.8 A public service on expedition

Expeditions help you to develop your leadership skills, whereby each member of the group is given the opportunity to take a leading role in the group and, using the map, compass and route card, guide the group to the next checkpoint. You begin to recognise the needs and strengths of others as you are all involved in supporting each other in completing the expedition. While on the route and during camp, you will all make decisions and accept the consequences for the good of the group and to complete the tasks set. These skills are highly regarded in the public services. Leadership, self-evaluation, teamwork and communication skills are the main qualities required by each and every one of the services and by any employer looking for suitable recruits or trainees.

Ask yourself!

Immediately after the expedition is over is the time to start reflecting and reviewing how things went. Think about your personal performance and that of the team. What were the strengths, the problems and the areas for improvement? Talk to your colleagues and leaders and ask how they thought the expedition went. Write down all the feedback you receive. Was the expedition a success or could more have been done by those involved? What needs to be done before the next expedition takes place to make it more successful? Consider the planning, preparation and participation elements of the whole event in your review.

Grading tip!

P4 For P4, you need to produce a route for an expedition.

P5 For P5, you should carry out an expedition,

identifying your own roles and responsibilities.

M3 For M3, you need to analyse the benefits of expeditions to the public services.

Reviewing an expedition

Individual performance from the expedition

P6

Once you have had time to reflect on the expedition, it is necessary to provide an account of your personal experiences and be prepared to feed back to the group all the relevant points. You need to specify how well you think you performed. Do not be afraid to detail your strengths and what you could have done better, your 'areas for improvement'.

Questions to consider:

- Did you have the correct clothing for the expedition or were you wet or cold at any time on the expedition? What can you do next time to eliminate any problems?
- Were you cooperative within your team and did you help out when navigating or solving a problem? How can you help to make the team work better together?
- Did you have the opportunity to lead part of the route or are you not yet confident to do so? Will you lead next time if given the chance?
- Do you think everyone played their part and did their share of the work? If not, how could you make each individual aware of their roles and responsibilities?

Then you can ask others, your peers and leaders, what they thought you did well and also what could be improved. Ask them to be honest and give constructive criticism rather than just saying 'good' or 'OK'. It may be that you thought that you had particular strengths in certain roles but others may have seen these as areas in which you could do better. This feedback can be carried out verbally, or even better in writing, so that you can gather all the feedback, analyse all the information and set yourself an action plan for future expeditions.

Key term

SMART targets are targets that are specific, measurable, achievable, realistic and time constrained.

The action plan will require you to set yourself targets and the best way of going about this is to be SMART – setting targets that are specific, measurable, achievable, realistic and time constrained.

Team performance from the expedition

P7

Now that you have reviewed your own performance on the expedition, it is time to look at how the group performed and gather all the information for feedback. This can be carried out amongst the small groups on the expedition, such as tent groups or cooking groups, before opening it up to the whole group – including the leader(s). Although you may have evaluated the planning of the expedition for a previous criterion (D2), it is important that you review all the processes involved with the expedition at this point so that the strengths and areas for improvement can be highlighted and addressed from the very beginning of the process to the end.

Start with the first ideas about the project through to the safe return.

- Who decided where to go for the expedition? Was it a good choice?
- Who split the group into smaller groups? Did it work?
- Who did the planning of the route? Were the route cards precise enough?
- Did everyone have the correct clothing, footwear and equipment? If not, how did they cope on the expedition and what should they do next time?
- Was navigation successful by everyone? Who needs more training?
- Did everyone help with the setting up of camp, cooking and cleaning?
- Were there any injuries, mishaps or problems? How were they dealt with?
- What evidence was collected – photographs, route cards, observation records, diary or log entries?
- Did everyone return home safely having had an enjoyable experience? If not, why, and what could have been done differently?

Once you have collated all the necessary evidence and feedback from everyone involved with the process, you are required to set up a group action plan, which should link nicely with your personal action plan (P6).

What did not go as planned?	Why did it not go as planned?	Action required	Date set for completion	Date completed

Table 15.1 Action plan

Strengths and areas for improvement

The presentation of the feedback – from individuals, small groups, the whole group and the leader(s) – will naturally lead to the strengths associated with the expedition, as well as areas for improvement, where either more, or better, things could have been done by yourself or others. It is never easy to say what you are good at, or what your strengths are, but we can all point to the weaknesses in our planning, preparation and participation because you have the benefit of hindsight. However, try not to be too negative and set too many targets that you may not achieve.

Figure 15.9 Teamwork on expedition

If there are only two or three areas for improvement, then that gives you something to work on when you start preparation for the next adventure, as long as you maintain the strengths of course. Evaluations are normally made by measuring results against objectives. If the evaluation is carried out at regular intervals throughout the appointed task, then objectives can be altered or modified to fit the progress of the task, but if the evaluation is carried out at the very end, then you can only measure it against the main aim and its objectives.

Activity

To practise writing up strengths and areas for improvement, set yourself the task of listing ten things not related to expedition skills that you think you are good at and ten that you need to improve on. You will find that the second list is completed before the first one because we are all proficient at noting our faults and not so clever at boasting about what we are best at. Go on, give it a go!

Once you have identified the group strengths and weaknesses, compare them with the strengths and weaknesses from your own evaluation and see if any of them are similar in any way. Try to understand why there are similarities and decide what you can do better next time. The strengths need to be retained for any further expeditions and the areas for improvement need to be highlighted and eliminated before the planning starts for another visit into the countryside.

A presentation of the strengths and weaknesses highlighted from the expedition, along with photographs and other evidence, upon returning to the centre will help to trigger memories and incidents that occurred, which can then be added to the action plan and help to set the recommendations for further expeditions.

Recommendations of the expedition process from start to finish

D3

(g)   **Grading tip!**

D2 **D3**   Use your evaluation from D2 to help with the D3 grade and add to it everything that has happened since the planning was concluded and the expedition took place.

The action plan derived from the individual and team performance reviews should point the way to improving and making recommendations for future expeditions.

Questions to consider:

- Did you achieve the aims and objectives?
- Did the expedition take place on the original dates set?
- How effective was the planning process?
- Were there any safety issues that were not addressed correctly?
- Were all environmental considerations taken by all members of the party?
- Was everyone involved in the planning and participation of the expedition?
- Are there any skills or techniques that need to be mastered before venturing out again?

These questions, and many others that you will think of, will enable you and the group to decide upon some recommendations for the next expedition to ensure it goes much better. Hopefully, upon achieving the BTEC Level 2 First Public Services qualification, you will decide to study on the next level of the Public Services course at your centre, so that you can put your recommendations into practice for the Outdoor and Adventurous Expedition unit at BTEC Level 3 National Public Services.

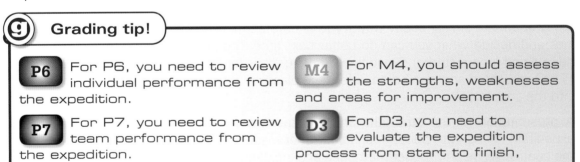

(g)   **Grading tip!**

P6   For P6, you need to review individual performance from the expedition.

P7   For P7, you need to review team performance from the expedition.

M4   For M4, you should assess the strengths, weaknesses and areas for improvement.

D3   For D3, you need to evaluate the expedition process from start to finish, making recommendations.

End of unit knowledge check

1. List three safety factors to be considered when using cooking stoves.
2. Describe the 'layering system' of personal clothing.
3. What factors do you need to take into consideration before buying a tent?
4. List the different types of 'Ordnance Survey' maps and describe the best one to use for expeditions and why.
5. List the five points of the Countryside Code.
6. Describe why a route card is an important part of an expedition.
7. What factors would you take into consideration when choosing a campsite?
8. List the benefits of expedition skills to the public services.
9. What benefits would you gain from an overnight expedition?
10. Why is it important to review your last expedition?

Grading criteria

In order to pass this unit, the evidence that the learner presents for assessment needs to demonstrate that they can meet all the learning outcomes for the unit. The assessment criteria for a pass grade describe the level of achievement required to pass this unit.

Grading criteria		
To achieve a pass grade the evidence must show that the learner is able to:	To achieve a merit grade the evidence must show that, in addition to the pass criteria, the learner is able to:	To achieve a distinction grade the evidence must show that, in addition to the pass and merit criteria, the learner is able to:
P1 Demonstrate the equipment needed for an expedition		
P2 Describe the use of safety equipment	**M1** Demonstrate the use of safety equipment	**D1** Evaluate the purpose and function of all equipment required for a day and overnight expedition
P3 Explain the planning needed for an expedition	**M2** Explain in detail safety and environmental considerations for an expedition	**D2** Evaluate the planning of the expedition
P4 Produce a route for an expedition		
P5 Carry out an expedition identifying own roles and responsibilities	**M3** Analyse the benefits of expeditions to the public services	
P6 Review individual performance from the expedition		
P7 Review team performance from the expedition	**M4** Assess the strengths, weaknesses and areas for improvement	**D3** Evaluate the expedition process from start to finish making recommendations

Introduction

Why should anyone want to give up their time to carry out work without getting paid for it? Thousands of people in this country do so every year by carrying out voluntary work for various organisations. Why do they do it? How do so many people benefit from volunteering and why is volunteering so important to the organisations involved?

It is a fact of life that the more you put into something, the more you will get out of it. This certainly seems to apply to voluntary work. Although most people would be happy to occasionally give up some of their spare time for nothing in order to help others, they may be pleasantly surprised to find out that they actually enjoy volunteering, find it very rewarding and experience a real 'feel-good factor' afterwards.

Many public service employers, particularly the uniformed services, expect new recruits to have gained some life or work experience and skills, and they will look for evidence of this on an applicant's CV. This can be difficult for many applicants as 'real' work experience placements with the uniformed services are very difficult to arrange, due to issues of confidentiality, for example.

You may not be aware of just how many opportunities there are for volunteering. These include helping with a youth group, visiting the elderly or going overseas to a third world country to help build a school! The skills you learn and develop during your voluntary work will be invaluable in any future career.

In this unit, you will learn about the many volunteering opportunities available and about the different skills you can develop from carrying out voluntary work.

Figure 20.1 Volunteer police specials

Learning outcomes:

By the end of this unit, you should:

1. Understand the importance of volunteering in public services

2. Know the different types of voluntary work available

3. Understand the skills required for voluntary work

4. Be able to undertake voluntary work.

What is volunteering?

Volunteering means giving up some of your free time to do something useful to help others, without getting paid for it. This does not mean that you should be 'out of pocket' – if you have to pay expenses, such as travel or meals, you should usually be able to claim these back.

> **Key term**
>
> **Volunteering** means giving up some of your free time to do something useful to help others, without getting paid.

There is a vast range of opportunities available for volunteering, both home and abroad. Ideally, you should choose some sort of volunteering activity which interests you, or which is related to the area of work that you wish to enter. For example, if you love animals, you could volunteer to help out at your local veterinary practice, or at a stables or kennels. There are many other opportunities available to work with animals. If you enjoy being with children, there are also many opportunities available to you – for example, helping children to read, helping out with children in hospital, fundraising for children's charities and helping at your local Beavers, Brownies, Cubs or Scouts.

Remember, if you are working directly with children, then you will probably need to have a Criminal Records Bureau (CRB) check. Voluntary organisations will usually organise this for you but it can take some time to process so you need to allow plenty of time to arrange this when thinking of applying to do voluntary work.

Figure 20.2 If you enjoy being with children, you could volunteer at your local Brownies

If you are hoping to join the police or fire service, there are specific volunteering opportunities available that may give you the valuable experience and skills that these services are looking for. For instance, the police specials are a voluntary police constabulary. Police specials work alongside regular police officers and they have exactly the same powers and same uniform – the only difference is that they do not get paid. Similarly, many fire and rescue services have cadet schemes where volunteer helpers are always welcome.

> ### Assignment tip
>
> Remember not to cut and paste or copy work from other sources into your assignments. This is known as plagiarism, which is stealing someone else's words or ideas! Read the text, and then write about the subject *using your own words.*

Why is volunteering so important in the public service sector?

P1   M1   D1

There are many people in this world who need help in their everyday lives for one reason or another. There are also many other deserving causes involving animals, buildings or communities. Governments and other organisations try to meet everyone's needs, but there are lots of demands for public taxpayers' money and it is impossible to do everything that needs to be done. There just is not enough money and manpower to go round!

For this reason, many organisations rely on volunteers to help them to achieve their aims. Some organisations rely completely on unpaid volunteers and are funded solely by donations from the public. These include organisations such as the Royal National Lifeboat Institution, search and rescue services such as mountain rescue, and many other charities.

Other organisations receive a small amount of government funding but then have to rely on public donations for their main source of income. Organisations such as the Citizens Advice Bureau and the Samaritans fall into this category.

There are other organisations who employ paid employees to carry out the main business of the organisation but also use unpaid volunteers to work alongside, often carrying out the same roles. The police service is one organisation where this happens. Police specials are unpaid volunteers who work alongside regular police officers, carrying out many similar duties.

> ### Ask yourself!
>
> **Can you think of any uniformed public services where volunteers are used?**

Volunteers provide a number of things that are valuable to many organisations. Some volunteers act as fundraisers. Others provide their time, skills and expertise at no cost to the organisation. Volunteers can be called upon to respond to emergencies or to provide new ideas, or sometimes just to be an extra pair of hands to help out!

Because volunteering is so important to the public service sector, it is often something they will look for when they are recruiting paid staff. If an applicant has experience of voluntary work on their CV, potential employers will recognise that this person is someone who is willing to help others, and that is exactly the type of person public service employers are looking for.

ⓖ Grading tip!

P1 To achieve P1, you should explain why volunteering is so important in the public service sector. You should explain about lack of public funding, resources and manpower.

How to upgrade to M1

M1 For the M1 grade, you should focus on two or three different public service organisations that use volunteers (e.g. hospitals, schools, police) and you should examine how the organisations benefit from this. Discuss the different roles that are carried out by volunteers in these organisations and describe what could happen if there were no volunteers. Also discuss why it is important that anyone who is hoping to go into a public service career should carry out voluntary work.

How to upgrade to D1

D1 To achieve the D1 grade, you could carry out research relating to organisations that use volunteers (many charitable organisations will have their own websites and also printed literature that you can send for). You could discuss the barriers to volunteering (i.e. what would prevent a person from carrying out voluntary work). This may include lack of time, lack of motivation and not knowing how to apply for voluntary work.

Volunteering in the public service sector

Volunteers are involved in many different public sector settings, in schools, police stations, hospitals, prisons and private homes.

The courts are another area where volunteers are used regularly. Victim Support is an agency that trains volunteers to assist victims of crime and also witnesses to crimes when they have to attend court. Even the magistrates in the courts are usually unpaid volunteers! There are many other important volunteering roles in the public service sector, such as school governors and representatives on youth offending panels. All of these voluntary roles are unpaid, but you will usually receive expenses for such things as travel, telephone calls and postage costs where appropriate.

Case study

Figure 20.3 shows uniformed public services students taking part in a sponsored 24-hour 'Run, Ride, Rowathon'. Students gave up their spare time to row, run and cycle for a period of 24 hours non-stop to complete a total of 1,600 miles for charity.

Figure 20.3 Uniformed public services students taking part in a charity fundraising 24-hour 'Run, Ride, Rowathon'

Why volunteer?

P2

Why do so many people choose to do voluntary work? There are lots of reasons. Many do so because of a desire to help others, to help out in their community or to give something back. Other reasons include the following:

- To support an organisation whose cause you think is worthwhile. This could be a charity or group that you have a connection with or which you just feel is a worthy cause to support.
- To make a difference. Many students who want to join the public services do so because they say they 'want to make a difference'. This is why many people become volunteers: because they can make a difference where someone or something needs help.
- To help others who are less fortunate than yourself. If people only care about themselves and never help anyone else, the world becomes a sadder, crueller place. When people volunteer their time, money or skills, they help to make the world a better place, where people can work together to make life easier for all. Fortunately, many people are willing to give up their time simply to help others.

Benefits of volunteering

As well as the benefits to others of your volunteering, did you realise that there are also many benefits that you can gain from doing voluntary work?

Gain important new skills and experience

By doing a variety of different tasks when carrying out voluntary work, you will gain valuable experience and additional skills, which you may be asked about in any public service job interview.

Develop existing skills

You may find that you will be using and developing the skills that you started to develop at college or in your part-time work.

Make connections

One big benefit of carrying out voluntary work is that the company or organisation could offer you a paid job after getting to know you as a volunteer. This could be very useful as a 'stop-gap' while waiting to join the uniformed public services. Voluntary work is also a good way of 'networking', which means you meet new contacts and people who may be useful to you later when looking for a career.

Make new friends

You will meet new people and make new friends – maybe open the doors to a whole new social life!

Build self-confidence and self-esteem

Any activity that helps to build self-confidence and self-esteem is obviously very beneficial to the person concerned when applying for a public service career.

Have fun!

You may be pleasantly surprised to find that you actually enjoy the work that you are doing, which will be an added bonus!

Work with different people

Working with people of different ethnic origins or people with different disabilities increases your awareness of diversity and is a valuable experience. You will almost certainly be asked questions regarding any such experience if you attend an interview for a public service job.

Gain work experience

This is one of the main benefits of carrying out voluntary work if you are on a uniformed public services course. Gaining a work placement in the uniformed public services can be difficult for reasons of confidentiality and the necessity for CRB checks, etc. Carrying out voluntary work is a very good alternative to work experience.

Volunteering also allows you to try out a potential career area to see if this would be something you would enjoy doing full-time. You can use the experience and skills you gain from volunteering to prove to a future employer that you can work hard and do a job well. This is particularly important if you are applying for a job in the uniformed public services.

Become more active and fitter

This may be a benefit that you have not thought of before! When working with people with disabilities or with children, you will probably need a certain level of fitness and being more active will mean you become fitter.

Feel needed and useful

A benefit that you may not expect is to be appreciated and valued by others. This brings a real sense of satisfaction and fulfilment.

See more of your community or the world

You may decide to carry out your volunteering in your local community, or you could decide to travel, either in the UK or overseas, to do your voluntary work.

◯ Case study

'Claire Flack and Chris Austin are Race for Life volunteers and say, "Everyone knows someone close who has been affected by cancer and we are no different. Losing friends to cancer spurred us on to find out what we could do to help such a fantastic charity.

Volunteering at Race for Life was a spontaneous decision a couple of years ago. We wanted to use our work–life skills and help Cancer Research UK deliver a Race for Life event.

It's such a fantastic and electric feeling when you're there, in the thick of it. Volunteering is not only personally rewarding for us, but is also so important to the success of Cancer Research UK events that rely on volunteers like us.

Being a volunteer is extremely enjoyable, hard work and great fun. Cancer Research UK also listens and supports its volunteers so well. We are both so proud to be part of the team and continue to offer our support as much as we can."'

Source: www.cancerresearchuk.org

Figure 20.4 Claire and Chris – Race for Life volunteers

Volunteering is good for you!

If the benefits described above do not convince you that volunteering is a good idea, you may be interested to know that a survey carried out by the Carers' Association discovered that:

● nearly half of all volunteers (47 per cent) say volunteering improves their physical fitness
● a quarter (25 per cent) who volunteer more than five times a year say it helps them lose weight
● half of people (48 per cent) who have volunteered for more than two years say volunteering makes them less depressed
● up to 63 per cent of people say volunteering helps them feel less stressed.

Source: www.carersinformation.org.uk

That is the secret of volunteering! People who become volunteers usually lead richer, happier and more satisfying lives than those who do not volunteer.

(g) Grading tip!

P2 To achieve P2, you should talk about the benefits to be gained to the individual by carrying out voluntary work. Talk about the benefits that are listed above.

Volunteering opportunities   P3 M2 D2

When thinking about carrying out voluntary work, you should choose an area of work that really interests you. If you like animals, you could help out at a local stables, kennels or veterinary practice. Most kennels depend on volunteers to keep the dogs happy and well exercised. Remember, while walking the dogs, you will also be keeping fit!

If you have a friend or relative who has a medical problem (cancer, heart disease or diabetes, for example), you might be inspired to donate your time to help an organisation that raises money for research into the disease or that offers other help to people with the illness.

If you like children, there are lots of volunteering opportunities out there – helping out in an after-school club or helping out with groups like the Brownies, for example. If you do want to work with children though, even in an unpaid capacity, you will usually need to have a CRB (Criminal Records Bureau) check.

The following is a list of just some of the things that volunteers and volunteer groups do to help others.

- Provide food for hungry people.
- Help the homeless.
- Find clothes for those who need them.
- Make neighbourhoods safer.
- Protect wildlife and natural areas.
- Help care for pets and other animals.
- Speak up for people who are unable to speak for themselves.
- Visit the elderly.
- Help to find cures for diseases.
- Help people learn to read or do better in school.
- Preserve buildings or monuments.
- Help to raise funds.
- Join the police specials.
- Become a magistrate.
- Become a Samaritan.

The possibilities are endless! You can find local volunteering opportunities by visiting your local library or by contacting your local Volunteer Bureau, which is an agency dedicated to providing volunteers in the community.

And if you have more than one thing you enjoy doing, you could combine the two. For example, if you enjoy working with children and are good at arts and crafts, you could visit your local children's hospital and offer to lead art activities for young patients.

What sort of voluntary work can I do?

Case study

Vitalise Skylarks
'I spent a week volunteering at Vitalise Skylarks in November 2007. The trip was set up for a group of us by my college in Oxfordshire. As health and social care students we are interested in careers in nursing and care, but for many a week at Vitalise was our first experience of caring for another person. I had very little experience of working with disabled people, so spending a week at Vitalise Skylarks was very daunting.

When I arrived, I was so nervous about everything I was going to have to do, but as soon as I met the guests and got into the swing of things I had the most amazing week of my life. My time was spent interacting with the guests, making cups of tea and just being there to support the staff. I assisted on trips out and worked to make sure guests received the best holiday possible. I would say that a highlight was helping guests to enjoy using the on-site swimming pool.

The support from Vitalise staff and other volunteers is overwhelming. If you are having problems with any aspect of being a volunteer they are there to help and they emphasise that no question is too silly to be asked. Knowing that many of the staff started off as volunteers themselves helps you realise they can relate to the emotions you are dealing with.

The experience was personally life changing for me. I developed into a better person and the joy of helping people enjoy a holiday overtakes all the other hurdles you have to overcome. Making sure guests have a brilliant week is so rewarding and the thanks that you get at the end of the week makes the tiredness you are feeling all worthwhile.

I would recommend volunteering to anyone that has a week to spare and loves to help people. I wouldn't change my experience at Skylarks for anything – it was one of the best experiences of my life.

I enjoyed myself so much the first time that I have already been back for another fun filled week. Once again I had the experience of a lifetime and it was great to meet some amazing new guests. And this time I was the support for volunteers who were there for the first time.

Visiting for a second time just reinforced the positivity I feel for Skylarks, its staff and all the services it offers the guests. I now think of Vitalise Skylarks as a second home, and I already have plans to visit for another couple of weeks later in 2008. I have gained lifelong friendships and memories that will live with me forever.'

Source: www.vitalise.org.uk

Figure 20.5 Vitalise volunteers

There are no qualifications or other requirements to become a voluntary worker; all you need is to be able to provide some of your time and dedication to your chosen cause. Some volunteer positions do require some training that they will usually provide free of charge. This would look very good on your CV!

There are no limitations on what kind of voluntary work you can do, as long as you are prepared to help out where needed. Voluntary work can be in your local youth club, community centre, mother and toddler group, hospital, hospice or charity office – the list is endless. You will probably gain the most benefit if you choose an area of work that interests you.

If you find an opportunity that you are interested in, you should find out as much as you can about it. Many voluntary organisations will have a volunteer manager or coordinator and they should be able to give you a good explanation of what your role would be. If you are under 18 years of age, you will need to check that you are allowed to do the voluntary work of your choice.

What time can I spare?

When considering what volunteering activity to do, you should think about how much time you have to spare. How big a commitment are you willing to make? How much of your day, week, month or year do you want to spend on volunteer activities? Do you have just a few hours now and then or are you looking for a bigger project?

For example:

- If you have a couple of hours each week, you could visit people in hospital or at a home for the elderly.
- If you have several weeks to spend volunteering, you could plan a bigger project, such as helping out at a summer club for children.

What skills do I have already?

Are you a good organiser? If so, you could use your skills to organise a fundraising event for a charity of your choice. It is advisable to think long and hard about the type of volunteering work that you would like to do.

How can I volunteer my time?

If you wish to offer your time to any organisation, the first thing you should do is contact them directly. Most organisations – again, especially those dealing with children – will ask that you provide a Criminal Records Bureau (CRB) check. This is so that it can be demonstrated that you are not a risk to children, the elderly or any other group that may be categorised as vulnerable.

You should remember to arrange your CRB check early on so that you can commence volunteering as soon as possible. The law says that you must not start work with children until the check has been made.

Types of volunteering opportunities

The following section will give you some ideas about the different volunteering opportunities that may be available to you. There will be many others, depending on the area where you live, but the ones listed here may be enough to whet your appetite and to start you thinking about the type of volunteering work you could do in order to complete this unit.

Working with animals

If you enjoy working with animals, there is a range of volunteering opportunities available to you. You could offer to help out at a local kennels, stables, cattery or animal sanctuary where volunteers are usually welcomed to help to exercise the animals or to clean out the environment where the animals live.

Figure 20.6 Volunteer kennel worker

Working with young people or children

There are many types of volunteering work that involve working with young people. Many organisations – especially those providing services for children – will have a need for volunteers who are good with children and can have a positive influence on them. Community groups, youth clubs and other organisations that exist to offer help and support to young people could be at the top of your list when it comes to deciding what type of voluntary work you wish to do.

There are many different kinds of clubs where children can go to be looked after, entertained or educated. There are playgroups, toddler groups, nurseries and crèches. Other groups include music groups, dance and gymnastics clubs, arts and crafts groups, and language groups. Some of these are run privately; others are run by the local authority. Many of them will welcome help from volunteers once they have undergone the appropriate criminal record checks.

Helping children to read
There are several organisations that exist to help children to read and they use volunteers to help them to do this. Volunteer Reading Help is one such organisation that trains volunteers to go into schools and help children to read.

Case study

'Mary has been volunteering for five years. She says, "I have seen the children I work with grow and flower during our sessions. One little girl barely spoke or looked me in the eye. Now she devours books and loves reading, and is a real live wire in class."'

Source: www.vrh.org.uk

Youth groups

Youth groups such as Brownies, Scouts, Girl Guides and youth clubs are all run mainly by volunteers. Without people who are willing to give up their time for no pay, such groups would cease to exist. Volunteers are always needed to give up some of their time to help out.

Cadet schemes

Most of the uniformed services have their own cadet schemes. There are Fire Service Cadets, Police Cadets, RAF Cadets, Army Cadets and Navy Cadets and, depending where you live, there may be any or all of these in your area. Maybe you are already a serving cadet. Such schemes are usually run by serving officers and volunteer helpers. By offering your time and services to help as a volunteer, you could gain valuable experience and skills before applying to the service of your choice.

Reservists

The Army, Royal Navy and the Royal Air Force all have reservist schemes where civilians can join and train to be part of the armed forces on a part-time basis. Reservists can be called up to fight on the front-line. Although classed as volunteers, reservists usually get paid a fee, are given a uniform and receive expenses.

Police specials

Police specials, or special constables, are part-time volunteer officers who have all the same powers as regular police officers.

Volunteering to be a special gives you the chance to give something back to your community while learning useful life skills. Police specials provide a vital link between regular police officers and the community and enjoy all the same powers. If you are successful in applying to become a police special, you will receive full training, have a similar uniform to that worn by regular police officers and have exactly the same powers as regular officers. You will need to give a minimum of four hours of your time each week but, in return, you will gain the valuable life skills that the uniformed services look for in new recruits.

You can apply to become a special once you are 18 years of age. Every police force in this country has a special constabulary and the duties of a special constable vary from area to area.

Helping the elderly

There are a number of ways in which you can carry out voluntary work to help the elderly. Organisations such as Help the Aged recruit volunteers to visit the housebound elderly in their own home or care home. Volunteers need to be checked and vetted and you would need to carry some identification to show to the person you are visiting.

There are also other agencies, such as the Volunteer Bureau, where you can register to do this type of work and they will arrange for you to visit someone, usually for an hour each week. Priority is given to those who live alone and/or have no family contact. Alternatively, one charity invites you to donate a small sum of money each week and 'sponsor a granny' overseas!

Case study

'Jim is 80 years old and lives alone in Walton-on-Thames with his pet dog, Rex. Jim has some mobility problems and has trouble walking. Even though he has an electronically powered vehicle, he doesn't manage to get out often so a visit from a Friends of the Elderly volunteer is a real highlight of his week.

Anne spends one hour a week of her time visiting Jim every Friday. She spends time chatting, reminiscing and the friendship has grown considerably. The friendship is mutual with Jim being full of praise for his weekly visitor: "Anne coming into my life through Friends of the Elderly has been an absolute blessing. She treats me as a friend and I know I can rely on her. It really helps me not feel isolated. It might only be officially an hour a week, but she has gone beyond that so many times."'

Source: www.fote.org.uk

Hospital visiting

There are many reasons to volunteer at a hospital. People who are in hospital and dealing with the stress of illness really appreciate the company and assistance volunteers offer them. When you work with children, it can be especially rewarding. You can brighten their day and give their parents a much-needed break at the same time. You could also gain a lot from hospital volunteering, particularly if you are considering a career in the paramedic service.

Working with people with special needs

Many volunteers work with people who have disabilities or other special needs. This can involve accompanying people on shopping trips or helping with care so that permanent carers can take a break. There are also charitable organisations that run centres where people with special needs can take a holiday or respite care. These centres rely on volunteers to assist the paid staff and ensure that the guests enjoy the time that they spend there. The type of skills and experience you would be likely to acquire doing this type of work would be valued by many employers.

St John Ambulance Service

Volunteers are trained in first aid to treat all sorts of injuries, ranging from headaches to heart attacks. They use these skills to provide first aid treatment at a wide variety of public events.

Over half of St John Ambulance's 43,000 volunteers are under the age of 18. Youth leaders play a crucial part in the development of thousands of young people by broadening their horizons and helping them to realise their potential.

Rescue services

There are many different rescue services in this country but they all (apart from the statutory fire and rescue services) have one thing in common. They all rely on volunteers and voluntary donations to ensure provision of the service. Services include mountain rescue, cave rescue and the Royal National Lifeboat Institution (RNLI).

Figure 20.7 Air ambulance volunteers in action

Conservation projects

Are you interested in the outdoors and preserving the countryside? Many conservation projects are run and funded solely by volunteers. Voluntary work may include spending a day picking up litter from trails or clearing out a pond or canal area. Other tasks could include repairing walls and fences.

Voluntary Service Overseas

Voluntary Service Overseas (VSO) sends volunteers to developing countries where they can work to improve health, education and the quality of life of the people living there. If you are 18 or over, you are eligible to apply for this work.

Charity shop volunteers

Many of the larger charities have their own shops in high streets around the country. These shops sell second-hand items, which are donated by the public, and they are mainly run by volunteers, although they are usually managed by a paid employee of the charity.

Charity fundraising

Charitable organisations rely on voluntary donations as their main source of funding. Thousands of volunteers carry out fundraising events for their chosen charities every single day. Fundraising can take many forms, ranging from standing in a street collecting with a tin, to jumping out of a plane with a parachute! Sponsored events, such as marathons, swimming, walking and even waxing legs or chests, are good ways of raising money. You could volunteer to organise such an event yourself or you could help out at an organised event, acting as a steward, running a stall or selling raffle tickets.

Figure 20.8 There are all sorts of ways to raise money for charity!

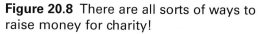

Activity

Make a list of all the different ways you can think of to raise money for charity.

Ⓖ Grading tip!

P3 To achieve P3, you should write about several different types of voluntary work and explain a little about the work and what would be involved.

How to upgrade to M2

M2 To achieve the M2 grade, you should look at the different types of voluntary work. You should explain what the work would involve and then compare the different volunteering activities by looking at what commitment of time would be involved, what skills may be required and any other things you would need to consider before undertaking the activity.

How to upgrade to D2

D2 For the D2 grade, you should assess the different volunteering opportunities and evaluate the skills and qualities required to carry these out. Carry out some self-evaluation to see what types of work you would enjoy, what skills you already possess and what you may be good at doing.

The skills required for voluntary work   P4 M3

Different kinds of voluntary work require different kinds of skills and qualities. There are generic, or general, skills that are needed for a wide range of voluntary work and then there are specific skills that are required only for particular kinds of volunteering. You may already have some of the required skills; others you may need to develop. In this section, we will look at these skills in detail. We will also look at the qualities needed for voluntary work. Although qualities are naturally developed within a person, sometimes people may be unaware that they have these qualities until they do something like volunteering. It is also possible to acquire leadership qualities by watching others.

The following are the skills and qualities that the uniformed public services look for when interviewing applicants. Applicants will often be asked to give examples of when and how they have demonstrated such skills and qualities. Having carried out voluntary work, you should be able to relate back to the work and give necessary examples.

Qualities required

Some of the qualities for voluntary work are general qualities that would be needed for any type of volunteering. These include honesty, commitment, reliability and empathy.

Honesty

Honesty is an obvious requirement for any volunteering activity. Volunteers frequently handle money – for example, when collecting sponsorship money – and many volunteers need to be trusted in order to enter people's homes.

Commitment

This is one of the most important qualities required by volunteers. Being committed means doing what you say you will do, not giving up on a task until you have completed it and not letting people down.

Reliability

Reliability goes along with commitment. People need to know that they can rely on you to carry out your part of the task.

Empathy

Being able to show empathy means being able to show some under-standing of another person's problems. Being empathic can mean listening to someone and being sympathetic and understanding, but not patronising or condescending.

Generic skills

Communication skills

Good communication skills are absolutely essential for anyone who is considering volunteering in any situation. There are many reasons for this. If working with children, the elderly or people with special needs, the way you communicate with them is extremely important and your communi-cation style needs to be adapted in order to suit the particular situation.

Some of the time spent volunteering, partic-ularly with elderly people, may simply involve listening to them talk. Many elderly people love to reminisce about their youth and young people may be surprised to hear about the lives they have led and the things they have done. This can be a two-way process where both people benefit and gain something from the experience.

Figure 20.9 Good communication skills are vital for carrying out voluntary work

When carrying out other types of voluntary work, such as collecting for charity, volun-teers need to be polite and friendly at all times when communicating with members of the public, otherwise they will just walk away and you will be left with an empty tin!

Teamwork

Most volunteering activities involve teamwork. Teamwork is extremely important in most situations, but especially where people are giving up their free time without getting paid. Everyone needs to contribute and pull their weight to share the workload. Volunteers need to encourage and support each other or they will soon become discouraged and disillusioned and will give up on the volunteering.

Leadership

Leadership skills are required by many employers, particularly in the uniformed public services. Volunteering is an excellent way to acquire some leadership skills. Good leaders usually have a number of particular qualities and these are the same qualities that can be found in people who volunteer successfully.

Some of the leadership qualities that may be demonstrated when volunteering are:

- charisma
- embracing responsibility
- altruism (unselfishness, concern for others)
- enthusiasm
- assertiveness
- consistency
- sense of humour
- experience.

Organisational skills

Many volunteering activities require some form of organising. When planning and arranging your volunteering activity, you may need to apply and go through a particular process. This means you will need to be fairly organised. When you start to carry out volunteering work, you may be working to a rota, along with other volunteers. You will definitely need to be organised so that you turn up for volunteering at the agreed time. If you fail to turn up, you could be letting down the rest of your team and, if you are working with vulnerable people, they could also be seriously affected.

Time management skills

Skills in time management are necessary in any type of employment. Punctuality is an essential requirement in any uniformed public service. Volunteering could help you to develop your time management skills.

Problem-solving skills

It would be very easy to develop your problem-solving skills by doing some voluntary work. If you choose to organise a charity event, you may come across all sorts of problems that need to be overcome. You may need to find ways of obtaining prizes for a raffle or tombola, or you may need to think of ways of obtaining sponsorship for an event. You may find yourself having to think 'out of the box' to solve some of the problems you encounter.

Administration skills

Many voluntary activities require administration work of some kind. You may need to send out letters to local businesses to ask for sponsorship or to produce posters, leaflets or tickets. You may need to keep records, use a database or produce a spreadsheet. All of these tasks would help you to develop your administration skills, which could come in very useful in later employment.

Specific skills

Certain types of voluntary work demand particular skills. For example, any of the following skills may be required for different kinds of voluntary work: driving, cooking, computer skills, sign language, physical fitness and first aid.

How can you demonstrate these skills?

For the P4 grade, you need to prove that you have demonstrated a number of the above skills. How can you do this? Think of all the things you do in your life, such as studying at college, working part-time, looking after smaller brothers, sisters or relatives and socialising. How many of the above skills or qualities do you think you have already demonstrated when doing these things? Think about the activities you do on your course that involve outdoor activities, team development and team leadership. Which skills do you use during these activities?

Ask yourself!

Which skills and qualities do you think you have already demonstrated?

(g) Grading tip!

P4 For P4, you should identify areas of your life where you have used different skills. Keep a log or diary to record these.

How to upgrade to M3

M3 To achieve the M3 grade, you need to not only demonstrate the skills that you would need for volunteering but also write some notes to explain in detail which skills are needed for certain types of voluntary work, and why.

Carrying out your voluntary work

P5

Once you have decided what volunteering work you would like to do, you need to find out how to go about it!

If you are considering working locally, you should contact your local Volunteer Bureau who will try to organise this for you. Or, if you want to do your voluntary work at a hospital or home for the elderly, for example, you could write a letter to the manager, stating your interest. You may be asked to go for an interview – you should treat this like any job interview. Any volunteer work provider needs to be sure that any volunteers they appoint are honest and trustworthy individuals. It is, therefore, very important that you present yourself well at the interview.

If you choose to carry out voluntary work for a national registered charity, you will probably be able to do this by registering via their website. Many national charities have a volunteering policy. The box below contains Cancer Research UK's volunteering policy.

Volunteering policy – Cancer Research UK

Our commitment to volunteering

We are committed to giving our volunteers the best experience possible and we believe that the volunteer relationship is one of honour, trust and mutual understanding. Here's a summary of what we expect from our volunteers and what you can expect from us.

Our expectations are that you will

- Maintain and uphold the good name and reputation of the charity.
- Aim for high standards of efficiency, reliability and quality in all aspects of your contribution.
- Cooperate, listen to and learn from members of staff.
- Respect the need for confidentiality whenever you have access to restricted charity information.
- Take reasonable care of your own health and safety and that of others.
- Encourage two-way communication with other volunteers and paid staff, fostering a pleasant and friendly atmosphere.

What you can expect from us

- Celebrate success and recognise loyalty and dedication.
- Recognise that successful volunteer involvement incorporates your motivations, aspirations and choices.
- Respect you as a volunteer, listen and learn from what you have to say, consistently encouraging two-way communication.
- Attempt to match the needs of the charity with your skills, knowledge, experience and motivation as a volunteer.
- Ensure the health, safety and welfare of all Cancer Research UK volunteers whilst undertaking volunteering activities.
- Foster a friendly and supportive atmosphere – aiming to make volunteering fun.'

Source: www.cancerresearchuk.org

For more information, you can read the full volunteering policy here: http://supportus.cancerresearchuk.org. For general enquiries about Cancer Research UK please contact volunteering@cancer.org.uk

g **Grading tip!**

P5 In order to achieve P5, you need to undertake some type of voluntary work of your choice. There is no set length of time for this period of voluntary work, but you should discuss this with your tutor who will advise what would be appropriate. You should keep a record, i.e. log or diary, of the work you do and also, for P4, remember you need to note which skills you use while carrying out the work.

Finally, the following is a list of tips for when you carry out voluntary work.

- **Be selfless.** Selfless is the opposite of selfish. Do not think about what you can do to help yourself. Think about what you can do to help others.
- **Be well trained.** Know what you are doing as a volunteer. If you need some time to learn your job, take that time. If you are good at your job, it will be much easier to help others (plus you will have a lot more fun).
- **Be reliable.** Do what you say you will do and do your best. Do not show up late, and always keep your promises. People will be relying on you so you do not want to let them down.
- **Be enthusiastic.** Do not moan and groan your way through your volunteer work. If you really do not like what you are doing, find something else. Always have a positive attitude and show others that you are doing this because you *want* to.
- **Be open-minded.** One of the great things about being a volunteer is the chance to learn and experience new things. Keep your mind open to new possibilities and you will probably grow as a person.
- **Be respectful.** Always remember to show respect for other people and other cultures. Keep in mind that your way of thinking or living is not the only way there is.
- **Be a good team member**. Do not try to do everything yourself. Work as part of a team to make sure everyone gets a chance to participate and do his or her fair share of work. If someone asks for help, be willing to lend a hand. If you need help, ask for it politely.
- **Be understanding.** Try to see things through other people's eyes. Try your best to understand what other people are going through, even if it is something you have never dealt with yourself.
- **Be humble.** Humble people do not go around telling everyone about all the good things they have done just to get some attention or feel superior. They are happy knowing that they are making a difference and do not need to shout about it.
- **Be friendly.** Treat others like friends and they will do the same for you. Many people who volunteer meet new people with whom they want to stay friends.

You have now completed this unit. Good luck with your volunteering!

End of unit knowledge check

1. Why should public services students undertake some volunteering?
2. Name three benefits a volunteer can gain from doing voluntary work.
3. Name four different volunteer roles.
4. Name three skills required for volunteering.

Grading criteria

In order to pass this unit, the evidence that the learner presents for assessment needs to demonstrate that they can meet all the learning outcomes for the unit. The assessment criteria for a pass grade describe the level of achievement required to pass this unit.

Grading criteria		
To achieve a pass grade the evidence must show that the learner is able to:	To achieve a merit grade the evidence must show that, in addition to the pass criteria, the learner is able to:	To achieve a distinction grade the evidence must show that, in addition to the pass and merit criteria, the learner is able to:
P1 Explain why volunteering is important in the public services	**M1** Analyse the importance of volunteering in the public service sector	**D1** Evaluate the importance of volunteering in the public service sector
P2 Discuss the benefits to be gained from volunteering		
P3 Identify the different types of voluntary work available	**M2** Compare and contrast the different types of voluntary work available	**D2** Appraise the different types of voluntary work available
P4 Demonstrate skills required for voluntary work	**M3** Explain in detail the skills required for voluntary work	
P5 Carry out voluntary work		

GLOSSARY

Absolute discharge means that no further action is taken against an offender

Accident any unplanned event that results in injury or ill-health, or damage or loss to property, plant, material or the environment

Accountable answerable for your actions (or inactions)

Anti-social behaviour any aggressive, intimidating or destructive activity that damages or destroys another person's quality of life

Burglary entering a building without consent and stealing property; it is also burglary if you intend to assault someone or damage property there

Citizen a person who lives in, has loyalty to and contributes to a community

Citizenship a status that is inferred on citizens, the collective term by which people are known

Civilian public services employee, usually undertaking a supplementary role, who is not a full 'sworn in' member of the service

Commitment dedication, loyalty

Communication giving and receiving information

Conditional discharge the offender receives no immediate punishment, but may do at a later date if another crime is committed

Constable a citizen, locally appointed but having authority under the Crown, for the protection of life and property, the maintenance of law and order and the prevention and detection of crime

Cool-down relaxing the body and mind after exercise

Countryside Code a set of guidelines for those who use the countryside

Crime a violation of the law; a wicked or forbidden act

Dangerous occurrence a near miss that could have led to serious injury or loss of life

Diverse different

Diversity recognising people's different characteristics and making sure they are considered so that they can get maximum benefit from their uniqueness

Equality giving every person a fair chance according to their needs

ETA estimated time of arrival

ETD estimated time of departure

Evaluate assess the situation, consider advantages and disadvantages

Expand widen, develop

Financial means test is a system used to find out how much people can afford to pay for services

First aid treatment for the purposes of preserving life and minimising the consequences of injury and illness until medical help is obtained, or treatment of minor injuries which would otherwise receive no treatment or which do not need treatment by a medical practitioner or nurse

Fitness a general state of good health, often as a result of exercise and nutrition

Hazard the potential of a substance, activity or process to cause harm

Health in the context of employment, means the protection of bodies and minds of people from illness resulting from the materials, processes or procedures used in the workplace

Human rights rights set out under the United Nations Declaration of Human Rights 1948

Individual rights things that an individual is entitled to have or to do, based on principles of equality and impartiality

Inquiry investigation, examination of evidence

Lifestyle the particular attitudes, habits or behaviour associated with an individual or group

Lifestyle factors with regard to health and fitness, include stress, smoking, alcohol and family history

Litres a unit of measurement that refers to the internal capacity of an expedition backpack

Local authority, local council, local government all basically mean the same thing. They are the organisations that receive money from central government and from local council taxes to provide our local public services

Mission statement a declaration of the overall aims of an organisation

Nation may be defined as a collection of people having some kind of collective identity, recognised by themselves and others; a nation is a history of association

Near miss any incident that could have resulted in an accident

Nutrition the act or process of nourishing

Passive recreation leisure, often for pleasure, may be sedentary

Personal protective equipment (PPE) all equipment (including clothing) intended to be worn or held by a person at work and which protects him against one or more risks to his health or safety

Physical recreation non-competitive, undertaken by personal choice

Priority most urgent, main concern

Privatisation when an organisation that was 'owned' by the government and paid for by public money is sold to a private organisation. An example of this is British Rail

Purpose the overall aim of the service (laid down by law)

Responsibility a duty, obligation or liability for which someone is accountable

Risk the likelihood of a substance, activity or process to cause harm

Robbery theft and using (or threatening to use) force in order to steal

Role the behaviour or duty expected of an individual or organisation

'S' factors Stamina; Strength; Suppleness; Speed; Spirit; Sustenance; Skill; Sleep

Safety the protection of people from physical injury

Self-esteem sense of worth or belief in oneself

SMART Specific; Measurable; Achievable; Relevant; Time constrained

SMARTER Specific; Measurable; Achievable; Realistic; Time constrained; Exciting; Recorded

Sports competitive and have rules. The aim is always to win

Statutory required by law

Strategic calculated, deliberate

Stress the adverse reaction people have to excessive pressures or other types of demand placed upon them

Tactical planned, premeditated, intentional

Team a group of people linked in a common purpose

Teamwork the joint action of two or more people, where each contributes different skills, explores interests and is efficient in achieving common goals

Theft taking property belonging to another person

Volunteering giving up some of your free time to do something useful to help others, without getting paid

Warm-up preparing the body and mind for exercise

Welfare in the context of employment means the provision of facilities to maintain the health and well-being of individuals at the workplace

Well-being the condition of the body working well

Index